Tracking the Vanishing Frogs

Tracking the Vanishing Frogs

. . . .

An Ecological Mystery

Kathryn Phillips

St. Martin's Press • New York

Design by Basha Zapatka

Library of Congress Cataloging-in-Publication Data

Phillips, Kathryn.
    Tracking the vanishing frogs / Kathryn Phillips.
        p.   cm.
    "A Thomas Dunne book."
    ISBN 0-312-10973-3
    1. Frogs—Ecology.   2. Endangered species.   3. Indicators (Biol-
ogy)   I. Title.
    QL668.E2P53   1994
    597.8′04529—dc20   94-111
                                                            CIP

First Edition: June 1994
10 9 8 7 6 5 4 3 2 1

To Julie

CONTENTS

ACKNOWLEDGMENTS

I could not have written this book if many people, especially many scientists, had not been so generous in sharing their time and knowledge. Some who helped me understand amphibian declines are mentioned within the pages that follow. Many others aren't, but their assistance was no less valuable and is no less appreciated.

I am especially grateful to those scientists who allowed me to follow them during their travels in the field, and shared their enthusiasm for their work and their outdoor workplace. They also patiently answered more questions than any human should be expected to answer, even as they tried to concentrate on the work at hand. Fond memories of those field experiences sustained me during the long months at the computer that followed.

In my world, libraries are temples. I visited the temples regularly during the last three years to collect yet one more bit of information or a few more journal articles. The librarians who run these temples rarely disappointed me. Special thanks to the helpful librarians who oversee the science and engineering collection at UC Santa Barbara.

Editors at several magazines gave me assignments to write about amphibian declines early on, which fed my interest in the world of frog study. Susan Milius at *International Wildlife* and Joyce Miller, formerly of *The Los Angeles Times Magazine,* were especially helpful.

Many friends offered encouragement, support, and good humor. To all of them, a heartfelt thank-you.

Jeanne Hanson worked hard and found a good home for this project at St. Martin's Press. Frank Phillips offered enthusiasm and advice. Charles Phillips gave me an education, moral support, and wise counsel.

Julie Wilson deserves special thanks for going beyond the call of duty. She listened to every detail of my book adventures, remained convinced the book would get written, and read the manuscript enough times that I suspect she can recite it from memory. She even developed a fondness for frogs. She is a rare and valued friend.

KATHRYN PHILLIPS
Ventura, California
August 6, 1993

Tracking the Vanishing Frogs

1

. . . .

Lazarus

Mark Jennings spent a blissful long weekend in the summer of 1960 camping beside the Kern River and collecting any live animal he could catch in his four-year-old hands. Mostly that meant a lot of suckers, a bony fish cast up on the shore by the fishermen who wanted something more elegant on their lines. Mark put the suckers in a bucket and tried to keep them alive. They inevitably died under his care. He also now and then spotted frogs basking on the river's banks, but his hands and reflexes and coordination weren't quick enough to nab them as they hopped into the river for cover, and so he coveted them.

The Kern River was one of young Jennings's favorite spots. It was surrounded by wild creatures that fascinated him. The Kern follows the path of one of the longest faults in the Sierra Nevada, the mountain backbone of California. Most of the river's 164 miles wind through a national park and a national forest, protected on either side by the steep slopes of the Sierra. At its southern end it arrives at the flat, dry San Joaquin Valley, with its factory-style farming and boom-and-bust oil towns.

The Jennings family camped that summer weekend along the river inside the national forest, not far from an abandoned sawmill. To get there, Roy and Helen Jennings packed Mark and his two older sisters into their car and drove 150 miles from their Southern California home, through orange groves and farmlands and vast open spaces. Then they watched the landscape turn from flatlands to hills to distant granite peaks, from chaparral to oaks and cottonwoods to pine forests.

This was a time before *ozone* was an adjective for *hole,* or *greenhouse* a shorthand for an environmental malady. Life in the campground seemed untroubled, and being outdoors in the forest felt healthy and comforting. The family spent days fishing, relaxing, playing by the river. At night they slept in sleeping bags on the floor of a big green canvas tent that was so heavy and hot that under the afternoon sun it felt like a sauna.

On the last day of their vacation, the family folded up the tent and stowed the aluminum ice chest from J. C. Penney in the car. Mark helped where he could, but mostly stayed close to camp and waited to depart from a place he didn't much want to leave. When almost everything was packed, a boy Mark had befriended during the weekend came to the campsite to say good-bye. He carried one of the coveted frogs. Mark was impressed. Then the boy presented the frog to him as a going-away gift. Delighted, Mark carefully took the creature in his hands. Its back was bumpy and olive-colored and had some spots and mottling. It had a triangle of paler olive on its snout. Its legs were a bright yellow on their undersides. It was perfect.

Mark's parents, both schoolteachers who cheerfully tolerated their son's fascination with furless animals, found an empty mayonnaise jar to hold the gift. They put a little water in the jar. Then Mark held the occupied container on his lap on the long ride home.

The family deviated from their normal route home and went east over the mountains into the Mojave Desert for a change of scenery before they headed south and west. Scrub and creosote bushes and miles of sand and dirt that seemed to change color with the light lined the roads. The car had no air conditioning and the ride was hot. The hours were made hotter for the frog by the curious boy who held it in the jar. Occasionally, Mark would shake the jar to make sure the frog was still alive. The frog moved less as the hours passed. The shaking and the heat proved too much for the creature.

Roy Jennings pulled the car into the family's driveway in Santa Paula, a pinpoint on the map about an hour's drive northwest of downtown Los Angeles, and checked the frog's condition. It was still and limp. While Mark's mother tried to console the boy, his father opened the jar and dumped the poor frog's body into a patch of ivy beside the driveway.

Later that evening, Roy Jennings put the family dog on its leash and took it for a walk. As he came back up the driveway, he saw movement in the ivy. It was the frog, hopping and miraculously alive. The elder Jennings captured it and took the creature inside to his son. The next day, father and son went to a pet store and bought a five-gallon aquarium to become a home for the frog. They put gravel and some water on the bottom. Then Roy Jennings fashioned a screen for the top. He used brass screws and made the screen so sturdy that Mark still has it more than thirty years later. Helen Jennings made a net using an old nylon stocking that she sewed onto a hoop fashioned from a wire coat hanger. With that, Mark could catch insects to feed the frog. Helen also named it Lazarus after the biblical character whom Jesus raised from the dead.

Lazarus thrived in his glass home, which sat on a kitchen counter in the Jennings home. Mark regularly caught the insects the animal needed to live. Then one day, about a year after the frog joined the household, Mark noticed a moth weakly flapping its wings. It was so docile that he was able to catch it with his bare hands and promptly give it to Lazarus.

Frogs are notorious for snapping their sticky tongues out in a flash and grabbing virtually anything that moves. They are not picky eaters and have been known to kill themselves by overloading on gravel during a feeding frenzy. Lazarus needed no coaxing to eat the moth. Unfortunately, it proved to be his last meal. The frog was dead within hours. In retrospect, Jennings figures the moth must have been so easy to catch because it was dying from pesticide poisoning.

As I hear this story of Lazarus, I am sitting beside Mark Jennings in his white Ford Ranger pickup truck while he drives it along one of the highways near his hometown. We are headed to see if we can spot a certain rare toad along a stream in the hills not far from his parents' house. A steady but light rain falls, even though it is early July, the driest season in Southern California. It is the kind of weather that typically draws the toads and frogs from their damp hiding places as though in celebration of water and everything it means to them. I have heard parts of the Lazarus frog story before, but this time, as I listen to it from beginning to end, it seems almost prescient.

Thirty-two years have passed since the Kern River camping trip when Mark held his first frog, and many things have changed. Jennings is now six feet tall and sports a light brown mustache. His parents still live in the same Santa Paula house, but he moved long ago and now lives alone in a one-bedroom apartment that doubles as his laboratory and office in Davis, in Northern California. He continues to like frogs, but now his interest is scientific as well as aesthetic. He is a biologist. His doctorate is in ichthyology—the study of fish—but his interest is primarily in amphibians—frogs and toads, salamanders and newts, and caecilians. Though he once thought frogs were everywhere and forever, as an adult Jennings has become a chronicler of their demise and disappearance.

The chronicling began almost unconsciously with Lazarus and his kind. Lazarus was a foothill yellow-legged frog, whose scientific name is *Rana boylii,* one of the five frogs of the genus *Rana* that are native to California. Ranid frogs are often called "true frogs" and are represented by various species in practically every part of the world. More than thirty species of ranids are found in the United

States alone. Among these is the northern leopard frog, *Rana pipiens,* a creature often used in high school biology classes of the past. Another is the common bullfrog, *Rana catesbeiana,* the critter whose legs are served in certain restaurants.

Ranids look like what many people, especially Americans and Europeans, think of when they think of frogs. They have long hind legs, long toes with webbing on the rear feet, and their topsides are green or brown or some variation of either color. When fully grown, most average a size that fits neatly into the palm of an adult human's hand, but they can get even larger.

Foothill yellow-legged frogs like to live in riffling streams with rocky or cobblestone bottoms loaded with crannies in which they can hide to escape predators. They like it where the banks and water surfaces are covered by a mix of sun and shade, the same sort of idyllic setting that a weekend fisherman wants. The Kern River has lots of spots like that, and it is still popular for camping and fishing. But if Jennings camped there today, he wouldn't find another Lazarus. There have been no confirmed reports of any sightings of foothill yellow-legged frogs on the Kern River since the early 1970s. In fact, Jennings says, that frog is gone from 45 percent of the places it once lived in California.

When Mark was a boy, foothill yellow-leggeds could be found in streams in much of Northern California and part of Southern California. Jennings recalls one time he saw a foothill yellow-legged in the east fork of Santa Paula Creek in the hills above his hometown. It was May of 1970. "We have the date on Mom's little calendar," he explains. He was on a Boy Scout camping trip, and his mother routinely noted such occasions in calendars that she then saved after the year was out. Jennings returned to that stream and others nearby many times over the succeeding years. But that one trip stands out: "That was the last time I saw *Rana boylii* in Southern California."

Under normal circumstances, Jennings's story about the foothill yellow-legged frog might be interesting, but no cause for great concern. Papers noting an apparent disappearance or decline of some species of frog or salamander occasionally have surfaced throughout the history and literature of herpetology, the science that studies amphibians and reptiles. But since the late 1970s, and particularly since the early 1980s, stories recounting unquestionable declines like that of *Rana boylii* have become so common that scientists are alarmed.

In Australia, for instance, scientists discovered in 1974 a rare frog that actually regurgitated its babies. The mother frog's odd physiology held promise for use as a model for devising better treatments for stomach ulcers. Six years later the two known populations, harbored in an apparently pristine rain forest, disappeared. The frog hasn't been seen since. Researchers estimate that twenty-six of Australia's 202 species of frog are in trouble.

In Costa Rica, photos of the orange-colored golden toad, *Bufo periglenes,* have commonly been used on tourism posters promoting the country's wild attractions. As late as the summer of 1992, frog lovers were traveling to the mountain village of Monteverde, on the edge of the toad's protected forest home, in hopes of glimpsing it. But the toad hasn't been seen in significant numbers since 1987, and not at all since 1989. It disappeared almost overnight. At the same time, several other varieties of frogs and toads and salamanders disappeared or dramatically declined in the Monteverde area.

In the mountains of Oregon, Colorado, and California, several kinds of amphibians, including Yosemite toads, Cascade frogs, leopard frogs, and western toads, dropped in number in the early 1980s and have not recovered. Some of these animals were once so abundant that scientists and backpackers recall having to take care not to step on them when hiking in the high country. One informal survey of scientists in the northeastern United States suggests there may be declines there in as many as twelve types of salamanders and eight types of frogs.

Scientists report having a difficult or impossible time finding certain species of once-abundant frogs in the Peruvian and Ecuadoran

Andes. In Puerto Rico, one type of common frog has not been seen in a decade, even though there has been no obvious change made to its habitat.

The list of declines became so long and unnerving by the late 1980s that scientists who work with frogs slowly and cautiously began sharing their tales of frog-finding difficulty with their colleagues. Among herpetologists, particularly those who work in the field more than in laboratories, being able to find amphibians traditionally has been a matter of pride. If a graduate student returned from a summer field trip complaining about not being able to find animals, colleagues and teachers assumed the student was not very competent. So when the professionals began sharing their experiences of not finding frogs, it was almost cathartic, like releasing some horrible family secret.

The notion that something as common as a frog should be disappearing is a strange one, considering amphibian history. Scientists estimate that the first amphibians appeared about 350 million years ago. At the time, the planet Earth contained one huge landmass and one even larger ocean. Plants and insects lived on land, and vertebrates—animals that have backbones and nervous systems—in water. Among the vertebrates was a class of bony fish called *Osteichthyes,* and within that class there were, among others, lungfish and lobe-fin fish. Somehow, one of these two fish—which one is a matter of scientific debate—evolved into a creature that had legs where fins would normally be and a physiology that allowed it to leave the water and walk on land for long periods. This creature crawled out of some swamp somewhere and a new class was born: Amphibia. Animals in this class were mostly terrestrial but usually lived in water at some point during their life cycles.

Over the eons, amphibians have evolved from a single group of large animals into three groups or orders of small animals: Caudata, Anura, and Gymnophiona. The order Caudata includes salamanders and newts, the slender, four-legged, tailed animals that look something like lizards with scaleless bodies. There are about 390 species of Caudata, and most are found in the Northern Hemisphere.

Gymnophiona are caecilians, secretive creatures that live under leaf cover or underground. They look more like very large worms than anything else. Scientists know relatively little about caecilians, and the number of people in the world who study them could probably fit into a standard-size hot tub. There are about 160 known species of caecilians.

The third order, Anura, are frogs and toads. Anurans are the most abundant amphibians and are represented by about 3,960 species. They also are the noisiest amphibians, and the croaking or whistling call of males looking for mates is one of the harbingers of spring in many parts of the world. The distinction between frogs and toads is imprecise. In general, toads are wartier, have poison glands, and can tolerate drier conditions. Toads are types of frogs, but frogs are not types of toads. Herpetologists often use the word *frog* to refer to both.

Scientists estimate that the first frog evolved from the main amphibian lineage about 150 million to 200 million years ago. Researchers usually date the beginning of complex life on Earth at 600 million years ago. Within those 600 million years, at least five—and some scientists say six—major global mass extinctions stripped the world of many of its creatures. At least two of the mass extinctions occurred after the appearance of frogs. The most famous was the one 65 million years ago that some researchers attribute to the effects of an asteroid's collision with the Earth. The collision churned up so much dust, according to one theory, that the Earth was darkened, precipitating climatic changes and food shortages. The great dinosaurs disappeared during this period. But the frogs survived. Scientists estimate that during each mass extinction at least half of all animal species died. Yet through at least two of these events, frogs have endured.

But something is very different in the world today from the way it was 150 million or even 65 million years ago. Humans have evolved and become, in very quick order, the Earth's dominant and most destructive animal. Formerly, a set of naturally occurring events would prompt earthly environmental cataclysms like mass extinctions. No single creature could be blamed for these events; they just happened from a combination of geologic and atmospheric conditions. Now, though, environmental disasters are routinely created by humans, and real cataclysms are within our ability to cause as well. People like Mark Jennings worry that significant numbers of amphibian species are facing another mass extinction. This one, though, seems to be brought about by humans at a breakneck pace. And this one may be the one that the frogs fail to survive, unless someone does something soon to stop it.

Other animals that share the late twentieth century with humans and frogs are also in danger. Large mammals—bears, wolves, and the like—have declined dramatically as their habitats have been wiped out. Birds have suffered similarly. Any amateur naturalist can name at least one bird that has captured headlines because its numbers seemed to tilt toward extinction. Peregrine falcons, brown pelicans, bald eagles, California condors, and a list of songbirds are just a few, not to mention the famous spotted owl of the Northwestern old-growth forests.

Most people know about the plights of these feathered and furred animals because they have had strong advocates. They are, as wildlife managers sometimes call them, "charismatic megafauna." They are animals who touch a public nerve, draw attention, and get action. They are represented by groups such as the Audubon Society, first organized in the late nineteenth century to stop the wholesale slaughter of birds for their feathers, or the National Wildlife Federation, originally started to represent the interests of the gun-and-rod crowd, who wanted to make sure there would be plenty of wild land and wildlife around for recreational enjoyment. Even state and federal fish and game agencies have a history of advocating the preservation and protection of these megafauna.

Frogs and toads, on the other hand, haven't had such advocates.

They are hairless, slick, sometimes slimy, and even warty—characteristics that many people find aesthetically displeasing and even offensive. Most of them don't have any value as edible game; eating some would send you to your grave. You can't hug a frog. Unless you have a very unusual sense of style, you can't easily mount a dead frog and decorate a room with it—although in some parts of the world you can buy a small purse made from a giant toad's skin. But even that item seems more tasteless than valuable. So the frogs and toads, despite a long history of important roles in art, literature, folklore, and fertility rites, have arrived at the end of this century in dire straits.

Amphibians are facing what some herpetologists consider a crisis. Some even suggest that the frog declines may be indicators of greater environmental problems. By 1990, a decade or more after the crisis began for many of the species, a collection of scientists raised the first loud alarm that something was wrong. Then the scientists took on the challenge of responding to the crisis.

Different scientists responded in different ways. Some formed committees to oversee more committees to figure out how to respond, much like any bureaucracy. Some headed back out to marshes and ponds to actually count frogs and examine their living conditions in an effort to identify exactly which amphibians were declining and which ones were doing fine, and why. Some drafted grant proposals and received funding for multiyear studies that included lab experiments to answer some of the toughest unanswered questions about declines. Some worked harder to protect the amphibians they knew were in danger. One, for instance, spent many months battling motorcycle gangs, more politely called off-road vehicle enthusiasts, who routinely plowed their noisy vehicles through a rare toad's mating grounds with the U.S. Forest Service's tacit approval. Some did a little bit of everything.

The way each scientist has acted on the declining frog issue has usually reflected individual interests and philosophies. Some are mostly concerned about how the research should be conducted.

Others believe frogs could be a good vehicle for making other environmental and scientific issues more compelling. Some, like Mark Jennings, are simply passionately interested in frogs, particularly rare frogs. The single thread tying all these scientists together has been a desire to know why frogs are disappearing.

Sometimes their task is like piecing a mystery together. At other times it is simply acknowledging and then quantifying what seems perfectly obvious. All the while, some of the researchers worry that they are witnessing a global environmental disaster that merely includes frogs as early victims and could end with humans. If such a disaster is in the works, will the typically slow pace of science mean that they will identify the disaster's cause only after it is too late to be corrected?

I am a journalist, and for nearly three years I followed these scientists as they looked for answers. That meant sloshing through marshes and watching mud ooze up to my knees as I took one precarious step after another, trying to keep up with experienced field biologists. It meant traveling thousands of miles to see for myself that there was nothing now where once there had been hundreds of frogs and toads. It meant spending a glorious day in an isolated bog where there were still hundreds of frogs, as well as birds and insects and sounds of nature that are themselves becoming rare. It meant standing in warehouses on the edge of the Los Angeles International Airport, watching inspectors open styrene foam cartons packed with frogs destined for pet stores, many of them already dead from travel. It meant spending dozens of hours on telephone interviews and long days in libraries hunting down journal articles. It meant having some questions answered and some left unanswered because there simply weren't answers yet. In that way my experience was much like that of the scientists working on the declining amphibian issue—there were more questions than answers.

This is the story of the scientists and their search for answers. Appropriately, the search begins with a question: What happened to the famous golden toad of Monteverde?

2

. . . .

Costa Rican Gold

The golden toad was to other toads what Marilyn Monroe was to other Hollywood sex symbols. It was mystery and unmatched glamour. The first scientific paper describing it was titled "An Extraordinary New Toad from Costa Rica." That was in 1967. Even today the golden toad still stands out as one of the most extraordinary toads ever discovered.

Although most toads are tough and warty and earthy, this variety was shiny and brilliant. The males were an unbelievably bright orange in color. Herpetologist Jay Savage's reaction upon first seeing them was typical. "I must confess that my initial response when I saw them was one of disbelief and suspicion that someone had dipped the examples in enamel paint," he wrote in the paper describing them.

The females looked entirely different from the males, but, as Savage wrote, "equally astonishing." They were slightly larger than the tiny males, which measured less than two inches from nose to rear, and they didn't have a speck of orange on their bodies. Instead, they were a dark olive to black and had spots of scarlet encircled by yellow. Together the male and female toads were gaudy opposites, the yin and yang of color.

This extreme difference in appearance between the males and

females, an example of a phenomenon called *sexual dimorphism,* was unusual and fascinated scientists. But equally fascinating were the toads' living and breeding habits. They lived in only a handful of spots within a range of a few kilometers in the cloud-shrouded forest above the small mountain town of Monteverde. They bred only during a few weeks each spring, usually in April, when the weather was rainy, windy, and harsh at their ridgetop habitat. Then the males would gather in groups of hundreds at a time in small, temporary pools of water, waiting to court the females, who would emerge from hiding to select a mate and lay a string of two hundred to four hundred eggs—each egg barely the size of an infant's tear-drop. The breeding bout would last for a week to ten days. Sometimes the toads would have another breeding session within a few weeks. But once the brief season was over, the toads would disappear for another year. Herpetologists speculated that they spent the time out of sight underground, dug into cubbyholes and caverns. Rarely were they seen outside of this brief period.

Despite the toad's unusual characteristics, few scientists spent any time following the creature or exploring its habits in depth during the twenty years after Savage's description. This is not so strange considering that those years in the tropics were filled with new discoveries that competed for scientific attention. Researchers and conservationists realized from early on, however, that the golden toad was rare. Its range was so limited and its numbers so few that it was recognized as endangered.

Its beauty and rarity helped give the toad a certain status and public-relations power unusual for an amphibian. In 1972, one young scientist who had done research in the Monteverde cloud forest and feared its destruction used the toad as a centerpiece in a successful campaign to entice American conservationists to donate money to establish a nature preserve in the forest. The Monteverde Cloud Forest Preserve's birth seemed to secure the golden toad's future. It was protected from collecting for the pet trade. Its prime habitat, on a ridge called the Brillante, was secured from development. In time, the toad even grew to seem more widespread than it actually was, as its image became a common feature of Costa Rican tourism posters. The golden toad became famous even as it was poorly understood.

In 1987, Martha Crump had an unplanned meeting with the golden toad that would entice her to try to learn more than any other scientist knew about it. Crump, an ecologist and herpetologist who was a professor at the University of Florida, had traveled to Monteverde to do research on tree-frog tadpoles. She planned to collect information to help her understand how some tadpoles use cannibalism to survive their vulnerable stage of life. She was happy to have a brief break from teaching to do fieldwork in the tropics that she loved.

The mountains and rich, wet forests of Costa Rica are part of the New World tropics or neotropics that span Central and South America. These tropics are a gold mine for biologists. They are packed with plants, animals, and insects. Scientists estimate that Central and South America combined contain up to three-fourths of the world's amphibian species. Costa Rica, smaller in area than West Virginia, alone has more than 150 known amphibian species. By comparison, the entire United States has just over two hundred. Researchers say that there are still thousands upon thousands of plant, animal, and insect species waiting to be seen and described in the tropics. A patient and observant scientist's chance of discovering something new is great, and knowing that always made the tropics that much more exciting to Crump. "It's like Christmas, it's so new," she once said.

Research in the tropical forests near Monteverde has been made all the more attractive by the small town's quirky combination of Costa Ricans, American Quakers, and scientists. Scientists, for the most part, have been welcomed and encouraged. The town—which looks less like a town than like a scattered collection of inns, a few small restaurants, and a cheese factory at the base of a forest—

sits four or five kilometers below the Brillante. Until 1951 there were only a few Costa Rican families living in the area. Then a troop of eleven American Quaker families settled there. The Quakers came mostly from Alabama after four men in the group had served prison terms of one year and one day for refusing to register for the post–World War II draft. Monteverde appealed to the Quakers because it had land they could buy and clear for pasture, and mountain streams that could be tapped for water. Not insignificantly, it was also located in a country that had no standing army and no draft.

Biologists began coming to Monteverde in notable numbers to do research in the early 1960s. Savage was one of the first to encourage his graduate students to study tropical amphibians there. As the years passed, the preserve was created and expanded, ensuring that unlogged forest would continue to be available for study. By the early 1990s, the preserve covered 26,000 acres and was a sizable natural laboratory for tropical scientists. It was also, by then, an increasingly strong magnet for tourists. So many were visiting each year that the preserve's caretakers were struggling with how to accommodate visitors without damaging the community and the forest.

But those were worries that were just beginning to develop in 1987. In retrospect, that year seems like some naïvely innocent time. The pounding Crump heard on her front door late one windy, rainy April night seemed so much less important than it would years later.

Crump opened her door and found, standing on the stoop, Wolf Guindon, fit and rugged, dripping wet, smiling, and full of excitement. "Marty, the golden toads are out," he announced. "You've got to come see them!"

Guindon was one of Monteverde's original Quaker settlers, and he has probably spent more time than anyone else hiking in the mountains above the town. He was one of the first to see a golden toad in the 1960s, and his land was part of the parcel that formed the first bits of the preserve to protect the toad in 1972. He may well have seen more golden toad breeding sessions than anyone else living. And on this day, despite the spring storm beating down on the hills, Guindon had hiked up to the Brillante and gleefully discovered the toads were breeding again.

To view the golden toads breeding is like seeing the northern lights. The experience is brief and breathtaking. Crump had been to Monteverde several times, but had never witnessed this rare event. She didn't have to think twice about Guindon's demand. They agreed to meet the next morning to hike to the Brillante.

The Brillante lies in line with the continental divide, and is in the path of almost constant winds that drive up the lowlands on the Caribbean side of the ridge and pound the dense, wet forest. Here the trees are up to about thirty-five feet high, taller than a three-story building and certainly much taller than any mythical elf. Still, it is called elfin forest, and when compared with the towering canopy of the main forest only a few hundred yards away, where the winds are calmer, the reason for the diminutive classification is clear. Trees in the main forest reach to well over one hundred feet high.

The rain was still falling steadily, the wind was blowing, and it was bitterly cold by the time Crump met with Guindon the next morning. The trek up the Brillante was only a few kilometers, but the going was difficult. The ridge sits at about five thousand feet above sea level. That translates into cloud level in these mountains. It is almost always moist on the Brillante, either with rain or cloud droplets.

The trail was slick and muddy, and with each step, Crump's rubber boots sank ankle deep. The stunted trees on the ridge, their branches covered with mosses and epiphytes that soak up the cloud mist like sponges, creaked eerily as they moved in the wind. Their root tops sat exposed above the soil, like the claws of an antique bathtub, allowing the trees to bend and sway with the wind without being toppled. The roots' rise and fall created gaps, bowls, and small caverns in the terrain. The rains had filled some of these bowls and turned them into temporary pools. Guindon led Crump to one of these small pools, and any thoughts she had of the difficult trail vanished. Hundreds of the male toads, each one less than two inches long, gathered there in a tight pack. They sat like brilliant flashes of shiny porcelain among the ferns and heliconia.

"They've been described as little jewels on the forest floor, and that's really the impression you get," Crump recalled several years later. "And as long as you're still and quiet, you can just sit and watch them."

For a while, Crump did just that. Then she gave in to the biologist's urge to add new information to what was already known. She began to collect physical data on the toads. Holding a large plastic bag containing a little water, she grabbed toads and placed them in the bag as fast as she could. Then she removed toads from the bag, one by one, measured their length and weight, and released them to their pool. It took hours, and the wind continued blowing, the rain continued falling, and Crump shivered from the cold. By the end of the day, though, she was entranced by the odd little toad and wanted to keep studying it.

Crump was most interested in the toad's breeding habits. Some information about the golden toad's breeding had been collected by students during two seasons several years earlier. On those occasions the student scientists watched male toads gather in pools and wait for females to come near. When one did, she was often the unwitting victim of a gang attack. The males struggled, several at a time, to mount the female. When one male finally moved into the preferred position on the female's back and locked his arms around her, he was the victor. But other toads would continue to harass the couple, occasionally driving them temporarily from the pool. A couple would remain locked together for hours, sometimes even an entire day, until the female laid her string of eggs in the pool as the male released sperm over them..

Crump decided to try to add details about the golden toad's

breeding habits to a growing pool of information about toads worldwide. The details would help fill out the story of how toads evolved. For the next eight days, as long as the toads remained visible and active, she hiked to the Brillante and gathered data. She measured the water depth and temperature in the pools. She spent long hours just watching the toads' behavior. She became their unofficial diarist.

During that spring the golden toads had two breeding sessions, the first in April and another in May. Crump followed both and monitored the fate of the eggs. Golden toad eggs have been known to take about two months to develop from egg to tadpole to toadlet. This year, before that metamorphosis could be completed, most of the ponds dried, and few—if any—toadlets survived. The high mortality didn't seem particularly strange to Crump, since many toads and frogs lay a lot more eggs than ever make it to tadpole and toadlet or froglet stages. Also, the student researchers had observed egg dessication in 1977 and 1982. Crump knew, however, that she couldn't come to firm conclusions about typical golden toad egg survivorship unless she had more data. What she found in a single season might merely be an oddity. The rules of statistics, a supporting rib in science, dictated that her data would be more valuable if it reflected more than one breeding season.

Crump's research break ended in July. She returned to the University of Florida and began searching for a way to continue the golden toad work. There are only a few sources for money for basic research of animals—commonly called "whole organisms" by scientists. One is the National Geographic Society, so Crump applied to that organization for a grant to support herself and a graduate student for two more seasons of golden toad research. The grant came through, and by early 1988 Crump was back in Monteverde with her student.

The two researchers arrived several weeks before the breeding season started, but they began hiking up to the Brillante right away. "For a while we felt silly going up, because the weather wasn't appropriate. But we did it anyway, because you don't want to take a chance of missing them," Crump told me several years later. Then the seasonal rains began and the breeding pools filled with water. Everything appeared perfect for breeding, and Crump expected to see a bowlful of toads each day as she hiked the trail. Yet the toads never appeared.

"We kept thinking, 'Well, tomorrow.' The next day. And this went on for a couple of months and there was nothing." She leans forward slightly for emphasis. "Nothing! I just could not believe it!"

In the middle of this search, Crump had to leave for a week in Ann Arbor, Michigan, to attend a joint annual conference of the three national associations for herpetologists. She was scheduled to present a talk about golden toad breeding habits. She had hoped to have new data by the time of the meeting. Instead she had to present remnants of her 1987 data.

"It was at that meeting that I announced to this huge audience that the golden toads hadn't come out and we didn't know why. That was the first time that anybody outside of Monteverde realized this." But because the breeding season wasn't entirely over, Crump wasn't ready to raise an alarm. Her graduate student remained in Monteverde through the time of the meeting, continuing to monitor the Brillante. He had strict instructions to telephone Crump if toads appeared while she was gone. She expected a call any day. "Well, I never got the call from him, and I was a little bit worried. When I got back to Monteverde and found out nothing had happened, that was disappointing."

By the time the season was over, in July, Crump had seen only ten golden toads, and just one of them was in the primary breeding area of the Brillante. None were actively breeding. Wolf Guindon had walked the hills regularly for decades, and he could not remember a single year since their discovery that the golden toads had not bred. However, he had not kept notes on his observations, and Crump figured it was still possible that the toads might have missed a breeding year in the past. What she was witnessing simply might be one bad year. "I guess I didn't really think there was something wrong because in my experience, working with tropical anurans, there's just so much unpredictability," she says. "I guess I was just used to the fact that you can't count on anything, including a species breeding exactly when you think it's going to."

Still, Crump had a nagging feeling that something wasn't entirely right. Even if the toads didn't want to breed, she couldn't figure out why they weren't coming out in any significant numbers, at least to take a look around. "It just seemed to me that they should be checking out the situation. That's what other amphibians do. You find someone hanging around," she says. "And we just never saw that."

Crump returned to Florida and contacted the National Geographic Society to report the progress—or lack of progress—of her research. Her contact there assured her that the society understood that fieldwork with animals was unpredictable. She received her second year's funding, and again (with a different graduate student this time) she returned to Monteverde in early 1989. Again they regularly hiked up to the Brillante, anxious not to miss the first emerging toad. This year the weather appeared even wetter than it had been in 1988, so Crump began the season feeling optimistic. As the weeks wore on, though, they found only a single toad. It was on the Brillante in the same spot where Crump's student had found a lonely toad the year before.

Now Crump was truly concerned. "I had this really panicky feeling inside me that it might be something I did. That maybe I left a virus in the forest or something that wiped them out. I just had this really awful feeling that I personally had done something to these toads."

Marty Crump sits at a table in her dining room in her home in the foothills of northern Arizona as she tells me this story. The day is brilliantly clear, with a cool snap in the air, and the mountains due north of her house look close enough to touch. Her children's cat scampers by, and her husband, a biologist who specializes in hummingbirds, passes through to drop off mail before he returns to their home office in a converted barn next door. She is a slender woman of medium height, wholesome in both appearance and manner. She is hardly the image of the Typhoid Mary to toads that she had worried she had become.

Crump left Monteverde after the 1989 breeding season to begin a year's fieldwork in Argentina. But she continued to ponder what had happened in Monteverde. She also arranged for Guindon to look for breeding toads the following spring. Meanwhile, in September, she flew to Canterbury, England, to attend the First World Congress of Herpetology. The conference, attended by more than 1,300 scientists from around the world, proved to be a turning point for Crump and for declining amphibians.

In science, conferences are a weird combination of final exam, political convention, and networking party. The heart of any conference is the researchers' presentation of papers about their work. Often these papers are about research that has yet to be published. The conference becomes their first public unveiling, a chance to weigh their peers' responses and adjust their work to answer unanticipated criticisms. The papers give the gathering its aura of high-minded activity. But the real action, just as at any political convention, often occurs away from the podium. In conference center hallways, lobbies, bars, and restaurants, ideas are floated, lobbying is conducted, gossip is shared, and jobs are offered. Hundreds of papers were presented at the Canterbury meeting. A few reported on some amphibian declines. But it was the hallway chatter that began to change the way many herpetologists thought about the creatures they studied, and set the stage for alarm.

Crump was not scheduled to report formally on her golden toad work. But when a few friends asked her how it was going, she told them about the missing toads. Pretty soon, word of this spread through the conference, and other researchers started approaching Crump during breaks. Some just wanted more information about the toads' disappearance. Many, though, wanted to share their own stories of seeing a decline in the populations they worked with. Like Crump, some had secretly worried that they had caused the decline through something they had done. But now the problem was out in the open, and it was clearly more widespread and complicated than they had thought. They could put away their fears that they were, individually, the cause. "I think all of us felt an incredible relief," Crump says.

One of the people Crump talked to at the conference was David Wake, a biologist who would, within a few months, become a sort of spokesman for disappearing frogs. A proper and reserved man who got his first taste of biology from a grandfather who was a preacher and amateur naturalist, Wake has the kind of résumé that many academicians dream about. His 1964 doctoral dissertation analyzing the differences among species of lungless salamanders and their evolution was, by many accounts, brilliant. It became the foundation of a solid career in evolutionary biology that began with a teaching post at the University of Chicago in the mid-1960s. In 1969 he was hired away by the University of California, Berkeley, where, two years later, he became head of the school's prestigious Museum of Vertebrate Zoology.

These credentials, accumulated before Wake had reached his forties, gave him fair-haired-boy status in academia, and soon he was climbing more ladders of distinction. He became one of a special category of achiever who matches early scientific accomplishment with increasing skill in science politics. By the time of Canterbury, he was a president, past president, or soon-to-be president and member or past member of a number of science organizations and special boards, including the National Research Council's Board on Biology, an arm of the National Academy of Sciences. He was notable for being well connected in the world of biological science politics.

One thing Wake was not always noted for, however, was a driving interest in conservation or applied biology. One scientist who was a student at Berkeley during Wake's early years there recalls him complaining that such activities were intellectually stultifying. Questions about animal behavior, habitat, mating practices, feeding habits, and population trends—the stuff that is the underpinning of wildlife management and conservation—weren't high on his list of priorities. Wake was typically more interested in questions of how the Earth and its inhabitants evolved. An animal's habits, behavior, genetics, and morphology—the design of its body—were primarily interesting to him if they could shed light on evolution. For Wake, amphibians, specifically salamanders, were tools to explain one part of the Earth's genealogy.

Wake had been collecting and using salamanders in his work since the late 1950s. By the 1980s he was having trouble finding animals in places where they had once been plentiful. One of those places was Monteverde. One November day there in 1988, Wake found only three frogs and no salamanders where just a year before he had found more than four dozen amphibians, including four different kinds of salamanders. "Hard to understand," he wrote in his field notes that day.

Occasionally, Wake had heard casual reports of colleagues having trouble in other places finding animals. Then the reports started getting more frequent. Now, at Canterbury, Wake realized they were too common to be cast aside as anomalies. As the week-long conference progressed, he continued asking other scientists about their experience with declines, and talking about what could be done in response. By the time the conference was over, though, neither he nor anyone else had a clear idea of what to do. But he knew something needed to be done.

A few weeks after the Canterbury meeting, a scientist far from the world of frogs and salamanders helped Wake decide on a course of action. The help came while Wake was in Washington, D.C., visiting the National Academy of Sciences headquarters on Constitution Avenue.

The National Academy of Sciences is an unusual, private, nonprofit institution that was initiated by President Abraham Lincoln in 1863 and chartered by the U.S. Congress. It is funded mostly through endowments and contract fees. One of its primary purposes is to advise the government on science and technology issues. It typically does this through its National Research Council by tapping the expert scientists around the country to sit on various boards and committees organized to address specific issues. Scientists usually regard an invitation to serve on a board as an honor and a duty. And the committees and boards often produce major reports that become the basic texts of public policy debates about everything from cancer treatment to pesticide use.

Wake was a member of the National Research Council's Board on Biology and was in Washington to attend a board meeting. The board's members, all biologists from different fields with impressive portfolios, followed their meeting by enjoying dinner and drinks together. During the social hour, Wake casually mentioned to one of his board colleagues the stories he had heard in Canterbury about declining amphibians. He told about the missing golden toads and the salamanders that no longer seemed as abundant as before.

Harold Morowitz listened to Wake intently. Morowitz, a professor at George Mason University, is a biophysicist whose main scientific pursuits have been to examine the ways in which cells transform energy from one form to another, and to explore the origins of life. But he is also something of a Renaissance man. His writings span a broad spectrum of subjects and he is clearly excited by new information about the world outside the boundaries of his own research. What Wake told him about amphibians now astounded him.

Only a few years earlier, the Board on Biology had convened a special session on the loss of biological diversity—the threat to the vastness and variety of the world's animal, insect, and plant life, primarily from habitat destruction. The board then produced a widely read collection of papers about the subject. It continued to be one of the board's hot topics. Board members often chatted about the possible consequences of loss of biodiversity. They had speculated about whether some point would be reached where large-scale diversity losses would seemingly occur with little warning. If that happened, they wondered, where would the losses first be felt? Which animals would be hit first? Now Morowitz wondered aloud if the disappearing frogs were part of the lost-biodiversity story and if they could be a warning of some more serious ecological problem.

Wake knew from experience that nature and its characters could be unpredictable. He felt cautious about drawing any conclusions about the meaning of the decline. But as he talked to Morowitz, and as Morowitz grew more excited about the issue, Wake became excited too. By the end of the evening, someone among the group of people who joined in the conversation between the two scientists suggested that the Board on Biology convene a meeting to determine the nature and extent of the declines worldwide. There weren't many organizations that could respond quickly and convene a meeting to respond to what Morowitz said looked like "a very, very serious species extinction problem." But the board could.

Morowitz was so concerned about the declines that he could not sleep that night. Over the subsequent weeks, he and Wake talked many times by phone. With Oscar Zaborsky, then the administrator for the Board on Biology, they hatched a plan for the meeting. Wake would be in charge of recruiting people to attend. Morowitz and Zaborsky would take charge of finding money to fund the meeting and to fly scientists in from around the world to attend.

They figured they needed about $30,000. Typically, the board funded about 80 percent of its meetings with grants from outside agencies. This meeting, they thought, would be no different.

For several weeks, Morowitz and Zaborsky made the rounds of scientific institutions and agencies in Washington, D.C., asking for money. They were almost like lobbyists for frogs. Inside the Washington Beltway, Morowitz later joked, they became known as the "Herp PAC." They were looking for funds stashed away in uncommitted accounts that agencies or organizations were willing to share on short notice. But they kept hitting walls. Few had uncommitted money, and those that did wouldn't part with it quickly or easily—at least not for frogs.

Morowitz decided he would try to tap conservation organizations for help. Zaborsky arranged for him to attend a luncheon whose attendees included a few conservation group representatives. An incident at the luncheon convinced Morowitz that it would be even harder than he thought to raise money for the frog meeting. He saw how difficult it was for even experienced conservationists to believe that something as common as a frog or toad could be in trouble. As Morowitz began telling the story about declining amphibians, one of the conservation group representatives who had worked in Costa Rica quickly cut him off. The golden toad was not declining, the representative insisted firmly.

Morowitz was stunned. "That totally took the wind out of my sails in the rest of the presentation," he recalled. "I was so teed off and disappointed and all of the above. I'm usually a reasonably subdued human being. I didn't blow my cool at that meeting. But I really lost my concentration because I was worried that he might be right." Morowitz ended his presentation, and as soon as the lunch was over, he called Wake. Had he gotten his information wrong, he worried. Wake assured him that, hard as it was to believe, the golden toad had disappeared. Then Wake and Morowitz tracked down Crump by fax and got more reassurance that they had their facts straight.

Eventually, Morowitz got some commitments for funds from the Smithsonian Institution and the Brookfield Zoo in Chicago, whose director, George Rabb, was a herpetologist. But he still didn't have enough for the kind of meeting the board hoped for. Zaborsky decided to appeal to a special fund controlled by the presidents of the National Academy of Sciences and its sibling organizations, the National Academy of Engineering and the Institute of Medicine. The presidents gave Morowitz and Zaborsky the necessary $30,000. The meeting was scheduled at the National Academy of Sciences West Coast center in Irvine, California.

February 19, 1990, was a beautiful, almost smog-free day in Southern California. Dave Wake and about forty other scientists gathered in a conference room in Irvine, mostly unaware of those nearly idyllic conditions. The room had no windows.

The scientists sat at tables arranged to form a giant rectangle. When space at the tables ran out, several sat in chairs that lined three of the room's four walls. Most of the scientists were men, two were women. Many were herpetologists, but many were not. Some had worked on declining amphibian issues for years, but others had never considered the issue until this day. Still others were there as observers from wildlife conservation organizations or scientific institutions.

Wake let it be known, as he compiled his list of invitees, that he didn't want this meeting to be just a lot of herpetologists sharing stories. He wanted scientists from outside the field to attend as well, to provide perspective. He invited a geneticist, a climatologist, a population ecologist, a veterinary pathologist, and an ecosystems specialist. The outside scientists sat as an informal jury during the first day of the two-day meeting, and scientists who worked with amphibians in different parts of the world presented reports about disappearances.

"I made my first trip to the . . . high Sierra Nevada in 1959," Wake told his colleagues as he opened the meeting, "and in that place I found paradise for a herpetologist." He had been exploring for toads with Charles Walker, a well-known amphibian biologist. Hiking in Yosemite National Park, near the Tioga Pass, they had found so many mountain yellow-legged frogs, *Rana muscosa,* that it was difficult to walk without stepping on them.

Twenty years later he had revisited the same spot. He had still found frogs, but there were fewer than before and they were much harder to find. Then, in the late 1980s, he had returned once more, and the frogs were gone. Not even determined hunting could turn up any, and this was in a national park, a protected area. "Something was happening, and I didn't know what."

Now, he told his colleagues, they were brought together to begin to address the disappearances in a formal manner for the first time. The first question they had to answer was whether there were in fact declines.

For the next five hours, one scientist after another, thirteen in all, stepped to the front of the room and told of declines and disappearances. Australia, Canada, Costa Rica, Brazil, Panama, California, Oregon, Colorado, Wyoming, Central Europe, Germany, Switzerland—the list of places grew as the hours passed. Wake shared a log he had lately collected of disappearances or declines noted by others, both scientists and nonscientists, in Japan, Norway, Great Britain, and other places.

The scientists also suggested possible causes. The overriding one was habitat destruction, ranging from rain-forest deforestation in Brazil to the paving over of wetlands to build shopping centers in the United States; from logging in the Pacific Northwest to filling in rice paddies to build golf courses in Japan. But simple habitat destruction couldn't explain everything. Frogs were disappearing in areas such as the Monteverde Cloud Forest Preserve, areas which are protected from destruction. In some areas, too, some frog species were disappearing while others were doing fine. In California, for instance, tiny green Pacific tree frogs, *Pseudacris* (formerly *Hyla*) *regilla,* seemed as abundant as cockroaches in a garbage dump in areas where other native frogs were disappearing. Wood frogs, *Rana sylvatica,* and chorus frogs, *Pseudacris triseriata,* continued to thrive in the Colorado Rockies even as leopard frogs and boreal toads, *Bufo boreas boreas,* dramatically declined there. At one long-studied site in Panama, two species of native frogs had disappeared even as three others increased in number.

The scientists speculated that where obvious habitat destruction by bulldozer and chain saw wasn't a cause, other, less visible problems were killing the animals: acid rain, drought, pesticides, human exploitation (killing and collecting for food and the pet trade), and new predators, such as fish introduced for sportfishing. A few suggested that ozone layer depletion or global climatic change might be having effects, especially on high-mountain species or on species living on the margins of their natural ranges.

By the end of the first day, the jury pronounced itself convinced that frogs and other amphibians were definitely declining in some places. But the evidence was mostly anecdotal. Science thrives on numbers—data, hard evidence, and trends that can be quantified, especially over a long period of time. Researchers needed more data. Now, they wondered, what information should they collect and how should they go about collecting it? What should be their next step?

On the second day of the meeting, the scientists began to try to answer those questions. They seemed to agree on little. As an observer sent by a conservation organization later wrote in a report about the meeting, "I'm afraid there was some floundering around . . . when talk came to the final recommendations and prospects for continuing the momentum generated by this workshop."

Some argued that there was sufficient information to show that certain species were declining and that the research emphasis should be on finding out why immediately, while there was still time to save them from extinction. Others countered that more data had to be collected over a longer period on even those species before their disappearance could be fully understood.

Some said that conducting surveys—going out into the field and counting amphibians—was the best way to begin. Others said that specific sites should be selected and that entire ecosystems, not only amphibians, should be examined and evaluated. Conducting ecosystem studies, the latter group asserted, would be the only way to persuade scientists outside herpetology that funding for frog-decline research was worth backing. But, opponents countered, such studies were extremely expensive and site-specific. If the decline was worldwide, one intensive study in one site would answer questions only for that area.

The political reality now, Morowitz told the researchers at one point, was that the amphibian people had to "think big," just like the molecular biologists who successfully pushed the human genome project until it became a specially funded project within the National Institutes of Health. The scientists needed to generate public support to help free up funding for research. And one of the strongest arguments the amphibian biologists had for getting the public and other scientists on board was that amphibians could be good biological indicators of the environment's health. A frog, the amphibian experts stressed, could be viewed as a sort of living thermometer for Earth's environmental health.

Yet even the suggestion to increase public interest in amphibians drew some dissent. "My research is already threatened by the animal-rights movement," one scientist complained. "I'm a little bothered about a riot of publicity."

"Why are we here, then?" another retorted.

Wake wanted amphibian declines publicized. While putting the meeting together, he had decided that he wanted it open to the press, and had had to push the National Research Council staff to make sure it was open. He and Morowitz both believed that the amphibian decline, especially the loss of something as common as a frog, could enliven public interest in the whole issue of lost biological diversity. "We are losing lots and lots of specialists. We're homogenizing. We're losing diversity," he told reporters during a break in the meeting. "The name of the game in biology is diversity. Diversity in and of itself is the goal. Without diversity, we lose options."

But Wake understood his worried colleague's hesitancy about one of the prices of publicity. Many scientists who work with animals worry that one day their labs will be vandalized by animal-rights activists, destroying years of research. "I think we badly need public education," he told the colleague. "What we need is a system to educate them fully, not just alarm them."

As the meeting wound down, though, it became uncomfortably clear to the scientists in the room that the conference would end without such a system and with little consensus on how to proceed. One key problem, Wake believed, was that they lacked any institution or organization to take the lead. The Board on Biology's mandate was to compile reports and recommendations, not to create worldwide research projects, and the amphibian specialists didn't have a strong organization of their own to carry on the cause. Within the few scientific organizations specifically addressing herpetology, amphibian biologists are in the minority, since most herpetologists are reptile specialists. This lack of an organization, Wake told reporters, was one reason the amphibian decline had proceeded for nearly a decade unmentioned and almost unnoticed. Now, he lamented to his colleagues, the lack was especially troublesome. "We are all painfully aware that, once we walk out of here, we won't have any continuing organizational support." Wake worried that the decline issue would now fall by the wayside. A few among the group suggested future meetings or volunteered to organize presentations at other scientific conferences. Some of the researchers organized themselves into committees to spread the word.

To several of the active field biologists in the room, suggestions to build more organizations and conduct more meetings were especially frustrating. Many of the latest declines could be traced back to the early 1980s. At least eight years of inactivity had passed before the Irvine conference. Time was running out, they worried. Some of the declining populations could disappear entirely before their colleagues had finished organizing to discuss again how to proceed.

"I feel all of a sudden a sense of procrastination here," complained one herpetologist who had witnessed rain-forest destruction in Brazil. "We know there is a problem right now. We should be moving on that problem. It's very urgent to get moving, not to keep having meetings, not to keep having congresses."

3

. . . .

In the Field I

It is late on an April night, and Mark Jennings and I are standing stone-still on the edge of a slow-moving creek, trying to be as quiet as possible. The creek is stepped and flows down a gully, occasionally ballooning into deep pools, then flowing some more. Grasses and low-growing bushes hug the banks. Tall willows clump around the edges in some spots, creating a canopy over the pools. The strong aroma of sage spikes the air. In the dark, this seems like a hidden wilderness, a classic example of what naturalists call riparian habitat. The footprints of cattle that have grazed here recently are invisible, the willows they have gnawed appear untouched. A paved road runs just ten yards from the gully, and the sound of a passing car occasionally creeps down to creekside. We barely notice it, however, because we are concentrating on the edges of a pool in the creek where a crescent of reeds grows thick and straight.

A few feet in front of us, Marc Hayes is standing in the water pointing a light beam at the reeds, playing it off the place where the plants emerge from the pool surface. The light comes from a small round lamp of the sort that a miner would wear on his helmet. It is attached by a cord to a book-size rechargeable battery pack that hangs on Hayes's belt. Jennings is holding a similar light, and points it at another spot in the reeds. Occasionally a frog croaks some-where in the darkness, but both men ignore it because they can tell by the pitch of the two-beat croak that it is a Pacific tree frog, the most common frog in California and not one they are interested in right now. The sound is familiar to me because this creature's voice has been used for background night music in thousands of Holly-wood movies. I point my light at a clump of grass to try to catch a glimpse of the animal, but the sound stops.

Hayes, a herpetologist and ecologist, has flown for six hours from Miami to California, and then ridden two hours with Jen-nings and me in the crowded cab of Jennings's truck to get to this place called Corral Hollow. It is located about thirty-five miles east of San Francisco Bay, as the crow flies. Both men believe this pool in the hollow may hold something much more unusual than the mouthy tree frogs. They think they may find California red-leggeds here. That frog favors a habitat of creeks with deep pools into which it can dive for safety. It needs overhanging banks under which it can hide, and floating reeds to which it can attach its masses of jelly-coated eggs.

Hayes motions with the light toward a spot at the edge of the reeds that would provide just the right mix of freedom and cover the shy red-legged prefers. "See, it's more open just on the other side there," he says quietly as he steps farther into the water. He is wearing Neoprene chest waders, which look like spongy overalls. He is trying them out for the first time. They are designed for fishermen who are determined to wade into cool mountain lakes to get closer to some perfect near-shore fishing hole, but Hayes is hoping they will work to keep him dry during frog hunting. He is over six feet tall, so with the waders he can venture into about five feet of water without getting soaked.

Tentatively he walks forward, carefully planting each foot on the fallen reeds that form an unstable mat on the pond's floor. His boot soles are made of rough felt to prevent slipping, but they won't be much help if the reeds break through. Within just a few steps, the water is above his thighs. He figures there is another five feet of water below the mat that holds him. The willow leaves and flower seeds that coat the top of the pond now cling to his waders. He stops for a moment, strips off his old brown jacket, and tosses it to Jennings. It's an unspoken signal that Hayes could find water deeper than he expects before he reaches the reeds.

"Just watch him when he goes under," Jennings whispers to me. Jennings has been on dozens of frog hunts with Hayes, and they seem to know instinctively what to expect from each other. Jennings knows, for instance, that Hayes will risk a full-body drenching if he thinks it will help him reach a single small frog. By the time we all gather on this night in 1991, they have spent nearly a decade collaborating on research to figure out why California's native frogs are disappearing.

Jennings and Hayes are sort of a "Cagney and Lacey" of biology; they challenge convention and are loyal friends. Single-minded and determined to the point of abrasiveness, they care about science, both the way it is done and the way it is used, and scorn anyone they think has deviated too far from a standard just short of perfection. And they care about frogs.

Jennings and Hayes both hold doctorates, but neither has a tenure track position at a university or a full-time position with a federal agency, the typical credentials of active researchers. A few months after the Irvine meeting, Jennings even abandoned a job working on fish toxicology for the U.S. Fish and Wildlife Service so that he would be free to put in more time on declining amphibians. Now the two researchers are freelancers in a discipline whose members often look with skepticism on freelancing, and distrust anyone not tied full-time to an institution. Sometimes Jennings and Hayes take on projects funded by government agencies. Sometimes they work on projects they fund themselves by scraping together whatever money they can save from consulting jobs, teaching, and other projects.

By going their own way, Jennings and Hayes became pioneers in contemporary frog-decline studies before the topic became a general news item. Their main frog of interest is the California red-legged, and they have managed to identify a suite of causes, some more certain than others, that have combined to push that frog's population to dangerously low levels.

We are here in Corral Hollow on this night because Jennings and Hayes are trying to finish one of their biggest tasks, a statewide survey of California reptiles and amphibians that seem to be in trouble. They have been working on it since 1988 for a single paycheck that could barely cover the cost of a stripped-down, no-options compact car. They have communicated by phone, by letter, and in person with 135 scientists and others who have actively noted the presence or absence of frogs, toads, and salamanders in California. They have searched museum collections and examined thousands of pickled amphibian specimens, dug through yellowed pages of dead scientists' field notes, and tapped into the hidden veins of university library systems for hints of historic sightings of any of the eighty reptiles and amphibians native to California. Then Jennings and Hayes have gone into the field.

They have waded through creeks, mucked around in marshes, and climbed up more hills than either of them can remember, looking for the amphibians to count, and occasionally to weigh and measure. Their territory is daunting; it covers all of California, which spreads over more than 158,000 square miles. That is more area than New York, Pennsylvania, and Ohio combined. It includes the highest mountains and the lowest deserts in the contiguous forty-eight states, a vast network of rivers and streams, and so many mountain lakes that many are unnamed. Jennings has accumulated about fifty thousand miles of road travel for this survey alone.

Tonight is my first chance to watch Jennings and Hayes at work together. My impression so far is that it is slow, tedious, wet, cold work, but the two scientists seem nearly immune to the discomfort and tedium. They appear almost giddy at times, relieved to be away from telephones, word processors, papers, reports, and journals, and happy to be doing the kind of research that first attracted them to science.

Hayes slogs to within a few feet of the edge of the reeds, where the water reaches to just above his waist. He stands frozen for a moment. In his left hand he holds the lamp at eye level. He focuses the beam on the surface of the water at the reeds, hoping to catch the shine of a frog's eyes. Like a cat preparing to grab a grazing bird, he keeps his right hand poised in a ready position at chest level. Suddenly he jams it into the reeds. His body rocks, and he just barely keeps his footing.

"Oh, shit. Goddamn," he hisses. A splash sounds as a frog dives deep into the water for cover.

"That's a miss," Jennings explains on the sidelines. "If there's no cussing, that means he got it."

Hayes ignores the comment and moves farther into the pond until the water is nearly chest high. "He had his head sticking out above the water," he says, not quite believing the frog's lack of caution. After a near miss, sometimes a red-legged will pop back up several feet away from where it went under. Hayes shines his light, quietly waiting. He paddles his hand across the water. "Ooh, that water's cool," he mutters. After a few minutes he wades back to the bank. "That can't be the only frog in there," he grumbles. Even if it isn't the only one, Hayes knows that the frog is probably one of only a handful still living along this creek.

Corral Hollow sits on the inland side of the coastal mountains that make up the western border of California's Great Central Valley. The streams and creeks here are part of the drainage system for the big valley. Historically the hollow has been used for cattle and sheep grazing. The cattle, at least, still use it. Part of the land now also includes a state-owned playground for people who enjoy their free time in the outdoors by carving tracks into the terrain with motorcycles and other noisy off-road vehicles. Another part of the hollow is home to the Lawrence Livermore Laboratory, where brainy men and women have spent decades conceiving and testing nuclear products, particularly weapons, for the federal government. In the early 1970s the lab decided it had surplus land, and gave the state about one hundred acres to become the Corral Hollow Ecological Reserve. Before it became a reserve with tight restrictions on collecting, the area was a popular place for amateur herpetologists to catch reptiles and amphibians, particularly snakes. On weekend nights, the main road through the hollow would be busy with nightriders who would use their vehicles' headlights or hand-held lamps to spot snakes and lizards that gathered on the warm asphalt after dark.

"This is the first place I ever saw a red-legged frog," Hayes says as he steps out of the water onto the bank. "It was in '79. There must have been thirty frogs in this area." He had spent the previous six years using his spare time trying to find Central Valley locations that still provided a home for red-leggeds. Until Corral Hollow, all the historic frog habitats he had visited in the valley were devoid of red-leggeds. He remembers seeing that first one at the hollow as though it happened just yesterday. "When I saw that frog, I got the equivalent of what's called 'blood fever.' I just sat there and stared at that frog for maybe fifteen minutes." A large female, it floated in a pool, barely moving. Hayes caught it and took it back to the University of Southern California in Los Angeles, where he was a graduate student and spent two rolls of film photographing it. Two weeks later he drove back to Corral Hollow, about six hours north of USC, and released the frog.

Hayes returned to the same three-hundred-yard stretch of creek and pools in 1983 and 1984, and both times he saw ten frogs within a half hour. That was the last time the hollow's red-legged population looked healthy. In 1986, 1989, and 1990, Hayes checked the creek and found nothing; not a single frog popped its head above water or stared straight into his shining light. The statewide statistics for the California red-leggeds are almost as grim. Jennings and Hayes estimate that the red-legged frog has disappeared from 75

percent of its historic range, and about half of that decline has occurred in the last twenty-five years.

For about two hours we slowly walk the stretch of creek. It is
almost an inch-by-inch matter. Walk a few feet, scan the bank with
the light, walk a few feet more, scan again, wait and listen. Hayes
does much of his walking in the water. Jennings stays mostly along
the opposite bank. Sometimes he walks ahead, then turns back and
retraces his steps, all the while keeping an eye on the edge of the
creek. Jennings wears a hat with a broad brim that pushes tree
branches and large bushes away from his face. He also wears rubber
hip boots that reach to mid-thigh, allowing him to walk in and out
of the shallow stream without getting wet. Occasionally the two
chat about what they see.

The trees here aren't doing very well. The grazing cattle are
taking their toll, eating the young saplings before they have time to
grow to replace the older trees. There are signs that the cattle have
also trampled parts of the overhanging creek bank. Break an overhanging bank, destroy a red-legged hiding place. The creek also
looks sandier than it once did. It is filling in with silt contributed
from the stirred-up ground of the off-road-vehicle park upstream.
The broken ground, when hit by rain, becomes a silt factory that
pours its goods into the streams and creeks. Broken banks, damaged trees, and silt all add up to the kind of subtle habitat alterations
that have helped wipe out frogs and toads throughout the western
United States, and possibly elsewhere.

As we come to another pool on this stretch, Hayes stops in his
tracks. "There's a red-legged frog," he says in a stage whisper.

"Now if you can get to him," Jennings answers.

The frog is sitting near a willow log in the middle of the pool, far
from the bank where Hayes is now standing. Slowly Hayes
crouches and even more slowly positions himself on the edge of the
bank, with his feet stretched in front of him, trying not to draw the
frog's attention. He slides carefully into the pool, where the water
reaches to his stomach. The frog still hasn't seen him, or at least

doesn't feel threatened, and remains motionless in the pool. Its face and bulging eyes are above water, its front limbs spread casually in front of it, as though for balance. The rest of its body dangles below the surface. It looks serene, content, anything but alert. Jennings holds a light on the frog, and it sits as though hypnotized. Crickets sing, but the humans here are silent. Hayes moves forward, planting his foot firmly on the pool bottom. But suddenly it gives way, and like a born-again at a baptism, Hayes is up to his shoulders in water.

"Oh, God, that's cold," he blurts. "Jesus."

To varying degrees, frogs will respond to approaching humans. Some, such as Pacific tree frogs, will simply stop calling and freeze. If the human likewise freezes, the frog will soon resume calling. Others, like the California red-leggeds here in this hollow, are very cautious and are likely to dive underwater with any movement a nearby human makes that is swift or sudden. The response is triggered by fairly advanced hearing and peculiar vision.

A frog's hearing is designed to pick up the specific mating calls of loved ones and rivals, but a frog can usually detect predators, intruders, and other noisemakers as well. Frogs hear and feel vibrations through the tympanic membrane that, on most frogs and toads, resembles a tiny drum face on each side of the head. The membrane covers the small, tubular middle ear and leads to a fluid-filled inner ear. Exactly how much they detect, how wide the variation in the sounds they can pick up, varies from one species to another.

Visual acuity can also vary among species. Most frogs and toads have a 360-degree view because their eyes typically protrude on either side of their heads. Usually this broad view is useless unless a frog is looking at something that is moving. The scientific dogma on frogs holds that their retinal processing excludes all information except movement. If a frog sees something small and moving, a few retinal nerves fire and the frog darts its tongue out and eats the small item. If a frog sees something big, a lot of retinal nerves fire and the frog knows to run for cover. They are generally better at detecting the movement of small items within a few feet. Large items at a distance, such as a slowly moving man in waders, are harder to see.

A fast-moving man in waders who is sinking into a pond and cursing stimulates all of a frog's senses. By the time Hayes regains his footing, this particular red-legged has dived deep into the water. Jennings and Hayes begin to laugh. "You're going to weigh a ton," moans Jennings, who knows that it will be his job to help hoist his soaked buddy out of the pool.

Undaunted, Hayes decides to make the most of his predicament. "Well, now that I'm in," he says, "I might as well check the edge." He slowly begins to tread toward the overhanging bank opposite from where he entered, but soon changes his mind as the water gets deeper. "I'm touching, but just barely," he says after about two steps. The water is nearly at his shoulders, and at the center, where the red-legged was, it is probably about nine feet deep. "This is the shallowest I can get," he says, turning back to the bank, and Jennings prepares to help him out of the pool. Jennings plants his footing on the bank and reaches his hand down to Hayes. "God, you're going to weigh a ton," Jennings repeats. Hayes grabs hold, and while Jennings leans back, he attempts to scramble up the sheer, muddy side of the pool, but makes no progress. The scene, a sopping wet Hayes dangling at the end of Jennings's arm, suddenly strikes them both as absurd, and they begin to giggle. "Just hold on a second. I want to rest," Hayes says as he catches his breath. Hayes is husky and fit, but the water is chilly, probably in the low fifties, and he has been standing in it for about a quarter of an hour. He is cold now and, just as Jennings predicted, his soaking clothes and the water trapped between his body and the waders have added many pounds to his weight. Jennings begins tugging again, and with effort, Hayes manages to flop back onto land. "Well, that got my adrenaline going," he says as he stands up and pulls on his jacket.

Two frogs tonight. The count is better than last year, when

Hayes found nothing. The one that got away in the last pool was a female, Hayes says, and the one he missed earlier was probably a male. As if on cue, a male red-legged calls in the distance, confirming that at least one adult pair still survives here.

The California red-legged frog, *Rana aurora draytonii,* is one of two types of red-legged frogs in the state. The other is the northern red-legged, *Rana aurora aurora.* The California red-legged could once be found from the middle of Northern California to northwestern Baja, below the U.S.-Mexico border. Its northern cousin's territory melds with the *draytonii*'s somewhere above San Francisco, and then ranges up to Canada.

Both red-leggeds are large frogs. The northern variety measures up to four inches long from its nose to the end of its rump. The California can grow up to about five inches long. Their main body color ranges from brown to red-brown to gray-green, and they usually have an ink-spatter of spots on their backs. Their hind legs are long and slender, with defined, muscular thighs. Flashes of color, varying from a hint of pink to a fluorescent red, run along the inside edges of their legs. The northern's legs are usually redder than the California's legs. Finding a red-legged in the wild and turning the muddy-colored animal over to peek at its rosy legs is like opening a battered shoebox and finding a polished ruby inside. The color can be dazzling. It is tempting to keep picking up the frogs and turning each one over, looking for brighter and brighter reds.

California red-leggeds were once one of the most abundant frogs in the state. They were also the most famous. After searching through books and old newspaper clippings, Mark Jennings concluded that the frog in Mark Twain's story "The Celebrated Jumping Frog of Calaveras County" was a California red-legged. Twain may not have been aware himself of the frog's species, and he never clearly defined its type in the story that gave him his first taste of worldwide fame.

Twain based his tall tale, about a frog whose jumping was hindered by swallowing lead shot, on an anecdote that had been circulating through California's gold-mining region since the 1849 Gold Rush. Twain heard the story while he was trying his hand at gold-panning in the 1860s. It had already been published in different versions in at least two newspapers in the 1850s, but Twain was apparently unaware of these. By 1865 he had committed his version of the tale to paper, naming the frog Daniel Webster, and it was published in *Saturday Press,* a New York magazine.

Over the years, the story has been accompanied by illustrations, and artists have drawn everything from bullfrogs to toads to represent the famous jumper. Toads tend to walk or scurry rather than jump, so it was easy for Jennings to eliminate them as the original inspiration for the story. California does have bullfrogs, though, and they now are the biggest frogs in the state. Many people, including some scientists, have assumed over the years that the bullfrog is the Calaveras County creature. However, Jennings argues, the bullfrog is an alien species that wasn't introduced into the state until 1896. The only frog available to the early gold miners that would have been big enough to jump like Daniel Webster is the California red-legged. For that reason, Jennings says, the California red-legged is more than just another frog. "This frog is just as important to our heritage as the much more visible big, furry, or feathered creatures such as whooping cranes or timber wolves," he says. "It would be as much a shame to lose this animal as it would be to lose the condor or grizzly bear."

Cultural heritage is not the only reason this animal is important, though. All amphibians, including the red-legged, play a critical biological role in their natural environment just by going about their day-to-day lives. One of their most obvious functions is as a living pest-control machine. Frogs consume insects the way kids consume candy—as often as possible, and with little discrimination. Hayes once examined the stomach contents of thirty-five red-legged frogs, including adults and subadults, the frog equivalent of teenagers. On average, the frogs had about seven prey in their stomachs, but one gourmand's gut contained forty-two items. That's evidence of a hearty appetite. In human terms it would be like eating seven or more hamburgers at a meal. The prey in the frog stomachs included beetles, water bugs, spiders, and snails. But Hayes also found mice (consider eating half a side of beef for dinner), other little frogs (consider eating your neighbor's children), and gravel, dirt, and stray plant material.

Red-leggeds are as determined as they are voracious. Hayes once witnessed a frog in the wild grab a mouse's head and then vigorously use front limbs and hands to push the mouse farther into its mouth. When it could push no more, the frog pressed the mouse's rump against the ground to finally get the little victim all the way down its throat. A delicious meal, no doubt, although the mouse's rump picked up a lot of sand that the frog also swallowed. The sight, Hayes later wrote, was further proof that California red-legged frogs "are poor discriminators and generally feed in an unrefined manner."

Other studies of amphibian eating habits support Hayes's experience with the red-legged. One small study of the contents of ten Yosemite toad stomachs found ants, aphids, butterfly larva, wasps, three kinds of beetles, four kinds of flies, fly larva, spider mites, spiders, stink bugs, thrips, springtails, and—adding more evidence that toads and frogs are more alike than different and one is no more refined than the other—a collection of leaves, grass seeds, and rocks. The bullfrog has been described as willing to eat anything that moves and is smaller than it is. The same could be said of many other frogs and toads. Hayes has seen lounging red-leggeds snap up windblown willow catkins just because the catkins happened to be moving. However, bullfrogs have outdone most others in adventurous eating. They have been known to eat baby alligators and whole colonies of stinging wasps, as well as other frogs, salamanders, crayfish, snakes, lizards, and birds—beak, feet, and feathers included.

What goes around eventually comes around, though, and a whole array of creatures end up eating amphibians, expanding their value from mere pest controller to staff of life. The things that prey upon frogs and toads include many of the things that frogs and toads themselves prey upon. Beetles, flies, snakes, birds, mammals (such as raccoons and opossums), alligators, horsefly larvae, fish, crabs, and even the Venus's-flytrap plant are known to dine on frogs. Other frogs, newts, and salamanders also eat frogs and toads. Every age group or life stage becomes a delicacy for someone, too. Freshly hatched tadpoles, for instance, are favored by certain fish, while other fish and some snakes have been known to prefer amphibian eggs. Bats like their frogs fully developed. Many creatures, including bullfrogs, like to eat bite-size froglets.

Under natural conditions, unhindered by human interference, all of this eating and being eaten makes for a nice balance that efficiently and perpetually cycles nutrients and energy from one level of the forest ecosystem to another. It would take a raccoon all day and more to eat enough insects to meet its nutritional needs. By consuming a single frog, which has itself spent a good while consuming insects, the raccoon can get its nutrition in just a few seconds.

Just how important amphibians and their role in the food cycle are in a typical forest is hard to measure. Yet in some places, scientists have tried to give an objective value to amphibian importance by figuring how much of the total animal biomass in a given area is represented by amphibians. Biomass, in this sort of calculation, is the weight of all the vertebrate animals found per unit of a defined area. The most famous biomass study considering amphibians was conducted in the early 1970s in the Hubbard Brook Experimental Forest in New Hampshire. The two scientists who did the study, Thomas M. Burton and Gene E. Likens, looked at the forest— including its streams and pools—as though it were overlaid with a grid of large squares. Then they randomly selected a number of the squares and counted every amphibian within each one. In this case the amphibians they found were salamanders, including the red-back salamander, *Plethodon cinereus,* one of the most common in the eastern United States. The redback is a land-based critter that spends most of its time hiding under leaf litter, emerging at night to forage for food.

Burton and Likens learned in their study forest that there were almost three thousand salamanders per hectare (a hectare is an area a little smaller than the size of two football fields). When weighed, the salamanders represented twice as much biomass as birds in the forest, even at the peak of bird-breeding season. The salamander biomass was about the same as the biomass of shrews and mice, the common small mammals in that forest. "This finding is somewhat surprising," the two researchers wrote, "as most ecologists have ignored amphibians in ecosystem energy flow and nutrient cycling studies while considering birds and mammals in detail." Other studies have shown that anurans—frogs and toads—are significant ecosystem members as well. Where they aren't disappearing, that is.

Marc Hayes was first inspired to track and try to understand frog declines in 1973, after reading a paper by a fish biologist about red-legged frog disappearances from the Central Valley. Although still abundant in selected coastal areas, the frog was gone from the valley floor by the 1950s. Nobody was studying the frog at the time, so the actual disappearance event was missed, and it was left to later scientists to try to piece together why it had occurred. The fish biologist concluded that the red-legged had been pushed out by the introduced bullfrog.

That explanation seemed too simple to Hayes. He had grown up in a small town at the north end of the valley, and he knew the bullfrogs were abundant. He had even caught and eaten bullfrogs there. But he was also a young scientist-in-training and, as such, was developing a skepticism for single-cause answers. Too many other factors seemed to be at work in the valley to lay all the blame on bullfrogs. Hayes decided to find out for himself whether the red-legged was indeed gone from the entire valley, including its foothill edges, and why.

"I've always been attracted by something that's really rare. It was sort of a challenge, sort of a puzzle, to find red-legged frogs," he recalls. "If they were dirt-common, I'd be less interested in them."

For about six years he spent weekends and other spare hours tracking down places in the Central Valley where the red-leggeds were once seen. "I started talking to everybody about where they had seen this frog, and then I started striking out and going to locations and not finding them. I'd find bullfrog after bullfrog after bullfrog. Everybody would tell me the same thing—in their entire lifetime, they'd never seen any red-leggeds or they'd seen them only along the coast."

Anybody else might have concluded at this point that the fish biologist's paper was right. Hayes can be stubborn, though, and he felt there were too many other possible causes that hadn't been considered enough. Nonnative fish that dominate many of California's lakes and streams, for instance, were known to eat native frogs and native frog eggs. Hayes thought they might be part of the Central Valley cause, but he didn't have the data he needed to prove that. He also speculated that perhaps simple habitat destruction had driven the red-legged into decline while creating habitats more favorable to bullfrogs. Again, he had only part of the proof.

Even after Hayes found a rare Central Valley population in Corral Hollow, he still didn't have the answers. Finally he concluded that he would never understand the decline fully until he knew more about the frogs and their habitat requirements. Very little was known about either. So he found an abundant population of California red-leggeds along the Central California coast, not far from William Randolph Hearst's famous castle at San Simeon. He began driving up once a month from USC for three-night stretches of watching, weighing, and measuring red-leggeds.

Hayes had decided, meanwhile, that he would do his doctoral

dissertation on red-legged frogs, and he arranged to study a population closer to his college. But when the owners of the property on which the frogs sat decided to sell their land, they forbade him from working there. He scrambled to find another project, and in short order, his adviser, Jay Savage, helped him arrange to do work on frogs in Monteverde. So, in 1982, Hayes had to drop his red-legged work to begin a year-long study of how glass frogs care for their young. It was fascinating work, but Hayes knew he wanted to continue working on red-leggeds. He had collected so much data that he was becoming a minor expert on the creature. He was also, as he soon learned, becoming somewhat territorial about red-leggeds.

One day in 1983, while Hayes was still working in Costa Rica, he received a letter with an Arizona postmark from a fellow named Mark Jennings, whom he did not know. Jennings explained in his letter that a mutual acquaintance had suggested Hayes might be interested in reading an early draft of a paper Jennings had drafted. Jennings was about to enter a graduate program in fish biology at the University of Arizona, but he had spent nearly a year counting amphibians and reptiles for a California Department of Fish and Game study on the impact of a state water project. He noticed that foothill yellow-legged frogs and bullfrogs didn't seem to live in the same streams, even when stream conditions indicated the foothill should have been there. But he also noticed that yellow-leggeds were absent where certain fish were present. And he started wondering why he found no California red-leggeds in the Central Valley.

Hayes began to read Jennings's paper, and he was shocked to find that many of Jennings's ideas about the disappearance of red-leggeds and other native California frogs corresponded to his own. In particular, Jennings thought fish might be one of the culprits, and he had new data to support the idea. "It was uncanny how identical the thinking was," Hayes says. "And of course my first reaction was a defensive one—'What is this guy doing?' " His second reaction was to write back to Jennings and see if he would be willing to collaborate. "I figured, if this guy's out doing this stuff, I might as well join him."

If Jennings had not become a scientist, he would have become a historian. An inveterate collector of biographical information about early biologists, particularly those who made their mark studying amphibians or fish, he can recite long anecdotes about the ways in which some of the famous field biologists carried out their work, what kind of field notes they kept, who trained them, and whom they in turn trained. He uses these early researchers as mentors, and often adopts and adapts their habits. For instance, he once read an obituary notice about a famous Harvard naturalist who left behind a lifetime of correspondence and had numbered in sequence each of the letters he had written over the years. Soon, Jennings began numbering his own correspondence. (By one day in July 1992, when he showed me his correspondence file, he had written 3,488 letters.)

On August 10, 1983, Jennings wrote letter number 548 to Marc Hayes. "As for your suggestion to undertake a joint venture on a paper dealing with frog-fish interactions, I would be more than happy to undertake such a project with you," he wrote. A collaboration was born.

During the first two years of their work together, Jennings, who was living in Tucson, and Hayes, who had moved to Miami, corresponded by letter and telephone almost constantly. They would exchange data and drafts of papers and the letters, which ran several pages long, and detail points and references that needed to be checked. "Please give me the stream order on all localities that will make sense for the Sacramento Valley," Hayes wrote in one letter. "I finally got an address for Phil Nelson, and have written to him concerning locality #3." They continued to work on their respective doctorates, but they thrived on their frog-decline work. Jennings brought to the table his knowledge of fish and his avid interest in history and historical research. Hayes brought skills in ecology and statistical analysis, as well as longer experience watching red-leggeds in the wild. They both brought a passion for the frog and an interest in conservation. By the end of those first two years, they had written three significant papers that, taken together, logically explain the factors that caused the California red-legged to decline.

The decline began well before obvious habitat destruction, such as the damming of rivers or the paving over of wetlands, became a factor. It began, in fact, in the late nineteenth century, and was aggravated by several introduced predators. The most damaging of these predators was the human being.

The year 1849 marked the beginning of the California Gold Rush and the beginning of the decline of the California red-legged frog. Until the Gold Rush, only about ten thousand people lived in the state, most of these in Southern California. Within a year of President James Polk's official announcement that gold had been found in California, the state's population ballooned by 100,000 people. The gold seekers came from everywhere—two out of three were born in other countries—and included everyone from restless young adventurers to well-established gentlemen. Most were men, and most must have gone out to eat, rather than cook, because a plethora of restaurants opened in San Francisco, beginning that city's reputation as a culinary center. As the century wore on, and Californians tired of their state's international reputation for ruggedness and violence, all things French became popular, especially French cuisine. At one point, a prominent San Franciscan imported forty chefs from Paris to boost what one historian has called "the city's feverish interest in French cuisine."

The Francophilism was bad news for frogs with long legs. "Californians had a complex about basically being a hick state," says Hayes, a native of the state. "That's why there was such a big move to change the image. The unfortunate consequence is that frogging really came into vogue fast."

The frogs with the longest legs in California were the California red-leggeds. Records don't exist for determining exactly how abundant they were before 1880, but based on what they know about habitat requirements, what habitat existed, and a few other published reports, Hayes and Jennings are certain the red-legged was abundant. The San Joaquin Valley, the portion of the Great Central Valley closest to San Francisco, was about one-third marshland. Bands of tule marshes were from two to seven miles wide, and the bulrushes there grew higher than a man sitting on a horse, making an ideal home for frogs.

In short order, the California red-leggeds became a commercial item as local restaurants began including them on their menus. The marshes became the prime hunting ground. Hunters equipped with gigs—long poles with sharp points—could pick up easy money tromping through the marshes, spearing red-leggeds to sell in the big city as the "French frog," a marketing tag that made the animal even more desirable. Early records from the U.S. Bureau of Fisheries—documents that Jennings stumbled across during his almost habitual perusal of historical data related to frogs and fish—draw the clearest picture of how the hunters devoured the red-legged population. By the late 1890s the U.S. Commissioner of Fish and Fisheries was characterizing the marshes of the Central Valley as one of the nation's major frog-producing regions. And the marshes closest to San Francisco were plundered the most. In 1888, about 48,000 frogs were taken, each one worth about twenty-five cents to its hunter. The number captured grew each year until the peak year of 1895, when more than 118,000 frogs were taken. That year, the value per frog declined to only about a dime, perhaps because the market was glutted. After 1895, the numbers of frogs captured declined dramatically and the price rose.

Among red-leggeds, females are the biggest and meatiest and were likely to be captured first, guaranteeing that frog hunting could not go on indefinitely. Removing the females first essentially robbed the red-leggeds of their breeding stock. By 1900, frog harvesting had declined as the battered red-legged population declined, and U.S. Fish and Fisheries reports on frog harvesting diminished as well. "In just eight [years], California went from being the leading supplier of market frogs in the United States to that of a supplier of quantities too small to report," Hayes and Jennings wrote in a 1985 paper on overharvesting of red-leggeds.

The decline of the red-leggeds didn't mean that Californians were suddenly willing to abandon their taste for amphibian legs. There was still a demand, and some unidentified entrepreneurs decided that the best way to satisfy that appetite was to import live frogs. The natural frog to import was the bullfrog, a large, leggy animal that, like many of California's residents at the time, was native to the eastern United States. One entrepreneur established in 1896 what was probably the first frog farm in California. The farm was in El Cerrito, a town across the bay from San Francisco. It began with four artificial ponds and thirty-six bullfrogs that had been shipped from Florida and Maryland. Jennings and Hayes figure that some time after this first frog farm began operating—and most likely between 1900 and 1930, when there were a number of other attempts to raise bullfrogs around the state—bullfrogs worked their way into the wild in California, either through intentional release or escape.

Bullfrogs have been known to eat other frogs. Only recently a graduate student studying red-leggeds in Northern California confirmed that bullfrogs will eat their smaller cousin. However, Hayes says, it is still hard to know how much bullfrogs are to blame for the red-legged decline. There are many places in the state that once harbored red-leggeds but now have only bullfrogs. It would be natural to assume that the bullfrogs simply pushed the red-leggeds out by gobbling them up. However, the places where bullfrogs now dominate are almost all less pristine than they once were.

Bullfrogs can withstand conditions that red-leggeds can't. The former have more tolerance than the latter for dirty water and high temperatures, and they don't require the same kind of heavy riparian cover. It is possible that the real culprit in many of the places now dominated by bullfrogs is habitat destruction. Bullfrogs may simply have been able to survive conditions that red-leggeds have not.

Some of the most obvious habitat destruction pushed red-leggeds out of the Central Valley after their populations were already weakened by commercial exploitation. That destruction began in the marshlands at the turn of the century, as frightened residents looked for ways to diminish the incidence of malaria. They began destroying the marshes to suppress what they believed was one of the disease's main causes: bad air over the marsh. Later, most of the remaining marshes were drained to make room for farmlands, irrigation projects, and other water projects in the Central Valley. One of those projects dried Tulare Lake, a seasonal lake that at times exceeded Lake Tahoe in size and supported large populations of birds, reptiles, and amphibians. Today, marshes make up only a small percentage of the Central Valley. The dominant open waters are irrigation ditches and thousands of acres of evaporation ponds that hold the pesticide-laden waters that drain off the farmlands.

The next big round of development and habitat destruction came after World War II, when California, particularly Southern California, grew up and out. Californians diverted or dammed rivers without thought of environmental consequences. Today there are more than one hundred major dams in the state. The big priority was to get water to the new urban and suburban areas. Hayes and Jennings figure that half of the 75-percent decline in California red-leggeds has occurred since the mid-1960s, after new towns, housing tracts, water diversions, and cattle grazing replaced or damaged most of the animal's remaining habitat. Clearly, the red-legged's downfall was its choice of habitat—a choice shared by its human predators.

It is the day after the Corral Hollow frog search, and Hayes and Jennings and I have driven to Berkeley to interview a pair of U.S.

Forest Service biologists about foothill yellow-legged frogs and what they think is causing their decline. The interview was one of dozens that "the two Marcks," as they are often called by their colleagues, have conducted for their statewide amphibian and reptile survey. The interviews help the two men clarify information that researchers have already reported on questionnaires sent to them when Hayes and Jennings began their survey. Interviews like these also give them a chance to catch up on general trade gossip about who is doing what, and why so-and-so isn't talking to some colleague or other.

We meet the biologists in a small Forest Service office in a downtown building. While Hayes asks questions, Jennings takes notes in a red-bound notebook and occasionally contributes a question of his own. Over the previous two years, as they have talked to scientists up and down the state for their survey, Hayes and Jennings have found many who were eager to help, and who willingly shared notebooks and records. But they also encountered others who hedged or outright refused to cooperate. They didn't want to share information, plain and simple, no matter how important it might be to the future of the animals. "People collect information and sit on it for years. It's their information. What are you going to do?" Hayes says with a shrug.

Sharing information is a touchy subject with many scientists, in and out of herpetology. Ideally, data should flow among scientists freely and in a timely manner. Considering that most data is collected with some government funding, it seems reasonable to expect scientists to share information vital to understanding what appears to be an environmental crisis. But many scientists live in constant fear that they will be "scooped" or won't get proper credit for work they have done. Credit for work done can mean the difference between employment and unemployment, between promotion and stagnation, between getting funding and not getting funding. In academic science, especially, the pressure to get credit is strong. In herpetology the pressure has helped create a field divided into a variety of competing camps. There are academic researchers who won't share data with biologists working for federal and state agencies. There are state and federal agency biologists who won't share with each other. "On paper they should cooperate, but in actuality they have certain requirements they have to fulfill," says Hayes, who has worked on contract for agencies. "If they release their information to other agencies, they risk the other agency taking the credit for it."

Over the three years during which I followed the amphibian-decline issue, I was privy to only one incident of a researcher intentionally taking data and an idea and claiming it as his own. Only one scientist—an academician, no less—actually and intentionally lied to me, as far as I know. But considering the small size of the community of people working on amphibian declines, even a few such instances are disturbing. Hoarding may be the only legitimate defensive tactic available to protect against unscrupulous colleagues. On the other hand, without cooperation, there may be no more animals left—including animals the hoarders want to study.

Herpetologists, though perhaps no more so than any other group of scientists, are also prone to feuding, which ultimately hinders the free exchange of information. Camps can be built around loyalties to one side of the feud or the other. These camps relate to each other much like the Hatfields and the McCoys, and woe to the one who doesn't know the history of the feuds.

Jennings recalls being introduced at a conference to one of contemporary herpetology's senior practitioners. The senior scientist asked him what institution he was from. Jennings said he was associated with the California Academy of Science, an organization that sponsors natural history research and runs a natural history museum in San Francisco. Upon hearing this, the scientist developed a severe case of rudeness and talked to Jennings no more. Jennings, who is generally a noncombative, inoffensive character, was dumbfounded. Had he said something untoward? Later, when he returned to California and shared the story with a friend at the academy, the friend burst out laughing. The senior scientist had an old, simmering competitive feud with another scientist at the academy, the friend explained. As a result, anyone from that institution was treated like a pariah by the senior scientist.

Fortunately for Jennings and Hayes, the Forest Service biologists in Berkeley on this day are willing to share their knowledge. They collect several important bits of information. After two hours we hit the road again, heading for California's north coast logging country. Our first stop, six hours from Berkeley, will be Arcata. It is the home of Humboldt State University, one of Jennings's alma maters. We will stay there for two days, as guests of one of Jennings's former instructors, while Hayes and Jennings work another leg of their survey.

Most of the ride up is along a two-lane highway that, for much of the way, is slick with rain. Redwood and cedar forests border the road, breaking occasionally to reveal fantastic views of a rushing river far below the roadbed. It is a pleasure to see so much color and water. The state is in the fifth year of a drought, and in great parts of California, where there was once a predictable rainy season, rain is now almost nonexistent and water conservation is in vogue.

Jennings has told me many times in the last year that red-leggeds are especially abundant in this part of the state, particularly compared to the rest of California. He calls it "the fog belt" because of its typical weather condition, but for the longest time I thought he was calling it "the frog belt." Over the next few days I will come to believe that either description—frog or fog—is equally accurate.

4

. . . .

In the Field II

It is early afternoon on our first full day in the fog belt when Jennings, Hayes, and I climb back into the truck to head for the wild to look for frogs. We are like a giddy trio of kids. We spent the morning at an environmental conference sponsored by a student group at Humboldt State where Jennings gave a talk on the threats to California's native amphibians. Then, egged on by Hayes and me, Jennings decided to forego the rest of the day-long event to go look for frogs. There is something irresistibly enticing about going to work when the whole wild outdoors is your office.

The two scientists decide to check several sites within a quick drive of our college-town headquarters. We take a scenic route on a network of backroads and main drags until we end up at an overpass that crosses the Mad River. Then we pull on frogging gear—chest waders for Hayes, hip boots for Jennings and me—and hustle down a narrow trail on a steep bank that takes us to the river's edge and a small, pebbly beach where Maple Creek runs into the river. The river, moving at a rapid and steady pace, is wider than a four-lane freeway. The creek is less than half as wide, and narrows even more upstream. It drains slowly and lazily into the Mad. We begin to walk up the creek. Steep granite walls, thick with moss and ferns, border parts of the creek, and at some points the bank disappears. Before we get far along its length, we begin to find frogs.

I see a fast flash of brown out of the corner of my eye and do the appropriate thing. "Frog! Frog!" I yell, as the tiny creature hops along the beach toward the water. I expertly point to it. Hayes, who is a few steps ahead of me, quickly turns and grabs the animal.

He examines it carefully. It appears to be a juvenile foothill yellow-legged. Its eyes are golden, with a kind of glittery sparkle I've only seen before on the finish of souped-up automobiles. "I'm guessing this guy is about twenty centimeters long," Hayes muses. He takes an empty plastic sandwich bag from his daypack, scoops a small amount of water from the creek into the bag, then adds the frog. He blows air into the bag and seals it shut. It looks something like a plastic fishbowl now, holding the frog and enough water to keep it moist and alive.

"It's a shame to take a juvenile," I say, feeling a little sorry that I pointed it out in the first place.

"It's a shame to take anything," Hayes replies. "But it's better for tissue sampling to take an adult."

This animal, and several others we find at this stream, will become what scientists call voucher specimens. They will be knocked out and killed with an overdose of a fish anesthetic, pickled with formalin, and tagged with labels that indicate exactly where they were caught and when. Then they will be stored in jars of ethyl alcohol at the California Academy of Sciences' natural history collection in San Francisco. As vouchers, they will provide proof for future researchers that these amphibians actually existed at this site. They will also serve as whole examples of what each amphibian species from this part of California looked like. Finally, they will become sources of tissue samples for scientists who want to trace the genetic lines of amphibians.

Collections like the one at the Academy of Sciences have been a key tool for Hayes and Jennings's survey of the status of California's amphibians. The two men have gone through museum and university collections throughout the state and around the country; they have spent hours and sometimes days looking at thousands of amphibian specimens identified as having been caught in California. The specimens told them where the amphibians once lived and helped them identify sites to check to see if the amphibians still survived.

The practice of collecting live animals and pickling them predates the formal profession of the scientist. In fifteenth- and sixteenth-century Europe, wealthy hobbyists and scholars interested in natural phenomena created "curiosity cabinets," dominated by collections of oddities. Two-headed cows, one-eyed chickens, and other anomalies were gathered in these collections as gee-whiz items to be ogled for ogling's sake. Gradually, as world exploration increased, scholars and hobbyists shifted their attention from oddities and collected in order to show samples of animals, plants, and insects of the world. This sample-collecting became even more popular as efforts mounted to come up with a workable system for cataloging creatures. It thrived after the mid-eighteenth century, when Carolus Linnaeus published his plan for the systematic classification of plants and animals, which included the kingdom-phylum-class-order hierarchy of taxonomic categories still used today.

During the Victorian era in the United States and Europe, collecting natural items was a common and popular pastime among the middle class. In the United States, government-funded collectors routinely accompanied military units and other explorers venturing into the North American wilderness. By the end of the nineteenth century, many of the biggest and best private collections had been transferred to public and university museums; philosophers and general scholars had been replaced by professional scientists who used the collections as research tools.

Until the late twentieth century, a single standard dominated among scientists who collected amphibians for research. That standard dictated that if a scientist saw an animal in the field, he or she should collect it. Some held to this practice more vigorously than others, and a few biologists still active today earned reputations early in their careers for being "human vacuum cleaners" in the field. They would, indeed, take every amphibian they saw. If that meant taking 1,200 salamanders from one site in Oregon—as one prominent scientist did—then so be it. Researchers assumed then that for every animal they actually caught, there would be several others in the field that eluded them. They figured that whatever they caught wouldn't harm a population's long-term fitness.

In the last thirty years, scientists have begun to vigorously debate what is proper and improper collecting and what should be the dominant standard. At one extreme, there are still a few scientists who can't shake the habit of collecting all that they see; at the other, there are researchers who won't collect anything, believing that to do so would needlessly kill an animal. In the middle, there are scientists who still collect with a deliberate purpose in mind and in generally smaller amounts than in the past.

"People are far less inclined to collect without thinking," says John Simmons, the manager of the herpetology collection at the Museum of Natural History at the University of Kansas. Simmons is typical of many scientists today in that he uses a case-by-case approach to determine whether to take an animal from the wild. For instance, if an animal is living in a protected area such as a park or a preserve, it is difficult to justify collecting just for collecting's sake, he says. However, if an area is slated to be bulldozed, he believes a scientist is justified in collecting all that he or she sees in that area, so that after the wetland or forest is destroyed, there will at least be a record of what once existed there. Concern that future development would wipe out the living record of species native to California helped spur Joseph Grinnell, the founding director of the Museum of Vertebrate Zoology at UC Berkeley, to champion collecting during the early decades of the twentieth century.

Because of collecting, Simmons notes, scientists have been able to document reasons for saving and preserving areas that otherwise would have been destroyed. Scientific collections have helped identify which portions of tropical rain forest are particularly rich in different species and should be given top priority for preservation. Jennings and Hayes routinely take voucher specimens as they survey California's amphibians. One reason is their belief that the voucher may become important later, if a habitat is threatened with development. Sometimes, Jennings says, only proof as tangible as a pickled specimen can protect an animal population and its habitat from destruction.

Maintaining a collection is time-consuming and expensive. Dried specimens, such as bird skins, have to be regularly fumigated to keep pests from eating them. Wet specimens, such as amphibians, have to be stored in bottles and jars of ethyl alcohol. All of the specimens take up space. The collection that Simmons oversees is the fourth-largest herpetology collection in the country, with twenty thousand jars of animals that have to be maintained. In recent years, many institutions have begun selling off their collections to other institutions just to free themselves of the expense of storage and maintenance. This economic picture has influenced how scientists collect today. Now it is not uncommon for a scientist to consider whether a collection really needs an animal, and whether it can really afford to take care of a specimen, before actually nabbing the creature from the wild.

Laws and regulations governing animal collecting have also helped change collecting habits in the last several decades. In general, a scientist needs a good reason and patience with paperwork to collect more than a few native frogs in most states. The amount of paperwork increases as animals are included on endangered-species lists. Likewise, it is difficult for scientists to return to the United States from other countries with certain amphibians, dead or alive, because they are now protected by local or international wildlife protection laws.

Wildlife inspectors complain that the occasional scientist lawbreaker typically pleads ignorance of the law or hides behind a shield of scientific higher purpose to justify transgressions. Indeed, wildlife protection laws, especially international laws, are not always clear and easy to understand, and they can change rapidly. Scientists are not stupid people, though, and they know how to dial phone numbers and ask questions. Considering how important some of these animals are to their research, it doesn't seem unreasonable to expect researchers to bear the inconvenience of keeping up on the regulations protecting the animals they study.

I often asked scientists involved in the declining-amphibian issue whether scientific collecting could have contributed to the decline of some populations. Scientists are notorious for hedging. They are quick to point out uncertainties that make it impossible for them to give firm black-and-white pronouncements. Yet they rarely hedged about the impact of their collecting. It was, most insisted, negligible compared to other threats to amphibians.

"There's no question, when you go out and grab the animal and put it in a jar, that you've reduced the number. That's readily apparent," says Jennings. "I guess the thing that bothers me is that it's not even close to some of the other things that are horribly destructive."

Typically, a scientist takes a maximum of two or three dozen frogs from a limited area. A bulldozer turning a forest or meadow or streambed into a building site takes hundreds and thousands of amphibians from across a wide range with a few scrapes and scoops. It wipes out the habitat as well, ensuring that there will be no future population comeback.

There are about 3.5 million amphibian and reptile specimens in U.S. museums. "If you think of this as 3.5 million dead reptiles and amphibians in jars, it does sound like a lot of animals, and thus a lot of damage done to populations," collection manager Simmons contends. "However, in context, it is clear that this actually is a very low number. The context is this: These collections were made over the last one hundred years, from all around the world. When compared to the number of reptiles and amphibians that die annually from natural causes—from being run over on roadways, used for bait, and killed as nuisance animals; the incredible numbers of animals that die each year because of habitat destruction; and the number captured or killed during capture for the pet trade, food, and other commercial uses—it is a very small number."

The U.S. Fish and Wildlife Service keeps records of both live and dead amphibians that pass through U.S. ports, either as imports or exports. Most of the animals are destined for the pet or food trades. Many are caught in the wild. In 1992 alone, over 14 million amphibians passed through U.S. ports, more than four times the number of amphibians and reptiles that sit in U.S. museum collections.

Whenever I joined researchers in the field, I watched them leave far more frogs behind than they took. Also, I learned of only one case in which a researcher publicly suspected his colleagues' scientific collecting of causing a frog disappearance. Some scientists doubted that researcher's conclusions, and said that the frog, native to a small area in Puerto Rico, more likely disappeared because of a variety of problems unrelated to collecting, including habitat changes.

Yet as I listened to scientists dismissing the impact of their own collecting, I wondered if I had essentially asked the fox about the situation in the hen house. This is not a hundred years ago, and life for animals in the wild is much more precarious than it once was. If scientists were having an impact by collecting today, how would they ever know? They don't keep running tabs on who is collecting what; they don't set firm standards about what is and isn't acceptable collecting. For instance, if a scientist believes he has found the last California red-legged frog, should he take it or leave it?

"It has more value in a collection than it does in the field, where it will die alone," Jennings tells me as we wade along Maple Creek. "The value is that if it's in the collection, it's available for future work."

I quietly consider this idea. I'm more thrilled about watching a frog hop in the wild than I am in considering what possibilities a frog carcass may hold for understanding genetic relations or evolution. I know, too, that Jennings has a point. One frog, or even a pair of frogs, is not likely to be able to survive or keep a species going.

Scientists who study population dynamics—how individual characteristics such as breeding habits and growth rates work with factors such as the environment and behavior to determine the size and growth pattern of a population—believe there are minimum population sizes that a species must maintain. Below that point it is doomed. What that minimum is can vary depending upon the animal and the way it breeds and lives. Scientists have studied the population dynamics of only a few frogs, so they have only barebones information. For most species they can't answer with certainty how many frogs are too few to keep a population going. But two are probably not enough for any frog species to survive for long under natural conditions.

Most amphibians, particularly ranid frogs, lay large quantities of eggs that produce many young all at once. This breeding pattern allows them to suddenly increase their species' population with a smaller number of adult animals than most mammals or birds would need to cause a comparable population increase. But the sudden population increase can be temporary. The offspring of such explosive breeders typically have a tough time surviving to adulthood.

Frog eggs, tadpoles, and juvenile frogs are extremely vulnerable to predators, weather and water conditions, and other environmental factors. One study found that northern red-legged frogs lay about 680 eggs, and that those eggs have a 91-percent chance of hatching. But the tadpoles have only about a 5-percent chance of actually making it to metamorphosis, when they transform into tiny frogs. Only about half of those baby frogs survive a full year. All the numbers taken together mean that about 2.5 percent, or about seventeen of the 680 eggs laid, actually make it to the one-year-old frog stage. Considering that it takes three years of dodging predators and bad luck before a red-legged frog reaches adulthood, the odds are even smaller that one of those eggs will ever become a breeding frog. Add to this the fact that a single breeding pair will create a limited genetic pool that potentially increases vulnerability to genetic defects or disease, and you get an idea of why a single breeding pair would be hard-pressed to pull an Adam-and-Eve stunt and repopulate the world with frogs. Northern red-leggeds have one of the highest hatching rates known among amphibians. So the picture is even worse for many other frogs.

At Maple Creek, Hayes, Jennings, and I walk along a beach that turns into a bank and eventually disappears, forcing us to wade in the stream waters. It is cool and humid, and the air smells like rich soil and green plants. At one point I think I see a group of tadpoles. Hayes takes a closer look and tells me they are just caddis-fly egg cases that look like tadpoles underwater. This frog hunting is trickier than I expected.

Hayes usually leads the way up the stream. When we come to a spot where it narrows and deepens, he slowly makes his way across and through the channel to a beach on the other side. The water reaches his chest, but he keeps moving. He keeps his eyes moving as well, from the stream to the bank, looking for frogs or other amphibians. Jennings and I stay behind and watch.

The two men have a friendly rivalry when they are together in the field that reminds me of a couple of fishing buddies. Each likes to catch and handle amphibians, and they almost seem to compete to see who can spot the most. Jennings easily concedes that Hayes, who is six years his senior, has more experience. In their early years of working together, Hayes was almost always more successful at finding elusive creatures. He always moved fast, and was always ready to check one more spot. It was nothing for him to drive a thousand miles in a weekend just to see a couple of frog sites. "I've watched him in the field and I've thought he was going to kill me—it was go, go, go all the time," Jennings says, as Hayes wades even farther upstream. "After he got cancer, that changed."

Hayes looks healthy, with thick black hair and olive skin that hint of his Gallic heritage. After a few days in the field with him, I have learned to sort of skip and jog in hip boots to keep up with him. It is hard to imagine that he once moved even faster, pushing himself—and anyone tagging along—even harder. Cancer is no longer a death sentence, and thousands recover from it each year. But Hayes had one of the toughest cancers to beat, and as he leads us along the Maple, there is no sign that only a few years earlier he became a rare statistic. Among American men who are diagnosed with liver cancer, less than 9 percent actually beat it. His saving grace was a particularly early diagnosis that he can only attribute to incredible luck.

In early December 1987, Hayes was thirty-seven years old and preparing to donate blood for a routine blood drive in Miami. Initial screening turned up a problem. His white-cell count was abnormally high, and other counts were abnormally low. A medical technician advised him to see a doctor as soon as possible. He took the advice, and a whirlwind of medical activity began. Hayes was soon undergoing exploratory surgery as doctors tried to find out what was wrong with his liver. "I didn't think it was real scary at that point," Hayes says. He just wanted to find out what was going on.

His doctors found a tumor and removed it. The good news was that it was clean and intact and encased in its own membrane. The bad news was that it was malignant. But because it was encased, it appeared not to have spread. Doctors recommended that Hayes undergo chemotherapy, upon which he began six months of regular intravenous chemotherapy, and the cancer suddenly became real for him. His high energy level all but disappeared, he lost weight, and he had a hard time staying awake. For at least eighteen months, he recalls, he felt miserable, constantly exhausted. He was sure he was going to die, and he decided to set some priorities in his

work life so that what time he had left was used well. He wanted
to work on something he really enjoyed, and he wanted to leave
behind information that might help the red-leggeds survive. He
pushed aside his unfinished dissertation on the behavior of Costa
Rican glass frogs and everything else to work even more intensely
on California red-leggeds.

Hayes kept the news about the cancer to himself, and only
shared it reluctantly after he began chemotherapy. Jennings learned
about it in a letter dated May 8, 1988, several months after the
diagnosis. "So much has happened since I talked or wrote to you
last that it is difficult to know where to begin," Hayes wrote. "I
will not go into the details of it now, but a bout with liver cancer is
the primary reason you have not heard from me. I am behind on
everything—mostly from heavy doses of chemotherapy that drain
one's energy, and from which I am still recovering. I will only
attempt to deal with the most pressing orders of business here and
will fill you in on details when I call you." In the rest of the one-
page letter, Hayes discussed a paper about habitat and California
red-leggeds and foothill yellow-leggeds that the two men were
preparing, and for which Hayes was late in completing his share of
the writing. Then he closed with an apology. "I hope this finds you
in better condition than I am. I am sorry about all these complica-
tions, I hope this has not inconvenienced you. Your friend, Marc."

Jennings recalls that the news of the diagnosis simply stunned
him. "I remember thinking later, 'Oh, my God, am I going to have
to write an obit for him?' It was not a pleasant thing to think about.
. . . Then I started to think about all the fun things I did with him,
and wondered if this was the end," Jennings told me one day as he
flipped through a thick file of correspondence from Hayes he has
saved over the years. "Fortunately, he got better."

With time, Hayes returned to his routine of quick trips to California to study the frog situation. His strength and energy began to
return, and he stopped worrying about dying. So now, as we work
our way up and down a stretch of the Maple, Hayes is thinking

only of the next frog, what he wants to find, and where he can best find it.

Even among his critics, Hayes has a reputation for being particularly able in the field. He seems to know plants as well as animals. As we travel from one stream or marsh to another, he easily rattles off the names—both scientific and common—of the greenery. When he approaches a spot, he seems to watch the bushes, grasses, and trees as much as the water and mud patches in which he is likely to find a frog. Plants help him assess the condition of any environment and guide him to the animals. "You very soon find that many of the [amphibian] species can be tracked by the flora," he tells me. "You get good enough at understanding what the plants are about, and you get a very high predictability for the animals."

Jennings knows some botany, but usually defers to Hayes when I ask about some odd flower or bush. He knows frog habitat and habits, though, and is as dogged as Hayes about finding anything that hints of being rare or endangered. I've watched Jennings hike an hour up a steep hillside in hundred-degree weather and then scramble over a canyon of giant boulders just to reach a single pool no bigger than a kitchen sink, occupied by twenty tiny frogs that were only rumored to exist. What Jennings doesn't know about the flora that go with each amphibian, he makes up for in knowledge about the history of amphibian biology. Hayes usually defers to Jennings when I ask any question the answer to which touches on history.

Hayes and Jennings are as complementary as bookends, so familiar with each other's expertise and personalities that they know instinctively how to deal with the quirks. Each is the son of schoolteachers, and Hayes notes that they have to be careful not to get too much into a teacher mode themselves, explaining everything slowly and patiently, in greater detail than necessary—especially to each other. Hayes has an occasionally explosive temper, while Jennings is notoriously even-tempered. Jennings is cautious and conservative in style, not given to spontaneous decisions or actions. Hayes is generally earnest, but has a daring streak. He enjoys telling stories about small bouts with risk, like the time during his college days when he narrowly eluded a police patrolman while speeding through Los Angeles streets in his graduate adviser's borrowed sportscar.

During the three hours we spend at Maple Creek, Hayes and Jennings work quietly and efficiently and capture about twenty foothill yellow-legged frogs, a rough-skinned newt, and a tiny western toad. It is a good haul. "Any time you can catch twenty ranid frogs at an easy-to-reach point, it's pretty good—and rare," Hayes comments.

We trudge back up the steep bank to the truck. Hayes lays the plastic bags carrying the frogs on the truck's hood and then removes from his daypack a plastic ruler and a couple of metal scales that are about the size of pencils. One by one, he takes the frogs from their bags and measures their length and weight. To weigh each frog, he clips its leg to the scale, and for a brief moment the creature hangs motionless while the scale's springy dial bounces into place. Jennings records the lengths and weights in a red-bound notebook. It is the same notebook in which he recorded the results of the Corral Hollow frog search two nights before, and later recorded notes during the interview with the Forest Service biologists in Berkeley.

Hayes tries to handle the frogs as little as possible, to reduce stress. As I watch each one hanging to be weighed, I wonder if anything could be more stressful, short of being eaten by a snake or bird. Hayes has seen some tropical frogs that are so sensitive to handling that their legs will stiffen like hardwood twigs when they feel a warm hand around their bodies. The stiffening is the result of a chemical reaction to the stress. Temperate frogs, like these yellow-leggeds, appear less sensitive. They move their legs a little to try to escape. Mostly, though, they are placid.

Hayes finishes the measuring and decides to keep the newt and toad for voucher specimens. He also keeps five of the yellow-legged frogs, both for voucher specimens and for genetic studies. He puts the bags containing those animals in a chest of ice in the back of Jennings's truck. Then the two men take the other frogs back down to the water. They release each one at the same spot on the beach or bank where they first saw it, hiking halfway back up Maple Creek to do so. They hold each plastic bag on the ground, open it, and encourage its occupant to escape by tapping on the bag or gently touching the frogs. The animals take the hint and are out of reach again within seconds.

We pile ourselves back into the truck and head to another site several miles up the road. We continue stopping at sites and search for frogs until shortly before midnight. Then, feeling exhausted, we drive back to Arcata and retire.

The next morning, day four of our trip, is Sunday and we are up early, just as we have been every other day of this trip. We are still staying at the home of one of Jennings's former professors, Gary Hendrickson, a fish biologist who specializes in fish parasites. The house is large and homey and sits in a hilltop neighborhood just minutes from the Humboldt State campus. Jennings, Hayes, and I are the first adults awake in the household, although the two Hendrickson children are already perched in front of the television by the time I wander downstairs.

This morning, Hayes and Jennings will "process" the amphibians they captured at Maple Creek. "Processing" essentially means killing, dissecting, and pickling. It is not a pleasant chore, but it will be made easier for the two scientists by the peaceful setting of their makeshift lab. They will work on a large wooden deck that overlooks a bright green lawn surrounded by a small forest of towering redwood trees. It is cloudy but not too chilly, and being outside still feels good. I settle into a spot on the deck that will give me a view of the lab work.

Jennings and Hayes prepare their alfresco lab methodically and swiftly. They unload from the truck the ice chest that holds the Maple Creek take. Then they unload a heavy box carrying a metal container that looks like a bulging milk can. The can holds liquid nitrogen. They set the cargo next to a glass-topped table on the deck.

Jennings places on the table a plastic container of the kind normally used to store food. He lays a mat of paper towels in it, then pours just enough of a clear liquid from a plastic bottle to saturate the towels. I get a whiff of the pungent liquid. According to the large handwritten label on the bottle, it is formalin, a mix of water and formaldehyde. It is a fixative, a chemical that makes tissue harden and prevents it from disintegrating.

Next, Jennings pulls a pair of panty hose from a box and cuts the legs off. He sees me watching, and explains that he will use the panty-hose legs to hold the vials of amphibian tissue in the liquid nitrogen, where the tissue will freeze immediately. Panty hose don't disintegrate in liquid nitrogen, and they're cheap. "Mom really helps," he says. "It embarrasses me to go in a store and buy them."

Hayes sits at the table and prepares labels for the vials that will hold the tissue samples. Each label lists the animal species, an identification number, a date, and the tissue type—heart, liver, kidney, or leg muscle.

At last the lab is ready. Jennings removes from the open ice chest one of the plastic bags holding a juvenile foothill yellow-legged. The frog is barely the size of a half-dollar piece. Jennings gently folds his hand about the frog and transfers it to another bag, which contains a small amount of a clear liquid called MS-222, a methane sulfate compound commonly used in lab work to knock out fish. Hayes points out a pinkish patch, called the osmotic patch, at the tail end of the frog's stomach. The patch is thin and porous, so liquid and air move through it even more easily than through other parts of the frog's permeable skin. It is also linked to a key vein, and the potent liquid in the bag will be absorbed almost instantly into the frog's blood system through this spot.

The frog hops a bit in the bag and then its movement slows; it kicks gently once or twice. Within minutes it is dead. I imagine a small frog settling into a puddle containing water polluted with garden pesticides. With the permeable skin, including that absorbent osmotic patch, the frog would seem to have no chance against any toxic liquid some homeowner or farmer might spray on plants—or decide to dispose of by simply dumping it on the ground or into a pond.

By now, Gary Hendrickson and his son Scott, a Cub Scout, have joined us on the deck. Scott glances at what Hayes is doing, but is more interested in examining the live rough-skinned newt, *Taricha granulosa,* sitting in a plastic bag on the table. It has a charcoal gray back, an orange belly, and golden eyes.

"Was this one fast?" he asks.

"He doesn't have to be fast because he has poison glands," Hayes responds. He means that because of its poison glands, the newt has few or no predators. Understandably, Scott misses this unspoken meaning.

"So he poisons you?" the boy asks.

"Not unless you touch him and then put your fingers in your mouth," Hayes explains. "So you should wash your hands after handling him."

"But why would you want to touch him and stick your fingers in your mouth?" the boy inquires sensibly.

Jennings grins as Hayes acknowledges that there really isn't any reason to do such a thing. Then Hayes pulls the dead frog from the bag and lays it belly-up on a paper towel on the table. He proceeds to cut a small slit on the belly, using a scalpel and tweezers. He removes the liver, heart, kidney, and a piece of muscle from the left rear leg. He places each in its appropriately labeled vial. Jennings takes each vial and slips it into a panty-hose leg, knots the leg, then slips another vial in, creating a chain of glass-and-nylon sausages. When he opens the nitrogen container, a stream of white smoke spills out. He lowers the chain into the container.

Jennings and Hayes will remove and then freeze tissue only from the foothill yellow-leggeds and the California and northern red-leggeds they capture on this trip. Then they will ship the tissues to David Green, a Canadian herpetologist and curator of herpetology at McGill University's Redpath Museum. For about a decade, Green has been studying the evolution of ranid frogs in the western United States and Canada by looking at their genetic relationships.

Green can track which frog species are related and how closely they are related by analyzing enzymes from frog tissues with a technology called electrophoresis. To do the analysis, Green first grinds up a piece of a frog's tissue to create a solution of enzymes. Then he dabs the solution onto a gel-covered plate. He runs an electrical charge through the gel, and the enzymes move and scatter according to their own unique characteristics. The movement and scattering results in a pattern of dots that, like a fingerprint, are the same each time the same enzyme solution is run through electrophoresis.

Enzymes are a type of protein created by a creature's DNA, a two-stranded chemical chain that is central to every living cell. DNA contains genes, and the genes determine which proteins a cell makes. Creatures of the same species have essentially the same genes, and will produce the same enzyme pattern. By looking at enzymes through electrophoresis, scientists are able to look at the products of many genes at the same time. Comparing the electrophoretic patterns their enzymes make gives them a quick way to tell if two frogs have the same genetic makeup.

Herpetologists pioneered the practice of using electrophoretic analysis to distinguish between species, and have been applying the technology for more than twenty-five years. Bird scientists and mammal scientists could always fairly easily distinguish their species by looking at feather color or other obvious physical features. But amphibians—especially nontropical frogs—can be extremely difficult to tell apart. Two species may look essentially the same—share a similar color or spot pattern—but have different genetics and different habitat requirements. Until a scientist identifies them as separate species, nobody may notice the different living requirements. Using electrophoretic analysis to identify species has the very practical conservation advantage of making it easier for wildlife managers to identify and protect rare and endangered amphibians.

Green's primary purpose in analyzing whether two similar frogs are of the same species has nothing to do with conservation, though. He is principally interested in understanding amphibian evolution and how North American frogs have come to be where they are. His findings add pieces to the bigger puzzle of how the world came to be as it is. Still, the conservation benefits are a bonus that pleases Green, who has been active in Canadian declining-amphibian work. It is also one reason Hayes and Jennings add hours to their workday to provide frog tissue to Green. They hope his work will help clarify whether some isolated frog populations in California represent distinct frog species that deserve more protection.

It takes most of the morning for Jennings and Hayes to process specimens. As soon as they are finished, they decide to go looking for more animals, farther up the coast in a series of lagoons, creeks, and marshes that border coastal parks. They repack the bed of Jennings's truck, which has a camper top that protects its contents from rain and thieves. Then we load ourselves into the truck cab and hit the road again. Jennings drives, Hayes sits on the passenger side, and I am squeezed between them, taking care not to knock the stick shift out of gear with my knee or boot as we speed down the highway.

The time on the road gives the two scientists a rare chance for in-person discussions with each other. Their conversation ranges through various topics related to their work. They confer about exactly how to get to where they want to go, share tidbits about other scientists, debate how to collect the information they need to finish this project or another, and trade news about recent journal articles they have read or frog habits they have heard about.

After four days on the road with them, I realize that the one thing they never seem to discuss is food. They rarely have breakfast, never break for lunch, and often skip dinner. Jennings, Hayes claims, is the worst about not eating regularly on field trips, and I'm inclined to agree. Always the historian, Jennings tells me that some of the fathers of modern field biology worked around the clock for days at a time, never breaking to eat. I take this as a warning of what may come as this trip continues, and make a mental note not to pass up any opportunity to grab a bite.

Field notes from trips by some of the great field biologists of the last hundred years also show that they got little sleep on their expeditions. As I follow Jennings and Hayes, I see why. Many of the frogs and toads they track are active only at night. Others are active mostly during the day. To get a count of both groups, the two men need to be out looking during at least part of the night and part of the day. Then they have to dissect or preserve any specimens they capture, which adds another hour or two or longer to their workday. Finally, they must spend time at the end of each day compiling their own field notes, recording in a notebook what they saw and where they saw it.

"First stopped at the ponds on the east side of 101 at Clam Beach," Jennings wrote in his notes on this Sunday, April 21, 1991.

Had Marc lead the way and he had to bore a hole through the salmonberry/stinging nettles/willow understory (alder overstory) to get to the ponds from the road. Didn't notice any junk on the road, but certainly found it walking down the embankment to the ponds. (One piece of garbage pitched was an old hamster cage!) Mostly old cans, bottles, etc. made up the garbage.

As soon as we reached the bottom, Marc let out a yell of frog and then grabbed at another one at the surface. He got the second one.

Marc also spotted a Rana aurora but it dove into the pond. We saved Marc's R. aurora and then had to watch him work the pond as it was too deep for our hip boots! Marc made it out to an island of cattails in the middle of the pond, and scrambled about on his hands and knees (in his chest waders!) looking for frogs. Spotted a large female (which he doesn't think came to the surface but was sunning on the mats), but she escaped.

Jennings is a dedicated writer of field notes, and consciously tries to meet a standard set more than sixty years ago by Joseph Grinnell, the early twentieth–century naturalist. Others kept notes before Grinnell, but "he was the one who made it into fine art," Jennings says. Grinnell believed that notes should not only carry the who, what, where, and when of every animal sighting, but should also include observations about animal behavior and details about habitat conditions. The notes should be more than merely a listing, as notes had been before him. Grinnell's approach was holistic. He believed that a researcher's notes should reflect more about an animal than could be garnered by studying dead museum specimens. Future researchers should be able to pick up a previous researcher's notes and get a full picture of an area's natural history. He was particularly concerned about recording the natural history of California before it was devoured by development. Good field notes, Grinnell believed, were such important and accurate resources that he required that his Berkeley students leave theirs at the museum he oversaw when they graduated.

"There aren't many people who take good field notes anymore," Jennings laments. "It's just sort of a lost art." Many contemporary field biologists have tried to reduce their workload by dropping note-taking from their routine. Some have replaced notebooks with tape recorders. Recorders might seem like a reasonable compromise in the notes-or-no-notes debate. But often researchers never get around to transcribing their tapes, and the oral notes are useless for quick reference. "You learn so much by reading a person's field notes," Jennings says. You learn virtually nothing from an untranscribed tape.

By day seven of our trip, we are in Six Rivers National Forest, in Del Norte County in the northwest corner of California. This county covers an area almost the size of Rhode Island, but has a population of only about 23,000 people. Seventy-three percent of the land in Del Norte is owned by some government agency, mostly the U.S. Forest Service. Trees far outnumber people here, although logging is one of the region's biggest industries. Despite the loggers, there are still stands of old-growth forest with tall, wide trees that sprouted long before there was a Forest Service or a state called California.

On this day the air is cold, and it feels more like early winter than spring. Hayes, who normally gets by with a T-shirt and jacket, has borrowed a sweatshirt to add a layer of warmth. He, Jennings, and I are standing on the bank of Muslatt Lake with two U.S. Forest Service biologists, preparing again to look for amphibians. We have been on the go constantly, camping a short night in a campground, another in Forest Service barracks. Last night, Hayes fell asleep about midnight, sitting upright in a sleeping bag spread on a bunk in the big, simple barracks, reading a scientific manuscript. At 2:00 A.M., Jennings was still processing amphibians the two had caught the day before, and then, before turning in, he made another quick survey of a stream near the barracks. The long days and lack of sleep are beginning to take their toll. As they stand by Muslatt Lake, chatting with the Forest Service biologists, Hayes and Jennings look tired and seem in no hurry to begin their work.

Muslatt Lake is essentially a big, deep fishing hole, surrounded on three sides by wooded hillside, and decorated with fallen timber. There are no other people here today. One of the biologists comments that it looks nicer than when she was last up here. "Usually there's all kinds of trash," she says. Just as she speaks, I see a discarded McDonald's bag among some bushes. Jennings points out a collection of spent bullet casings at the base of some trees. The weekend recreationists have left their mark.

Beads of soft hail begin to fall, and then stop after just a few minutes. Before they tackle the lake, Jennings and Hayes decide to walk the length of a short dirt road to look for salamanders. Salamanders usually hide in moist, dark places, under rocks, logs, or leaf litter. Jennings and Hayes turn over and then carefully replace large rocks and logs beside the dirt road as they search. Almost immediately, Jennings finds a Del Norte salamander, *Plethodon elongatus.*

There are at least twenty-six species of the genus *Plethodon,* which is part of a larger family called Plethodontidae. They are found only in North America, where they make up the largest of any amphibian genus. Their most interesting characteristic is that they lack lungs, instead breathing through their moist, gas-permeable skin.

Jennings holds up the salamander for inspection. Its skin looks like slick rubber, and its four legs, with their handlike feet, seem too short for its body. The greatest problem this species faces lies in its choice of a home: old-growth forests, a disappearing fraction of America's forest stock. Like the red-legged frog and so many other amphibians, this salamander species is suffering from habitat destruction.

Its best friend may be the spotted owl, the creature who needs the old growth to reproduce, and whose plight has drawn attention to the ecological importance of the old, unlogged forests. As we stand in this forest on this day, there is a temporary logging ban in effect. Timber companies and environmentalists are battling in courtrooms over whether the owl's fate is enough to justify permanently halting old-growth logging, particularly on federally owned land. Logging proponents have painted the owl as a single expendable animal whose survival is unnecessarily harming economic stability in the Pacific Northwest. Clearly, though, the owl is a representative of many other things, including amphibians, that rely on these threatened forests for survival. Protecting the owl is protecting the same kind of biological diversity that Americans complain is being destroyed when other, poorer countries chop down their tropical rain forests. Biologists know this. But their voice is rarely loud enough to counter the rhetoric of economic self-interest.

Jennings bags the salamander as a voucher specimen, and after turning over a few more rocks, we head back to the lake. The biologists spread out to circle the lake's banks. I follow one of the Forest Service scientists through the wooded hillside, stumbling my way through tangles of branches and bushes. Occasionally I look under a rock or log and find nothing. More often, though, I just try to keep my eye on Hayes and Jennings as they wade along the edge of the deep lake, and I try not to get lost.

The scientists cover the whole lake's edge. Then we all gather on the bank again, and Hayes discusses weather conditions at a site higher in the mountains that he wants to check. The Forest Service biologists warn that there will probably be snow there. Hayes and Jennings consider whether they should try to reach the spot the next day. Hayes is leaning toward trying, Jennings is noncommittal. The word *snow* sends chills down my already chilly spine and induces an automatic craving for warmth and food and sleep. One of the biologists is headed back in the direction of the barracks, and I hitch a ride with her. Fieldwork is looking more difficult to me each day. Meanwhile, Jennings and Hayes, still eager to continue their search, head for yet another stream.

This trip was one of the last Jennings and Hayes had to make to finish their statewide survey. The results of their three years of research weren't encouraging. California has about twenty-six native salamander species and about twenty-one native frog and toad, or anuran, species. (These numbers are estimates because scientists are still considering whether some species are actually two rather than one species.) Of those, two salamanders had already been listed by the state and federal government as endangered by the time Hayes and Jennings began their work. An endangered animal, according to state and federal law, is one that is in serious danger of becoming extinct. Five other salamanders and one toad had been listed by the state as threatened, a classification for animals that will likely become endangered if something isn't done to protect them.

After they finished their survey, the two biologists concluded that, in addition to those already on state and federal lists, ten anurans and one salamander could be considered endangered; three salamanders and one anuran could be considered threatened; and seven salamanders and two anurans warranted watching because they might slip into threatened status. In short, more than half of California's native amphibian species appear to be in trouble or in decline.

At the Irvine conference, critics kept noting that the scientists attending provided many anecdotes but very little data to support their claim that frogs and other amphibians are declining. Three years after that conference, Hayes and Jennings completed the 335-page report. That report provided some hard numbers for one part of the world. But Hayes and Jennings knew from the beginning that the survey would only be a start and that they would continue, through other work, to try to understand declining amphibians. They also believed that the numbers would give them a powerful tool to use immediately to help protect some of the most endangered amphibians.

5

· · · · · · · · · · · · · · · · · · · ·

To Have and to Hold

The smell of dead and rotting flesh pushes its way out of the metal cargo container as Sheila Einsweiler, U.S. Fish and Wildlife Service inspector, peers into the container's doorway. Dozens of brown cardboard boxes fill her view.

"Yep, smells like frogs, all right," Einsweiler says with a grimace. "They don't smell too good."

The container, no bigger than a coat closet, is sitting in an airline warehouse on the perimeter of Los Angeles International Airport. It has just been unloaded from an airplane that arrived much later than scheduled. Massive tropical storms tied up flights for two days and left this cargo stranded between its Dominican Republic origin and its Los Angeles destination. By the smell of things, the cargo has suffered.

Einsweiler takes one of the toppled boxes and peers into nickel-size air holes cut into its sides. "They're definitely packed in there," she mutters, and then sits the box on the ground and gently opens it. Sensibly dressed in a khaki uniform and solid work shoes, she doesn't hesitate to kneel on the dusty cement floor to get a better look at the box's contents. No sooner does she lift one flap of the box top than a six-inch-long frog with equally long legs makes a break for freedom and hops across the floor. It passes by me and I manage to grab it. Its skin feels sticky, not as damp as would be normal. Einsweiler returns it to the box, where it has spent at least the last three days with about twenty other frogs, literally packed as tight as sardines. Most in the box are barely moving; many are dead. The boxes are moist, but not moist enough to keep the frogs properly hydrated during the longer-than-planned trip.

Einsweiler surveys the cargo container's arrangement before she takes another box to inspect. The boxes are toppled atop a wooden pallet. They weren't strapped in or otherwise secured, so during the trip at least half have fallen and look now as though they were simply thrown into the container. There were two thousand live bullfrogs in those boxes when they were packed. Perhaps as many as half have made the trip standing on their heads or upside down because of the toppling. "You can see that the airlines took great care," Einsweiler says without trying to hide her disgust. "That's not atypical."

Soon the cargo's owner, Cheng Lai, arrives and greets Einsweiler with a nod. He is clearly disappointed by the bullfrogs' condition, and calls over an airline official who helps him begin the paperwork to file a claim for damages. He has lost some money today. The frogs are useless to him dead. He is one of two people in Los Angeles who regularly import live frogs for the food industry. He sells his to ethnic restaurants, mostly Chinese, in Southern California. Depending on the time of year and how many other live bullfrogs are on the market, he can sell the animals for three dollars to six dollars a pound. A two-thousand-frog shipment could bring in $3,000 to $6,000, but only if they are alive.

As Cheng Lai waits, Einsweiler peeks through the air holes in the boxes. She uses a flashlight to get a clearer view. She is looking at the frogs' markings, to be certain that all are bullfrogs and nothing else. Her job is to make sure nothing that is protected by state, federal, or international conservation laws passes illegally through the Los Angeles port, either here at the airport or several miles south, at the harbor. She is one of eleven inspectors working out of the Fish and Wildlife Service's Los Angeles office, and one of about ninety working at ports around the country. They are a small group charged with checking a lot of cargo.

All kinds of stuff, ranging from shoes made from animal skins to live tigers for zoos, has come through the L.A. port in the four years Einsweiler has worked for the agency. Most of the live animals come by plane in the evenings or on weekends, their arrival dictated by airline schedules. Today is Sunday, one of the busiest days for fish, reptiles, and amphibians imported from the Pacific Rim. Einsweiler doesn't have time to open and inspect each of the boxes of bullfrogs individually because she has other shipments to inspect, and this is the smallest and most straightforward of the day. After a few minutes she has peeked into the holes on each of the boxes and is satisfied that there is nothing out of the ordinary.

At another airline warehouse, Einsweiler waits patiently while a truck just arrived from the airport unloads a couple of pallets stacked with Styrofoam containers. Two other loads, stacked as high, wide, and long as full-size pickup trucks, have arrived earlier and sit unopened, waiting for inspection. Most of those boxes contain bags of water packed tight with live tropical fish, and another inspector will take care of them. Einsweiler knows from shipping documents that the pallets being unloaded now contain boxes of frogs and toads.

A large, gregarious man, a regular fish importer, teases Einsweiler as she waits. There are, he jokes, several containers of very rare endangered fish buried in the middle of one of the larger loads. Einsweiler politely assures him she'll check on it. She is cautious as she responds because she knows, as he knows, that burying within legitimate loads is an obvious but common trick for smuggling. "Maybe a quarter of the time we find something in a shipment that's not okay," she tells me.

When the pallets are finally off the truck, Einsweiler and another inspector set to work checking the cartons' contents. In one she finds six gallon-size bags, half-filled with water. Juvenile Asian toads, dull brown and barely bigger than chocolate kisses, are float-ing in a heads-up position, their legs dangling in the water. Several appear dead. But they stay upright because there is no room to fall. There are anywhere from fifty to seventy-five per bag. All that survive are destined for pet stores.

Einsweiler opens another carton. This one contains boxes within which are stacked plastic containers of the kind that might be used by a bakery to hold a mini-éclair. A thin damp sponge sits on the bottom of each plastic container, and on top of that sits a single adult toad. It has little room to move. There are a dozen of the toad packs. The animals struggle to get out as Einsweiler lifts each pack.

"This is a good packing job, as packing goes," she says. "They look lively. Their noses aren't too banged up."

She opens a third carton. This one contains green tree frogs, also packed in the éclair packs. The frogs are a couple of inches long. As she pulls one pack out, it becomes clear that this batch of animals isn't doing well. They are barely alive. One is dead, one is flattened and looks like road kill, another is hardly breathing. They have dehydrated. There are seventy-two of these frogs, at least half of them dead or dying.

"You get them frozen, squished, dehydrated," Einsweiler sighs.

The U.S. Fish and Wildlife Service has written humane trans-port regulations for mammals and birds that specify exactly how the animals must be packed to protect them from injury or death. Hu-mane transport regulations for amphibians and reptiles are on the agency's agenda, but it is hard to tell when they will get done, since there are so many other tasks that have priority. Getting regulations for birds, which became effective only in 1991, was helped by the fact that the U.S. Department of Agriculture—concerned about controlling the spread of avian disease to commercial poultry—keeps mortality figures on birds transported into U.S. ports. No one keeps similar figures on how many amphibians or reptiles die in shipping.

. . .

After scientists publicly raised the declining-amphibian alarm, human trade in amphibians was not staunched. Instead it increased dramatically. More than four times as many amphibians legally passed through U.S. ports in 1992 as in 1990, according to U.S. Fish and Wildlife Service records. The increase probably had nothing to do with the alarm, and everything to do with a simple increase in human exploitation to meet a popular demand. People sell frogs for food, pets, purses, and wallets, now more than ever. And consumers continue to buy these products.

Like any other predator, people want frogs mostly for food. Many Asian cultures have included frog legs in their diets for centuries—or at least until they have run out of frogs. But the most famous frog eaters, and the people who inspired frog-eating in Europe and the United States, are the French. Alexandre Dumas, the French novelist and author of *Le Grand Dictionnaire de Cuisine,* a classic nineteenth-century reference for cooks, noted that frogs were not always so popular in his homeland.

> *In the Middle Ages, many physicians were against using this meat for food, though it is white and delicate and contains a gelatinous ingredient that is less nourishing than that of other meats. Bernard Palissy, in his treatise on stones in 1580, put it this way: "And in my time, I have seen very few men who would eat either turtles or frogs."*
>
> *Nevertheless, frogs were served on the best tables in the sixteenth century, and Champier complained of what he called a bizarre taste. A hundred years ago, an Auvergnat named Simon made quite a fortune in Paris fattening frogs sent from his countryside and selling them to the finest houses, where they were very much the mode.*

By the time Dumas was writing, frog-eating was firmly in vogue in France. Its popularity had also spread to neighboring countries, such as Germany and Italy. The animal was even being recommended as an ingredient in soup to cure consumption.

The preferred frog for the French was their own *Rana esculenta,* commonly called the green frog or—even more appropriately, considering its fate—the edible frog. But as local demand increased and frog populations declined, the French began moving across Central Europe and then into Turkey, grabbing other large frogs to satisfy their increasing taste for the creature. By 1977 the French government, so concerned about the scarcity of its native frog, banned commercial hunting of its own amphibians. At about the same time, the Central European and Turkish supplies were drying up. None of this, though, stopped human frog-eaters. So the French and Dutch (a major frog-leg wholesaler) turned to India and Bangladesh for frogs. A combination of efficient refrigeration and dirt-cheap (often child) labor in these countries made it possible to catch frogs, cut off and freeze their legs, and then ship them to Europe and still sell them at a price that made them appealing. They became an easy-to-find item in grocery store freezer sections.

The demand for frog legs surfaced in the United States in various parts of the country, not just California, and involved various frogs, not only California red-leggeds, according to Mark Jennings and Marc Hayes. Bullfrogs and pig frogs *(Rana grylio),* have been the most widely harvested American food frog because they meet a basic requirement: They have large, meaty legs. Other medium and large frogs, including leopard frogs *(Rana pipiens),* sometimes called grass frogs, have also been enthusiastically collected for food, especially in New York State.

At New York's large Oneida Lake, hunters perfected one style of mass frog-collecting in the late nineteenth and early twentieth centuries that helped make the area among the most productive in the frogging industry. Each year from July until winter, men and boys would "tramp the borders of the lake and swamps and upland fields, singly or in small parties, carrying clubs about three feet long," according to one paper published in 1916. "The frogs are flushed and as they alight a blow is struck with the club, killing them." Using this rather brutal method, hunters collected three types of medium-size frogs, including leopard frogs, green frogs *(Rana clamitans),* and pickerel frogs *(Rana palustris).* A hunter could collect on average six hundred to eight hundred frogs in a single day, although at least one hunter reported taking more than 1,200 during less than six hours of work.

In the fall, as the frogs migrated from the meadows back to the lake to hibernate, the hunters would set up along the lake shore cheesecloth screens that were too high for the frogs to clear. So, typically, a frog would wander along the edge of the screen looking for an opening. The only opening, though, was straight down into sunken cans the hunters had set as traps for the frogs. Along a half-mile length of shoreline, a frogger could collect about five hundred pounds of frogs in a night, according to the 1916 report.

It took about twenty-five to forty Oneida-area frogs to make a pound of frog legs. The legs sold for an average of just over one dollar per pound. It would, then, take a whole lot of frogs to make the frog collecting pay off. But even by 1916, frogs in the area were abundant enough to provide a hunter a decent living. One hunting team claimed an annual gross of about $15,000 from frogs alone— very big bucks at that time.

"They used to literally collect tens of thousands of frogs in a day. Just tremendous amounts of frogs," Hayes says of the Oneida area hunters. "You would think it wouldn't take terribly many years to decimate a population, but what was truly amazing about the way they operated was that the population didn't go down very fast. There must have been tremendous populations for them to harvest them as they did."

Louisiana and Florida swamplands were also prominent commercial frogging sites in the late nineteenth and early twentieth centuries. But as the technology for catching and storing frogs improved, the number of frogs dropped from overharvesting. Until the 1930s, according to Hayes, most commercial frog hunters in the southern swamps used elongated dugout boats that they slowly maneuvered with long poles through the stump-ridden waters. As they moved, they would catch the frogs by hand. There was no refrigeration, so the frogs had to be treated delicately and kept alive so that they wouldn't spoil before they got to market. This limited the number of frogs a hunter could nab and the amount of time he could spend in the swamps before having to return to shore. These hindrances to mass production kept frogging low enough to prevent any major damage to local frog populations.

Things changed in the 1930s, when block ice became available. Suddenly, froggers were free to use spears to nab frogs from the swamp because they could keep the dead animals from spoiling by placing them on ice. But what really revolutionized commercial frogging, according to Hayes and Jennings, was the invention of the airboat. Rapidly pushed by an aircraft-type propeller, the airboat allowed froggers to speed through the swamp and cover many miles in a single night's work.

"Commercial froggers expert at airboat use could easily harvest a metric ton of frogs in less than a week," Hayes says. "In the absence of any restriction on harvesting, airboat-assisted commercial harvest rapidly depleted frog populations." Commercial frogging peaked in the mid- and late 1930s. Within twenty years the bullfrog and pig-frog populations were so depleted that most commercial harvesting ended. However, sport frogging continued—and is still conducted—in Florida and Louisiana, as well as other parts of the country, including California.

As happened in France, when the local catch became harder to get and more expensive, American frog-leg fanciers and restaurants turned increasingly to frozen imports. In recent years the United States, Germany, and the Netherlands—which processes and sells frog-leg products to France and other countries—have been the top consumers in the international frog-leg trade. According to figures collected from government agencies by Traffic U.S.A., an arm of the World Wildlife Fund conservation organization, the

United States imported more than 6.5 million pounds of frozen frog meat each year between 1981 and 1984. This meat represents only the legs of the frogs, a fraction of their total weight. If you figure that one pair of frog legs weighs a quarter of a pound (a generous estimate), then about 26 million frogs were captured and killed during each of those years to serve the American frog-leg appetite. Ninety percent of those legs came from India and Bangladesh, according to Traffic. In 1987, India banned frog-leg exports after reports that the frog-hunting was decimating local populations of *Rana tigrina* and *Rana hexadactyla,* the two Indian versions of the bullfrog. Conservationists and one prominent Indian biologist charged that such decimation was causing an increase in mosquitoes and forcing India to become more reliant on expensive pesticides.

Two years later, Bangladesh also banned frog-leg exports. But by 1991 its government was considering removing the ban. The reason? The country was dependent on income sent home by Bangladeshi oil workers in Kuwait. With the outbreak of the Persian Gulf War, that income was severely cut at the same time crude oil prices rose. Incredibly, frog legs were viewed as one way to make up that lost income.

Since the India and Bangladesh frog-export bans, Indonesia has become the major exporter of frog legs to the United States and Europe. But no matter what country the legs come from, one thing is usually constant: The legs once belonged to frogs taken from the wild, not from farms. Frogs are nearly impossible to farm economically. It would probably be easier to develop a human demand for crickets, mealworms or ants—the preferred breakfast of captive frogs—than it is to farm frogs successfully and make money. Frogs don't withstand crowding very well, and have a tendency toward cannibalism. They are also expensive to feed, because they will eat only live creatures. And in the countries where frogs are commercially harvested from the wild, the harvester gets paid only pennies per frog. No farm can compete with that price.

Many dreamers have tried to farm frogs commercially. During the 1930s, a couple of clever scam artists hawked frog-farming as the way to riches in the United States, and unwary consumers spent their last dime trying to work their way out of a worldwide depression by setting up frog farms that ultimately failed. Even today, people occasionally make legitimate attempts to build a better frog farm, and herpetologists have told me of hearing about working farms in Brazil and China, where labor is cheap. Perhaps after the last populations of large, wild, palatable frogs are wiped out for commerce—as they eventually are sure to be in Indonesia—prices for legs will become high enough that farming will be feasible. A cynic might suggest that foodies everywhere should keep eating those frog legs. The species they help push into extinction in the wild today may become a farm animal tomorrow—if there are any left.

Connoisseurs describe frog-leg flavor as resembling that of a delicate chicken. Indeed, the legs are often prepared like chicken—soaked in milk, dusted with flour, then fried. Inquiring minds might wonder why leg fanciers don't simply eat chicken and avoid the consequences of knocking out wild populations. The answer probably lies within the mysterious ways of human taste buds. But it is worth noting that leg-eating can return to haunt, and after nearly one hundred years, scientists have attributed at least two famous incidents of unexplained ailments to the effects of eating frogs.

In the late nineteenth century, French doctors reported two separate cases of priapism among soldiers who were stationed in North Africa. Priapism is the rather embarrassing condition of having a prolonged and painful penile erection unassociated with any erotic pleasure. The French doctors noted that in both cases the soldiers had eaten frog legs and that the symptoms, as one recent science magazine noted, "resembled those seen in men who had overindulged in a drug called cantharidin—popularly known as Spanish fly—which is extracted from a particular beetle for its purported value as an aphrodisiac." The doctors found the beetle in the gut of local frogs. But despite all of these signals, the physicians couldn't conclusively say the legs had caused the ailment. Then, in 1991, some prominent entomologists did their own studies with frogs and the offending beetles and found that, indeed, frogs that dined on the beetles retained significant amounts of cantharidin in their thigh muscles for a few days. However, the drug seemed to have no effect on the frogs.

Theoretically, the scientists concluded, a person who overindulges in frogs that have eaten this exotic beetle could actually consume enough cantharidin to kill himself. Chances of that happening are slim, however. As Thomas Eisner, one of the scientists who made the discovery, told the magazine *Science News,* "I'm not saying, 'Watch out, don't eat frog legs'—although I'd like to say that, because frogs are endangered all over the world."

Humans also covet frogs and toads for their hides. In Brazil, toads—warts and all—are fashioned into purses, and in Thailand, street vendors sell wallets made from frog skin. Toad and frog leather goods began making their way into the United States from other countries in the early 1980s, according to Traffic. One U.S. Fish and Wildlife Service biologist recalls seeing whole orchestras composed of stuffed cane toads, *Bufo marinus,* holding miniature instruments, including cellos and violins, among the imported leather novelties. Raw skins have also been imported into the United States to be turned into products.

But increasingly, people covet frogs and toads for themselves, and have made them part of the world's pet trade. One pet industry trade group's 1991 survey of eleven thousand independent pet stores in the United States found that more than 41 percent sold amphibians and reptiles, two categories of animals that seem inseparable when pet industry statistics are compiled. In Los Angeles alone there are about five major reptile importers and twenty major fish importers, most of whom also deal in amphibians. Some of those importers sell amphibians in their own large retail stores, while others sell mostly to retailers and private collectors.

There are a few reasons why frogs, toads, and salamanders have increasingly become pet-trade items in recent years. First, amphibians are less protected from trade than are either mammals or birds. Fewer than one hundred amphibians are listed on the Convention for International Trade in Endangered Species, or CITES, the agreement that about one hundred countries follow to varying degrees to protect the world's wild animals. In contrast, CITES lists many hundreds of birds and mammals.

Also, in the last ten years, unusual and colorful amphibians, especially frogs and toads, have been brought out of the tropics and placed on display in stores and at pet fairs. A bright blue, inch-long frog that looks more like a porcelain figurine than a live animal is its own salesman. The pet trade has only had to show its supply to create a demand for some of these animals.

Finally, more people live in smaller quarters and want animals that are quieter and smaller than the proverbial family Fido. Pet dealers have set out to meet—and, some would argue, to help create—this demand by expanding their stock in amphibians and reptiles. (In fact, reptiles are even more in demand in the pet trade than amphibians, because amphibians are susceptible to dehydration and are harder to keep healthy in pet stores.)

The green tree frogs Einsweiler inspected as I watched one September Sunday were probably caught in the wild in Asia. The large toads were also probably caught in the wild. However, some amphibians are being bred in captivity for the pet trade. Hong Kong and Singapore both have captive-breeding industries. Successful captive breeding of parrots was one of the keys to slowing the U.S. trade in wild-caught birds. Some of the advocates of captive breeding say it could have the same impact on amphibian trade and help keep the wild animals in the wild—at least where they still have wilderness in which to live.

. . .

Philippe de Vosjoli and Robert Mailloux are among captive breeding's most visible advocates. Mailloux, a tall and slender man with
a cap of curly, sandy hair, looks boyish despite a graying beard. He
grew up in Southern California coastal towns, and as a youngster
he would catch local frogs and bring them home to an aquarium,
where they would lay eggs that he watched develop into tadpoles
and tiny frogs.

De Vosjoli, clean-shaven, with long black hair pulled back in a
fashionable ponytail, is the son of a French diplomat. He spent his
youth moving back and forth between the United States and his
hometown of Paris. He fell in love with the idea of captive breeding reptiles and amphibians almost the very second he walked into
a Paris shop owned by a former zookeeper. The shop was filled
with vivariums—small, realistic natural worlds re-created in glass
containers. The shop owner became a mentor to de Vosjoli, who,
at fourteen, bred his first lizards in a vivarium in a Paris apartment.

De Vosjoli and Mailloux met in the mid-1980s at a herpetological conference. By then, Mailloux was developing frog-breeding
techniques in his California backyard. De Vosjoli was in graduate
school at Harvard University, studying frog behavior. Specifically
he was interested in poison-dart frogs, members of the geni *Dendrobates* and *Phyllobates*. These tiny Central and South American tropical frogs come in a rainbow of brilliant colors. Their beautiful skins
are also quite toxic, and some South American hunters traditionally
rubbed certain Phyllobates frogs' skin on the tips of their blow-gun
darts to make their weapons more deadly. It takes only a small
amount of the toxin to kill a mammal.

Before de Vosjoli could finish his work on the poison-dart frogs,
his study animals died. By then, the pet trade demand for poison-
dart frogs was great in Europe and the United States. In addition,
the tropical forests in which they lived were being quickly demol-
ished. These two facts combined to persuade CITES signatories to
list the frogs as endangered species, and legal trade in wild-caught
poison-dart frogs all but stopped. De Vosjoli couldn't find enough

frogs to restart his study. Also, he was tired of school and wanted a change. So he left school and moved to California to begin captive breeding with Mailloux.

In 1988 the two men founded the American Federation of Herpetoculturists, an organization for people who captive-breed reptiles and amphibians. Within four years the organization had four thousand members, making it the largest herpetological organization in the country, and possibly in the world. The AFH's members are mostly hobbyists and commercial captive breeders, the cogs that keep the pet trade in amphibians and reptiles going, just through their own enthusiasm. Most of the members are interested in snakes and lizards, but some, like de Vosjoli and Mailloux, captive-breed amphibians as well. Today, de Vosjoli has little time for active, hands-on captive breeding or research; he spends most of his time administering the organization and writing books and manuals about the care of reptiles and amphibians.

Mailloux is the main keeper and breeder, and works out of his backyard in Redondo Beach, a crowded oceanside town about an hour's drive south of downtown Los Angeles. His house is a modest stucco one-story in a neighborhood dominated by remodels that have turned into mini-mansions. Its modesty belies the size and contents of its backyard. The yard seems to go on forever, even as its boundaries are visible. The illusion is helped by a zooful of lizards and snakes housed in an orderly arrangement of large, solidly constructed cages and pens. The animals are being bred, or waiting for whenever Mailloux can find an appropriate mate.

The centerpiece amid all these reptiles is a low, long building about the size of a three-car garage. On a late summer day, I follow Mailloux and de Vosjoli, who has traveled up to Mailloux's from San Diego, into the building. Half of the room is taken up by a pond, a deck that hangs over it, and a collection of tropical plants. A grid of sprinkler-system pipes hangs over the pond. During the breeding season, Mailloux tries to simulate the rainy season in the tropics by turning on the sprinklers each night.

"There are quite a few different types of frogs hanging out in this area," Mailloux says, pointing to the bank of plants along the pond edge. The frogs are invisible now, hidden among the leaves and in the water. "In the breeding season, they all kind of play off of each other. One type will start calling and the other will start calling. It sounds like a chorus, and they all sort of get into it."

Mailloux walks across the deck and turns a knob. Water sprays like a fine summer rain over the pond. "I try to turn the sprinklers on these guys for a few hours each evening, which is a bit scary because I always worry about the neighbors. This gets the frogs going all night and, you know, five or six species going full tilt all night . . ." He shrugs, leaving his sentence unfinished. His neighbors don't complain, he says thankfully. "Some of them say they hear it but they kind of like it. But I lie in there and think, 'Oh, God, they're going to torch my house.' "

Today the frogs are quiet. The only nonhuman noise we hear is an orchestra of crickets. Mailloux buys six thousand crickets a month, which lay eggs to produce more crickets. Ultimately he feeds all the crickets to the amphibians and reptiles. He also stocks mealworms for feed.

A bank of glass containers holding various frogs lines one wall and part of another. Dozens of small blue-green frogs stick like suction cups to the glass. They are White's tree frogs, *Litoria caerulea,* natives of Australia whose transport outside of that country, which is a strong adherent to international wildlife trade laws, has been restricted for more than a decade. However, people like Mailloux have mastered the methodology for getting these frogs to breed.

"In the early eighties, I purchased three White's tree frogs from California Zoological Supply. I'd seen one a year before at a show, and I just thought it was the greatest frog I'd ever seen," Mailloux recalls. "They were almost impossible to get, then. I got the three, raised them up, and they all turned out to be males. It took me a year to find a female." When he did, he started breeding them.

The White's doesn't breed well in the pond. Mailloux uses a rain chamber, which is essentially a fifteen-gallon glass container occupied by plants and rigged with a sprinkler to encourage breeding. He places several pairs of the frogs in the chamber, and after a day or two, a few of the pairs will find each other and amplect, the frog version of a sexual embrace essential to mating. One female White's can lay several thousand eggs at a time.

If you walk into any American pet store that carries frogs, there is a good chance the store will have in stock at least one White's tree frog. They are popular in part because they are bright green or blue-green, and colorful frogs sell better than brown ones. Also, White's tree frogs have prominent ridges that hang over their eyes, giving them an amiable look reminiscent of the movie alien E.T. Mailloux breeds and sells thousands of White's to wholesalers and large pet stores each year. He is probably the largest single producer of the frog in the country, and it is one of his biggest sellers.

Some frogs can be caught in the wild and imported so cheaply that captive breeding can't compete economically. The White's works because it can no longer legally be caught in the wild and exported. A wholesaler pays Mailloux about five dollars apiece for the captive-bred White's and then sells it to retailers for two or three times that much. By the time the frog reaches the store shelves, it is carrying a twenty-to-twenty-five-dollar price tag. In contrast, some species of imported frogs and toads that are still wild-caught cost the wholesaler less than one dollar apiece and still sell in stores for fifteen dollars to twenty dollars and sometimes much more.

Mailloux and de Vosjoli have mastered breeding methods for a number of frogs, but actively breed only a few. Time and space inhibit them from breeding more. "You have to work with things that are economically viable," Mailloux says. "There are a lot of other neat little frogs that we would raise, but they would be hard to sell or we couldn't get enough for them to make it worthwhile."

One of the frustrations that goes beyond economics is the

knowledge that no matter how healthy the frogs are that Mailloux and de Vosjoli cultivate and sell to pet stores, many if not most will be dead within weeks. Most pet-store clerks are "abominably ignorant" about how to care for reptiles and amphibians, de Vosjoli complains. And that ignorance gets passed on to the customer. Some estimate that fewer than half of the amphibians imported make it to the retailer alive. Of those, probably fewer than half live beyond a month or two once sold.

Most captive breeders of frogs work on a much smaller scale than Mailloux and de Vosjoli. The majority are hobbyists, and the results of their work are traded with or sold to other hobbyists. Europeans, particularly Germans, are among the most avid live amphibian breeders and collectors. Creating lush vivariums is a popular pastime in Europe that hasn't hit the United States with much force.

Drew Ready, one young American hobbyist I met at a meeting of amateur herpetologists, showed me his small collection of tropical frogs in three vivariums he kept in the corner of the bedroom he shared with his brother in his parents' home in a Los Angeles suburb. Tanks of tadpoles were arranged on a table along one wall. His setup was immaculate, and he had successfully bred and was raising tadpoles of tiger tree frogs, *Phyllomedusa hypocondrialis*. These one-and-one-half-inch-long brilliant green frogs have orange and black stripes on the insides of their legs. When they move, they raise their whole bodies up and move their legs with the steady, deliberate steps reminiscent of a walkingstick insect. Sometimes they are called "walking frogs."

Ready considers his frog breeding an interesting hobby that has the added benefit of helping to increase rare frog populations. To do it right requires a lot of attention to detail. He has had to experiment with the setup of tanks and terrariums, pipes, tubes, and misters to find the one that works most efficiently. Ready figures he spends an hour or two a day just cleaning terrariums and changing water for tadpoles. "There's no neglect. You're cleaning the water all the time," he notes. "And when neglect sets in, you get rid of the animals."

Another hobbyist I visited, Alan McCready, has a collection of glass containers located in different parts of his house and backyard. The type of occupants in each container doesn't remain constant. McCready, like most hobbyists, frequently trades with and buys new animals from other hobbyists as his interests change. If a certain species catches his fancy, he will try to collect enough to breed. When I visited, the containers held various exotic frogs, some destined for breeding, some still unpaired. They were from Ecuador, China, New Guinea, and the eastern United States. The most exotic was a large light brown toad from Madagascar, where deforestation is rapidly wiping out native animal life. The toad had blue and pink striped legs, blue and gray flashpoints on its side, a brown stripe on its mouth, bright green toes, and parkling golden eyes. It was beautiful.

One of McCready's most innovative creations is a simple seasonal pool he dug in his backyard to collect rainwater. During drought years he supplements the rainwater with tap water in the summer. The pool serves as an annual breeding ground for Pacific tree frogs. Almost singlehandedly, McCready has repopulated his suburban neighborhood outside of Sacramento, California, with that native frog. "It's sort of my way of trying to keep wild America still alive."

Keeping wildlife alive has become one of the latest arguments for captive breeding. Aside from helping to dissuade consumers from buying wild stock, breeding frogs may be one way to ensure that at least small populations of endangered amphibians are in safekeeping. Zoos have often stepped in as savings banks for endangered mammals and birds. However, they have been less than enthusiastic about amphibians in the past. Most amphibians are nocturnal or secretive and don't display well. They would rather hide behind a rock than preen in front of a glass window. They don't attract crowds to the gates. Also, many zoos perceive amphibians, especially frogs, as difficult to keep because many of the animals require perfectly clean water. Maintaining that high quality can be laborious. And exactly what kind of zoo environment works for many amphibians is unknown, so zoos have to become pioneers in habitat creation if they want to keep these animals. That pioneering can be labor-intensive and expensive.

Nevertheless, some zoos and aquariums have taken steps to try to keep and breed endangered frogs. For more than a decade, about a dozen zoos, including the Metro Toronto Zoo, have kept and bred Puerto Rican crested toads, *Peltophryne lemur,* a species endangered in its natural habitat. In the early 1990s the Sacramento Zoo began a breeding program for Yosemite toads, which are apparently declining in their Sierra Nevada mountain range habitat. Through their major trade group, the American Association of Zoological Parks and Aquariums, zoo curators and directors are trying to identify other amphibians that need immediate captive-breeding attention.

The National Aquarium in Baltimore has one of the largest captive-breeding programs for amphibians. The aquarium's collection includes twenty-four species of poison-dart frogs displayed in a rain-forest exhibit that about one and a half million people visit each year. The frogs have proved to be a great way to show rain-forest biological diversity, according to Jack Cover, the exhibit's curator. But the institution also has learned new things about the frogs, including some of the difficulties of captive breeding. The aquarium has been able to breed about twenty of the poison-dart frogs but they have found that none of the ones bred in captivity has poisonous skin. Cover figures this may be because something is missing in their diet in captivity. Or it may have something to do with lack of exposure to unfiltered sunlight. In any case, if these frogs were released to the wild, would they regain their toxic skin? Or, if they didn't, would they then be eaten by predators who once shunned them? In short, would returning them to the wild return a balance or destroy it?

Captive breeding is not a solution to stop amphibians from declining in the wild. It can only be a stop-gap, temporary measure to stop some creatures from becoming extinct. As Cover says, it can be an ace in the hole to protect some species from total decimation. Habitat is being destroyed at such a rapid rate around the world that it is almost guaranteed that more creatures will disappear than will make it into captive-breeding programs.

Some amphibian researchers and hobbyists believe that captive breeding might be used to strengthen or restore wild amphibian populations. But releasing captive-bred animals into the wild has its own set of problems, as the California condor restoration project has shown. Beginning in early 1992, eight captive-bred condors were released into their ancestral home in the Los Padres National Forest. Three of the birds died within one nine-month period. One drank antifreeze that had been dumped on the ground, one was electrocuted when it landed on power lines, and one collided with some object—either a car or power lines. The old condor habitat was no longer wild enough to sustain the introduced animals.

What will happen to captive-bred amphibians released to the wild if there is no real wilderness left? And even if there is a wild spot, unless the reason for the amphibians' decline in the first place has been accurately identified and corrected, there is no guarantee the introduced animals won't disappear as well. There is also a risk that captive-bred animals will take some new virus from captivity into the wild with them, and infect wild populations. The captive-breeding stock's introduction could change the genetic pool in the wild, possibly for the worse.

Finally, any captive-breeding program costs money. Even captive-breeding advocates routinely point to the high costs associated with the California condor breeding program. More than $25 million was spent on that program before any condors were released. Is anyone willing to spend as much on frogs?

. . .

Often it is difficult for people who are so passionate about frogs and toads and salamanders to explain why they like them as much as they do. It seems about as difficult as explaining to someone who has no eyesight how it feels to see color, or to someone who has no hearing how it feels to listen to music. De Vosjoli has found a single word he believes explains what makes some so passionate about amphibians. That word is *enchantment*.

"Enchant—one of the definitions is to delight to a high degree, to charm. And that's what they are," he says, "they are a charm." As de Vosjoli talks, we are sitting in Mailloux's living room, within an arm's reach of a long glass box filled with tropical plants. A turquoise and black frog, no bigger than a large cockroach, stares out at us. It is contained in its own damp, green tropical world as we sit outside in the California heat, staring back at it, enchanted.

Frogs and toads, which may repel or bore some people, open up for others a whole different way of looking at the world. If you think of an animal as a creature who has a different form of thinking and perceiving, then by developing a relationship with that animal, de Vosjoli says, a human can expand his or her understanding. "All of a sudden you realize that life can be richer and it's possible to have relationships, interactions with a great variety of forms of consciousness, and it can be anything from plants to animals," he says. "By doing that, by having that relationship, your whole relationship to the world has changed."

De Vosjoli distinguishes between the hobbyist and breeders on the one hand and scientists on the other. He believes hobbyists and breeders are more enchanted by these animals than scientists are. Scientists see them mostly as tools, and seem to have lost a deeper feeling for the creatures. I know what de Vosjoli means. I have talked to scientists involved in amphibian work who seem less interested in the creatures themselves than in the research project the creatures represent. Perhaps that is one of the prices of the high-pressure system of academic research. But I have also heard scientists in the field talk about the challenge of thinking like a frog, about the pleasure they get when they believe they have met that challenge. I have watched big, serious male scientists suddenly shift their booming voices into a sort of high-pitched, soothing talk as they approach and gently hold a toad or frog. They too seemed enchanted.

Human sentiment about frogs and toads has been a mixed bag through history. Anurans have appeared in art, literature, and folk culture as demons, connivers, saviors, good-luck charms, and simple goofy characters with kind hearts. The ancient Chinese credited a frog with holding the world upon its shoulders. Japanese legends gave the toad an all-knowing quality. More than one culture has believed toads and frogs could induce fertility in humans. Pre-Columbian art includes any number of carved and cast images of frogs, whose purpose was to ensure that a happy couple produced many children. Contemporary literature, especially children's literature, depicts frogs and toads as either courtly or, in the case of the very famous Muppet, Kermit, exceedingly cheerful and polite, with an outsize heart.

Toads generally have been vilified more than frogs, possibly because of the average toad's wartier appearance and toxicity. Recently, St. Lawrence University literature professor Robert De-Graaff published *The Book of the Toad,* a loving literary celebration of the toad, in which he traces the creature's history in world culture. This poor animal has been horribly maligned over the years by virtually everyone, credited with every evil known to man. In light of this history, it is almost surprising that there are any toads still alive.

Things got a little less dark for the toad's reputation during the late nineteenth and early twentieth centuries, according to De-Graaff, in part because people began recognizing some of its virtues. One key virtue is its nearly insatiable appetite for insects and other garden pests that rank even lower in human respect than the toad.

Some myths about frogs and toads seem to take forever to die. Only recently someone told me, seriously, that he had acquired warts from handling toads. For the record, toads do not cause warts. Many toads do have warty-looking skin, and some of those wart-like projections are glands filled with toxins that make them unappetizing or even deadly to predators. If you handle a toad, it is wise to wash your hands immediately so that you don't accidentally transfer toxin to your mouth or eyes with an innocent wipe or lick. But don't worry about warts. They aren't spread by this creature.

Toxic chemicals held within skin glands are not limited to toads. Some frogs, including the poison-dart frogs, and some types of newts and salamanders also have skin toxins. In addition, the eggs of various amphibians are coated with toxic chemicals. Many different chemicals are represented in these toxins. Some can cause heart failure; others affect the central nervous system. The toxins' obvious purpose is to make the amphibians unpalatable to predators. But humans have also adapted these toxins to their own uses.

One of the arguments for preserving biological diversity in the world is the hope that many of the Earth's creatures and plants may hold the chemical keys to solving human ailments. This is already proving to be true of amphibian toxins. For centuries the Chinese used a powder called Ch'an Su to treat heart problems. The powder was derived from toad skin secretions containing bufotenin, which, like digitalis, causes blood pressure to rise by strongly constricting blood vessels.

Now scientists know that poison-dart frogs and a few other amphibians have alkaloids in their skin. Alkaloids are a broad group of compounds that have in the past been extracted from plants to create useful pharmaceuticals, including drugs that fight malaria, cancer, and pain. One National Institutes of Health researcher has spent much of his career identifying and analyzing amphibian-based alkaloids because he believes they hold a great potential to become the models for important painkillers and other drugs.

Anthropologists have found that some indigenous people living along the Amazon River use frog toxins to get a satisfying feeling of superhuman strength and confidence before going out to hunt. They rub the toxins into self-inflicted open wounds. The confidence doesn't come without its cost, though. It is preceded by vomiting, drooling, and extreme discomfort immediately after the toxins make contact with the hunter's circulatory system.

Some toad toxins are rumored to cause hallucinations. These hallucinogenic qualities have become legendary among people who find sport in taking mind-distorting substances, and have led to a still-uncommon practice called toad licking. Toad licking—which is exactly what the term implies—is a dangerous business. The toxins in amphibians, including toads and newts, are extremely potent. Drinking bug spray would probably be safer. Studies to measure the potency of some of the toxins have found, for instance, that a single adult rough-skinned newt contains enough toxin to kill 25,000 white mice. That's easily enough to kill a few large humans.

David L. Martin, a young biologist who studies Yosemite toads, *Bufo canorus,* frequently speaks to community groups and conservation organizations about that toad's decline. After he finishes one of his talks, it is typical for someone in the audience to ask about the toad's toxins. The question is often awkwardly phrased in an effort to be discreet, but the intent remains clear. The questioner wants to know if the Yosemite toad's toxins are good hallucinogens. If they are, Martin doesn't know and, he says, he's not interested in risking his life to find out. He is also careful not to reveal the exact whereabouts of toad populations when he speaks to groups. He doesn't want the populations to be targeted by collectors, including the toad lickers.

The medical research value of frogs extends beyond their skin toxins. Like the white rat, the frog is one of the most common laboratory animals, and its system has opened many doors in understanding how cells and genes work, and how certain human ailments might be tackled or cured. There is probably not a biomedi-

cal scientist or medical doctor alive today who didn't dissect a leopard frog, African clawed frog, or bullfrog early in his or her science
training. In fact, leopard frogs were so heavily collected for biological supply houses that some blame that collecting for local declines
of those frogs in parts of the Midwest.

Today the frog most commonly used in labs is the African
clawed frog, *Xenopus laevis,* native to South Africa. One of its first
medical claims to fame saw it replacing the rabbit in pregnancy
testing. Urine from a woman would be injected into a female African clawed frog. If the woman was pregnant, within a few days the
hormones contained in the urine would prompt the frog to produce and lay eggs. The frog is no longer used in such tests, but it
remains a key tool in scientific research, including genetics.

The African clawed frog is a valuable lab animal for several reasons: It is hardy and easy to take care of, will eat practically anything, and can be induced with hormones to produce eggs many
times during most seasons. Its eggs are fairly large, and because they
are transparent, scientists can watch the frog embryos develop.
Some researchers and government agencies have recently begun
using a standardized test that includes the eggs of clawed frogs to
determine whether some chemical or compound will have a toxic
impact on pond life or even on human life. This test is considered
the tip of the iceberg and will likely be followed by other types of
toxicity tests using frog eggs.

One of the clawed frog's greatest assets—its hardiness—has also
proved to be one of its greatest hazards. When released into the
wild in parts of the United States, the species has been nearly impossible to control. It can live in the dirtiest water imaginable and
will eat anything that moves, including native frogs. It can do irrep-
arable ecological damage if let loose in a delicately balanced environment.

The research and biomedical value of amphibians has barely
been tapped. For self-interested humans, that alone should be reason enough to save them. Some scientists have tried to emphasize

amphibians' biomedical value in an effort to drum up public concern about declines. Australian Michael Tyler, an amphibian biologist, is one of those drummers.

Tyler is a lanky, middle-aged man who constantly seems to be peering over a pair of half-glasses. He speaks with an Australian accent softened by his English upbringing, and is renowned for enjoying a good laugh. Tyler has become a minor celebrity in Australia. One of his admirers describes him as the Carl Sagan of frogs. He speaks to anyone who will listen about frogs and the dangers of their decline—from local farmers' groups to ladies' clubs to conservation organizations to television audiences. In virtually all of these talks, he brings up the gastric brooding frog, an animal with clear medical research value that will never be fully explored.

A muddy brown creature, the gastric brooding frog, *Rheobatrachus silus,* was discovered in 1973. Its discoverer, an Indonesian scientist visiting Australia, had defied conventional local wisdom that declared that the continent had no aquatic stream frogs, and began looking for some. He found the gastric brooder in sites along remote streams in the Conondale and Blackall mountains in Southeastern Queensland.

Some of these mountain sites lie within a national park protected from hunters and loggers. All of the sites are covered with rain forest whose trees rise more than one hundred feet. The forest canopy is so dense that it blocks most sunlight from reaching the forest floor. Networks of streams and pools that contain what Tyler describes as "exquisite fresh water as clear as a bell" wind through the forest. It is, in short, a storybook setting for a frog.

The gastric brooding frogs were most active in these streams and pools at night during the spring and summer. Early on, they distinguished themselves with some unusual habits. Tyler recalls seeing them hanging in the pools in groups of three or four, touching each other's front fingers, like children holding hands in a game of ring-around-the-rosy. He commonly found frogs resting on the floor of the forest near the stream, back to the ground, belly and all four feet turned upward to a single stream of light peeking through the forest canopy.

At first, Australia's herpetologists were interested in the gastric brooder mainly because it was aquatic and resembled another species found in the southern part of South America and South Africa. They thought the frog might be a link that could tell more of the story about how Earth's landmasses moved and its creatures evolved. Then, about a year after it was discovered, the frog proved to be even more interesting than anyone initially realized, for reasons nobody ever would have imagined.

Two young men in Brisbane who kept some of the frogs alive in an aquarium were cleaning the enclosure. As they moved one of the frogs, it spit a tadpole from its mouth. The men were flabbergasted, and immediately called Tyler at the University of Adelaide. Tyler assumed from their description that the behavior was evidence that the frog was related to a South American frog called *Rhinoderma darwinii*. The male of that frog typically holds the fertilized eggs in its vocal sacs—the bags located in the throats of most male frogs and toads that amplify their call. When the eggs develop into frogs, they jump out of their father's vocal sacs and through his mouth into the world. Tyler knew he couldn't be sure whether the new frog was like the South American type unless he managed to get one of the new frogs while it still had babies in its throat. So he told the men to hang on to it and let him know if anything else happened.

As he tells what happened next, Tyler's voice takes on a tone of excited disbelief, as though he is telling it for the first time and still can't quite fathom the amazing thing he witnessed. "So they kept it until about three weeks later, when they found in the aquarium, sitting beside the parent, a baby frog," he says. "The next day there were two more. We talked about it on the phone and I said, 'Look, I've got to get the babies in the vocal sac, so hold its mouth shut, immerse it in chlorohydrate—if you've got to die, you might as well die painlessly—then I can look at the babies in the throat.' "

The men began to follow Tyler's orders. As soon as they grabbed the frog, it vomited twenty fully formed little frogs in staccato fashion, like a machine gun firing bullets. They again called Tyler, who told them to send the parent over right away. Soon he was at work on the euthanized frog. "I dissected the throat, looking for the vocal sac," he says, ". . . and I found that it didn't *have* a vocal sac!" Upon dissecting it further, he discovered it was a female and it had a huge stomach. Apparently the froglets were actually developing in the stomach before they were expelled. "I realized then that what I was looking at was a form of reproduction that was unknown in the world," Tyler recalls. "It was something totally new. It was one of those times when you feel very excited. It just blew my mind."

One of the most common misconceptions people have about frogs and other amphibians is that they all reproduce in the same way. The standard model, the one that becomes the topic of the earliest introduction to science in elementary schools, says that a female frog lays eggs in a pond or stream. Then a male frog fertilizes the eggs. Later the eggs hatch into tadpoles that are confined, like fish, to a life in water. Gradually the tadpoles develop into froglets, miniature carbon copies of their parents, which split their life between land and water.

The model is true for a lot of frogs, particularly "true frogs," members of the genus *Rana*. However, there are hundreds of frogs that deviate from this standard model. Few creatures can match the reproductive diversity of frogs and toads, a diversity that begins with the places where they lay their eggs.

Direct deposit into ponds and streams isn't for everyone. For instance, glass frogs, rain-forest members of the genus *Centrolenella* whose skin is so transparent that their internal organs are visible, usually lay their eggs on the undersides of leaves overhanging a pond or stream. When the tadpole hatches out of the egg, it drops into the water below and proceeds along a standard development course.

Dendrobatid poison-dart frogs, the colorful animal gems with the toxic skin, spend most of their time among the leaf litter on the moist forest floor, and that's where they lay their eggs. The male fertilizes the eggs and then stands guard for about ten days until they hatch into tadpoles. At that point a parent, usually the father, manages to coax the tadpoles into climbing onto his or her back. The parent then carries them piggyback to stream or pond. Sometimes the destination is a bromeliad, a plant with long, wide, stiff leaves that form a basket shape in which water collects into puddles. The mother or father dumps the tadpoles into the bromeliad puddle or stream or pond where they live until they become frogs. In at least one animal, the strawberry dart frog, *Dendrobates pumilio,* the mother periodically returns to the bromeliad where she carried her tadpoles and lays an unfertilized egg into the puddle. The tadpoles actually feed on these eggs while they grow into froglets.

One variety of toad, the Surinam toad, *Pipa pipa,* is most famous for its odd development. As a female toad lays eggs and the male fertilizes them, the couple flips and circles like a Ferris wheel to place the eggs onto the female's back. Her soft skin envelops the eggs into individual pockets. Eventually, fully developed froglets emerge from the pockets, like prairie dogs digging out of a sandhill.

An entire frog genus, *Eleutherodactylus,* has so many members (more than four hundred) that it is considered the largest single genus of vertebrates known to man. These frogs often don't have spectacular colors or a notable physical appearance. But their reproduction makes them stand out. Their offspring go through direct development. That is, after the eggs are laid, either on the ground, under a rock, or in a leaf, they hatch directly into frogs, bypassing the tadpole stage. A handful of frogs never actually lay eggs, but hold them internally in oviducts until a froglet develops. The mother then gives birth to a fully developed froglet through her cloaca, the opening to the passage that doubles as a waste tract and birth canal.

The list of different ways in which amphibians reproduce keeps growing as scientists discover new species, or simply study known species in greater detail. However, Tyler's gastric brooder's reproduction takes the prize for odd discoveries. For several years, Tyler tried to understand exactly what mechanism was at work, how the mother incubated the frogs. He never actually witnessed how the eggs ended up in the mother's stomach. Even after several attempts to get gastric brooders to breed in a lab setting, he never witnessed an actual egg-laying. Apparently, though, after a mother frog laid her eggs and they were fertilized by a male, she simply swallowed them whole. Immediately her stomach became an incubator. Normally, anything the frog swallowed would be digested by the stomach's natural chemicals. However, as Tyler learned through lab analysis, the mother gastric brooder's stomach was able to turn off its natural acid production. The entire time the brooder's stomach contained eggs, the mother could not eat. She simply grew fatter as the eggs and then tadpoles and frogs developed.

Tyler was so amazed by this discovery that he immediately wrote a paper that he sent to the prestigious English scientific journal *Nature*. "They sent it back straightaway. They said it wasn't of sufficient general interest to merit publication," Tyler recalls cheerfully, more than a decade later. "I understood years later—many years later I met the editor—that they thought it was a spoof." He continued to send the paper out until it was published in December 1974 in *Science,* the American equivalent of *Nature*. Still, his finding was not entirely accepted as legitimate. He received dozens of letters in response to the paper. "They were fairly evenly divided. Fifty percent said, 'Look, this is the most exciting thing since sliced bread,' and the other fifty percent said, 'Look, this is bullshit, there's no way it could happen.' "

Undaunted, Tyler put a research group together in Adelaide to start to figure out what mechanisms helped the brooder's stomach switch off its acid production. "We realized that people who suffer from gastric ulcers would love to be able to do what the frog could do," Tyler says. "It had very clear human benefits to it." The researchers found that the brooder's eggs were surrounded by a jelly that contained prostaglandin E-2, which inhibits gastric secretion. At about the same time, drug companies were experimenting with prostaglandin E-2 for treating human ulcers. Tyler's group was able to demonstrate that frogs had been using the compound successfully for millions of years to neutralize stomach acids. As often happens when scientists discover something new, this discovery prompted dozens of new questions and other paths to follow in research, and the scientists were beginning to go down those paths when something unthinkable happened. The frog disappeared.

Typically, gastric brooding frogs left the stream in winter and, presumably, sat out the season's cold temperatures by hiding in the cracks and crevices of rocks. When spring returned, the frogs would go back to the stream. But in 1980 they didn't return, and they haven't been seen since. That same year another, less notable frog commonly found in the same area as the gastric brooder also disappeared. Why either of these frogs left is an unsolved mystery that still plagues Tyler.

"I've explored every scenario I can. I even think about how we have earthquakes—could it be we had a rush of heavy metals through the water? It wasn't drought. I mean, I've devoted more of my thinking capacity to try to resolve this problem than anything I've ever addressed in my life," Tyler says. "And I still can't come up with a solution that sounds sensible to myself, let alone anyone else."

One thing that made the gastric brooding frog's disappearance so confounding was its abundance in the few sites it was known to exist. "You could have gone out, as somebody said, with a sugar bag and filled it in a night," Tyler recalls. Herpetologists had visited the area before, though, for many years and had never seen it. Apparently it wasn't always so abundant, which suggests it went through huge population swings. But Tyler is certain, after more than a decade of not seeing the creature, that something more than a cyclic population swing is at work. "We have to accept that populations go up and down naturally in a huge cyclic sort of fashion," he says. "However, when they disappear totally, we've got to say, 'My God, what's happened?' "

After the frog's disappearance, conservation organizations, anxious to expand the areas protected from logging in the forest where the frog had lived, used the issue to give weight to their argument. The government, particularly the forestry department, "went berserk," according to Tyler. The government sent biologists into the field with orders to find the frog, and night after night, for month after month, they never saw another gastric brooding frog.

Tyler has been back to the forest several times himself. "What I notice about it is not just the demise of that particular species, but the others have gone as well," he says. And with their disappearance, the very forest itself has changed character. You can still see the water running across the rocks. You can still smell the decomposition of plant material. But there is no longer any croaking of frogs, the heralds of spring. "It's now a silent forest," he says. "It's dead."

6

. . . .

Sunbathing

One spring day I followed Mark Jennings on a brief field trip up a mountainside above the high desert near Palm Springs, California. We hiked for about half an hour along an often invisible path through short shrubs and tall pines and oaks. The route was steep, and we were breathing hard by the time we got to a flat. Then we cut off into a rocky streambed routed through a gorge. Water didn't flow during this drought-plagued year; it simply sat in small puddles here and there. We climbed up and over dry falls. We maneuvered around giant boulders. Then, only halfway expecting it, we found a lineup of small brown frogs sitting on the edge of one isolated puddle. Jennings got to them first, and almost as soon as he spotted them, they dove off their rock ledge into the deep puddle. They were mountain yellow-legged frogs, *Rana muscosa,* and they had been sunbathing.

The temperatures that day were well above one hundred on the desert floor. Even at our elevation, somewhere above five thousand feet, it felt as if it were in the nineties. Jennings and I both wore hats to protect us from the merciless sun and heat. Yet here were these hairless, thin-skinned frogs, happily frying themselves in the midday sun, like winter tourists on a Caribbean beach.

This group of mountain yellow-leggeds was a rare discovery,

one of only three small populations that are known to exist south of the Sierra Nevada. Mountain yellow-leggeds were once scattered throughout California's high mountains. In fact, their taste for height distinguishes them from the foothill yellow-legged and California and northern red-leggeds. The mountain yellow-legged typically lives at elevations ranging from 4,500 feet to well over 12,000 feet. By the mid-1970s it was hard to find a mountain yellow-legged in Southern California's mountains. And then, in the late 1970s and early 1980s, the species began to decline dramatically in its Sierra Nevada strongholds.

One of the first to witness the Sierra declines was David Bradford. In the summer of 1977 he was a graduate student in ecology, taking a break from work by backpacking in Sequoia National Park. His destination was a collection of lakes near an area called Table Meadows. The lakes sat at an elevation of about eleven thousand feet, on the edge of the treeline, where the landscape is dominated by stark rock faces, and the plantlife ranges from lichen to wildflowers to heathers and willows. The views are broad and breathtaking, the light is intense, and the sun seems an arm's length away.

Bradford hiked by several lakes. Most didn't have names. But what they did have, he noticed, were frogs whose backs had color patterns of yellow and green or yellow and brown marbling. Their thighs were yellow, too. They were mountain yellow-legged frogs, and there were lots of them. He knew he was near the highest limit amphibians were known to survive in North America, and as he watched the frogs he became intrigued. In his graduate studies, Bradford was interested in how characteristics of an animal's physiology allowed it to adapt and survive in its environment. These yellow-legged frogs, he realized, were amazing examples of adaptation.

In the Sierra, the winters can be long and unpredictably cold and snowy, and the summers short. If a summer is too short, the mountain yellow-legged tadpole may hold off its own development a year or two and stay in its fishlike stage in the cool waters of iced-over lakes until another spring arrives. The adult frogs also spend the winter under the lake ice. They can lower their metabolism so drastically that, for up to nine months at a time, they can do without food or any air except that carried in the lake water. After seeing their abundant populations in Sequoia, Bradford decided to return and study the hardy mountain yellow-leggeds.

The following summer, on July 4, Bradford retraced his steps. The winter had been very snowy, and the spring thaw hadn't arrived at the lakes—they were still covered with snow. So Bradford set up camp and waited. The wait was longer than he ever anticipated, with the thaw failing to come until mid-August. There were tadpoles in the lake left from the previous year, but no adult frogs. Logically, Bradford speculated that the harsh winter had been the culprit. After doing lab studies on temperature and the mountain yellow-legged, he was convinced he had witnessed the results of a winterkill in which the lake had frozen so much that there wasn't enough oxygen in it to keep the adult frogs alive. It was an event he figured could be considered a natural occurrence that helped control overpopulation of the frogs.

In 1979, Bradford returned again to the Sierra, and this time he found two mountain yellow-legged populations in lakes near the lakes he had watched the previous summer. The thaw came earlier this time, and adults and tadpoles were plentiful at his new sites. Then, in August, populations started crashing. Bradford watched adults slowly die, pathetically groping along the ground as they expired. The population dropped from about eight hundred frogs to nearly none as a bacterial infection called red-leg disease spread like wildfire. At about the same time, Bradford later learned, researchers were seeing dramatic declines in Yosemite toad numbers in the Tioga Pass area of Yosemite National Park. Some of those toads were also suffering from red-leg disease. It had been the same way in the early 1970s, when a researcher began seeing red-leg disease and declining populations in boreal toads, *Bufo boreas boreas,* in the Colorado Rocky Mountains. By the early 1980s, few toads were left there.

Red-leg disease gets its name from its most obvious symptom. As it progresses into its advanced stages, the disease causes the capillaries in a frog's legs to swell and burst, giving the legs a reddish hue. The disease is caused by *Aeromonas hydrophila*, a bacterium that is prevalent in freshwater ponds and lakes, and can infect fish and humans as well as frogs. The bacterium can lie dormant within a frog's body until a frog's system is stressed. The disease is a secondary infection. That is, before it can take hold, something else has to be wrong and cause a breakdown in a frog's immune system that allows the bacteria to become active.

Bradford wondered at first if his presence, particularly his handling of the study frogs, could have been the stressor that made them vulnerable to red-leg disease. But since some of the populations he had handled remained healthy, he dismissed this as the probable cause.

Bradford left the Sierra frog sites to do other work, but he continued to be troubled by the massive frog deaths he had witnessed during his studies. In 1989, a decade after his previous visit, he returned again to the Sequoia National Park and checked the frog status at thirty-eight lakes that had once claimed mountain yellow-legged inhabitants. He found frogs in only one.

At the Irvine amphibian meeting in 1990, as David Bradford shared his story about the mountain yellow-legged and other high-mountain declines in the western United States, Marc Hayes began to think his way into a hypothesis that might fit all those populations. None of the high-mountain declines seemed to be in heavily logged areas. Most, in fact, were in parks or untouched forest. Introduced fishes had wiped out some populations and prevented others from recolonizing their old lakes. But, clearly, introduced fishes hadn't killed the frogs Bradford and others found suffering

The reason for population declines in the mountain yellow-legged frog, *Rana muscosa*, of California's Sierra Nevada mountains, remains a mystery. *Courtesy John S. Applegarth*

A Pacific tree frog displays its climbing skill. *Courtesy Marc P. Hayes*

A California red-legged, *Rana aurora draytoni,* that Marc Hayes found in 1979 at Corral Hollow. Hayes has watched frogs decline here over the years, victims of a variety of problems, including human abuses of the habitat.
Courtesy Marc P. Hayes

Researchers have noted declines of the northern leopard frog, *Rana pipiens,* in the Colorado Rockies and parts of Canada, among other places. This one was photographed in Nebraska.
Courtesy Stephen Corn, National Biological Survey

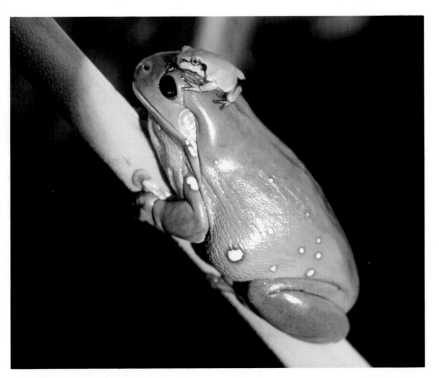

This large White's tree frog poses with a small friend. Note the White's broad toes that allow it to stick to tree branches and leaves. *Courtesy Robert Mailloux*

Yosemite toads, once so abundant in parts of California's Sierra Nevada ranges that they were hard to miss, are now difficult to find. *Courtesy M. L. Morton*

A golden toad of Monteverde, Costa Rica. This stunning toad hasn't been seen since 1989. The last time a researcher saw it in large numbers was in 1987. *Courtesy Martha L. Crump*

A harlequin frog from the Rio Lagarto River near Monteverde, Costa Rica. These frogs were last seen at this site in 1987. Other harlequin populations at other sites continue to thrive. *Courtesy Martha L. Crump*

A group of golden toads gathered in a small rain-filled pool at the base of a tree. At the height of their brief breeding season, dozens of toads would pack into such tiny pools. *Courtesy Martha L. Crump*

These blue poison dart frogs lose their skin toxicity when bred in captivity. Their shiny, colorful skin and tiny size make them appear more like porcelain figures than live animals. *Courtesy George Grall, National Aquarium in Baltimore*

The arroyo toad, *Bufo microscaphus californicus,* lives in flowing streams with sandy beaches, a habitat that has almost disappeared in its Southern California home-land. *Courtesy Spencer A. Weiner*

Not all frogs lay their eggs in ponds or streams. The strawberry dart frog, like other members of the genus *Dendrobates*, lays its eggs on the forest floor and then carries the newly hatched tadpoles to water. *Courtesy George Grall, National Aquarium in Baltimore*

from stress-related red-leg disease. Obvious habitat destruction seemed not to be the culprit. Something more subtle had to be at work, Hayes concluded.

Some scientists at the meeting who were more familiar with conditions in the eastern United States speculated that acid deposition, such as acid rain, might be plaguing animals in western mountains. Neither Bradford nor his cohorts working on the high-mountain toads had monitored acidity levels the years they had watched the animals die. And at least one study presented at the meeting suggested that "acid pulses" in the Colorado Rockies during snowmelt could affect salamander development. So, when the Irvine meeting concluded and Hayes returned to Miami, he began to dig through existing research about acid deposition in the western United States.

That search led to a dead end. Most of the acid deposition in the eastern United States comes from sulfur and nitrate released from coal-burning power plants and factories. The West has few of these facilities, and although there is some acid deposition from other air-pollution sources, the problem is less severe in the West than in the East. Also, the soils in western mountains (although not necessarily at the highest elevations) are composed of materials that tend to neutralize acid deposits. There is strong evidence that acid rain and other acid deposits have threatened and killed amphibians in eastern North America and parts of Europe. But similar evidence doesn't exist for western North America.

Hayes had only one more direction left to consider. During the Irvine meeting, a couple of scientists raised the question of whether increases in ultraviolet (UV) radiation caused by thinning of the stratospheric ozone layer could be affecting frogs. Almost immediately, an atmospheric scientist invited to the meeting nixed the UV idea. The increases so far, he said, were probably too small to have any discernible impact. In Miami, as Hayes rejected acid rain, he began to reconsider what he had heard at the conference about

UV. Again he began digging into existing research. As he probed and read, he recalls, "The UV stuff became very compelling as the next thing down the line."

Ultraviolet radiation is light emitted by the sun. Like all light, it is usually measured and defined according to wavelength. UV light is invisible, and most of it is harmless to humans and to other life on Earth. One type, however, called UV-B, can be deadly, and in recent years it appears to be reaching the Earth's surface at increasing levels as the ozone layer in the stratosphere thins.

The stratosphere, which begins ten miles above the Earth, is a layer of gases twenty miles thick, and one of its most important components is ozone. Each ozone molecule is composed of three atoms of oxygen as opposed to the two atoms normally found in atmospheric oxygen. Ozone wraps the Earth like a protective sheath that filters out most UV-B as the sun's rays pass through it.

In 1985, a team of British scientists discovered what could ultimately become one of humanity's most disturbing revelations. The scientists found that the Earth's ozone layer was thinning above Antarctica. Subsequent research has shown that the layer is thinning in many places above the globe at varying rates. The obvious cause of this thinning is chlorofluorocarbons, or CFCs, human-made gases used as refrigerants and as ingredients in a number of common products, including foam plastics and industrial solvents. Since the 1930s, millions upon millions of tons of these gases have escaped into the atmosphere. In the early 1970s, scientists discovered that the chlorine in these rising gases was gobbling up the extra oxygen atoms in ozone. But it took nearly a decade and a half for scientists to realize that CFCs had already caused substantial damage to the valuable ozone layer. After years of haggling, the world's political leaders, through the United Nations, agreed to end CFC production by the year 2000. However, the chemicals remain active in the atmosphere long after they have been released, and most scientists anticipate that CFC damage to the ozone layer will be seen for decades after the ban.

As noted above, one of the consequences of ozone damage is an increase in the amount of UV-B that reaches the Earth's surface. Exactly how much of an increase there will be or has been in any given locality is difficult to assess because ground-based UV measurement is still imperfect. Scientists can, however, estimate UV-B exposure based on how much ozone thinning there has been in the stratosphere over a given region. Colder temperatures enhance the chemical reaction that allows CFCs to gobble ozone. Therefore, the closer an area is to the freezing North and South poles, the greater the thinning of the ozone layer and the greater the increase in UV-B exposure.

Scientists say that UV exposure in Antarctica has more than doubled because of ozone thinning. In the United States, according to one prominent atmospheric scientist's work, UV-B exposure increased 5 to 10 percent from 1979 to 1989, and that trend is expected to continue in following decades. Indeed, in early 1993, new research suggested that UV-B exposure would increase by up to 16 percent above normal levels that summer in parts of North America. So far, there is no sign of ozone thinning over the equator. But the equatorial tropics, where the sun is particularly strong, tend to receive higher levels of UV-B radiation exposure than do other areas of the world. So scientists speculate that even a tiny change in ozone layer thickness over the equator could result in significant increases in tropical exposure to UV-B.

Researchers know that UV-B causes skin cancer and cataracts in humans, and can weaken the immune system. A United Nations Environment Programme scientific committee estimated in 1991 that UV-B increases would result in at least 1.6 million new cases of cataracts worldwide each year by the year 2000. Lab tests using various animals have shown that nonhumans are also vulnerable to increases in UV-B. Scientists have also found diminished growth of phytoplankton—single-celled ocean plants—in Antarctica because of increased UV-B. What, Hayes began to wonder as he sifted through the information, would the UV-B increase mean for wild frogs?

Frogs are ectotherms, which means their body temperature is controlled by their environment. If a frog is sitting in cold water, its body will be cold. If it is on a warm rock, its body will be warm. How much heat and cold any amphibian can tolerate varies among species. Taking all the species together, the temperature range they can tolerate goes from −2 degrees Celsius (about 28 degrees Fahrenheit) for certain land-based salamanders to nearly 36 degrees Celsius (about 96 degrees Fahrenheit) for some tropical frogs. This broad range of temperature tolerance helps amphibians live in extreme climates, from desert to mountain.

Their dependence on external environment to regulate their temperature has turned some frogs, including high-mountain species like the mountain yellow-legged, into hard-core sunbathers. During the warm summer months, when nighttime temperatures can drop into the forties and lower in their high-elevation homes, mountain yellow-leggeds will spend whole days basking in the sun.

Could basking atop a mountain under a cloudless sky during the era of ozone thinning somehow be killing frogs, Hayes wondered. Was the UV-B increase weakening the frogs' immune systems and making them vulnerable to maladies like red-leg disease? Laboratory experiments had shown that amphibian eggs and embryos wouldn't develop properly if they were exposed to high levels of UV-B. Were the eggs in the wild now becoming UV-B victims? Were populations being wiped out from the bottom up or from both ends of the age scale because of ozone thinning? If to any of these questions the answer was yes, what would that mean for humans and the rest of life on Earth?

By the time Hayes finished reading the literature of ozone depletion, he was convinced that UV might be one of the pieces of the amphibian-decline puzzle. Somebody needed to start studying the issue immediately, and he was willing and anxious to be that somebody. But there was a problem. Working part-time at an environmental consulting firm, and spending other time trying to finish the final draft of his doctoral dissertation, Hayes had no money and none of the professional clout required to get the kind of funding he would need to conduct a good study of the amphibian-UV link. He was trapped by the traditions and requirements of scientific funding that favor academic institutions and their employees over independent researchers.

Andrew Blaustein went through his undergraduate and graduate education giving little thought to frogs; he was more interested in mammals in those days. As a graduate student at the University of California's seaside Santa Barbara campus, he studied population dynamics of small wild rodents. It wasn't until he got his doctorate in 1979 and a tenure-track teaching job at Oregon State University in Corvallis that Blaustein switched to amphibians.

Blaustein's main interest is animal behavior and ecology, the branch of biology that looks at the ways living things relate to each other and to their environment. In the end, it doesn't really matter to Blaustein what animal he uses to study. What matters most is that the animal is available. Amphibians have long been very popular animals among researchers in various fields at OSU for that very reason: They have been available and abundant. All it has taken for some scientists to round up several months' supply of research animals is a quick trip to a nearby pond. Newts, especially, have always seemed to be everywhere in this rainy state. So, after Blaustein arrived in Corvallis, he decided to continue his animal behavior work by looking at amphibians. Specifically, Blaustein became interested in tadpoles and how they recognize their siblings.

The first time I heard about this work, I found myself repressing images of orphan tadpoles swimming around in search of someone—anyone—they could call family. It was a poignant picture, but it didn't seem to have a whole lot of scientific value. Then I began reading the research papers, including Blaustein's, and it became clear that once again amphibians were playing a role in helping scientists answer significant questions about how the world works.

Scientists who study animal behavior and evolution have wondered increasingly what makes some animals cooperate and do things for their own family that they won't automatically do for others. One leading theory explaining this holds that by practicing altruistic behavior toward relatives, an animal is working—doubtless more instinctively than thoughtfully—to ensure that its own genes, shared by the family member, will be passed on to future generations. In a sense, survival of the fittest becomes a family matter. But before an animal can know whom to be altruistic toward, it needs to recognize its relatives. That raises a number of questions: How are various animals able to recognize kin? Is kin recognition limited to only certain kinds of animals? And where and when in evolution did kin recognition begin?

By the time Blaustein moved to Corvallis, the whole field of kin-recognition research was just beginning, and researchers were trying to answer these questions for a variety of animals, from deer mice to quail to honeybees. Blaustein and a postdoctoral student, Richard O'Hara, took on the task of looking at kin recognition in Cascade frog tadpoles.

As their name suggests, Cascade frogs, *Rana cascadae,* are native to the Cascade Range, which runs from Northern California to Canada. The range spans Oregon like a ragged spine on the eastern edge of a chain of inland valleys that are bordered on the west by the Coast Range and the sea. The Cascade Range's highest peak, Mount Hood, reaches over eleven thousand feet. Cascade frogs have historically thrived throughout this chain in high mountain meadows where the sphagnum moss runs several feet deep, and water stands in ponds and potholes that are connected to each other by trickling springs and rivulets. They lay their eggs in shallow water that is easily warmed by the sun. The adult frogs are brown or greenish brown and have black spots on their backs. They are considered a medium-size frog, smaller than the red-legged, but still a good size.

In the early days of their kin-recognition work, Blaustein, O'Hara, and a few students routinely traveled into the Cascade mountains straight east from Corvallis, beyond central Oregon's broad Willamette Valley. A single Cascade frog can lay up to about eight hundred eggs in a mass that looks like a glob of clear jelly marbles, and in the spring the scientists could easily find and collect freshly laid frog eggs. Then they would return to their lab and raise the eggs into tadpoles, which would become study subjects.

The kinship studies relied mostly on watching tadpoles behave in special aquariums that controlled tadpole-to-tadpole contact. The scientists found that Cascade tadpoles relied on chemical cues to distinguish which tadpoles were their siblings and which weren't. They essentially smell or taste the chemical differences among tadpoles and recognize the chemicals that belong to their siblings.

Once Blaustein was finished with a batch of tadpoles, he would hold them in the lab until they matured to small frogs. Then he or his students would take the froglets back to the wild and release them at the site where their eggs were collected.

In the early 1980s, only a few years after beginning the tadpole studies, Blaustein began noticing an unwanted change in his routine. "I tried to find the animals and they were getting rarer and rarer," he recalled a decade later. "We started thinkin', 'Man, it's harder and harder to find these animals.' " By the time of the 1990 Irvine meeting, Blaustein and others in Oregon had been keeping track of Cascade frog and Western toad numbers at certain sites for about a decade. The numbers showed real declines. Blaustein's own surveys of about thirty sites where Cascade frogs were once abundant show that about 40 percent of the populations no longer exist.

"They're missing from logged areas, they're missing from unlogged areas. They're missing from destroyed areas, from pristine areas. We don't see any correlations there. We've also taken pH measurements [to test acidity] at every lake and pond we go to, and everything is normal, as close to [pH] 7 as you can get, which is neutral. And we've done water-quality tests on certain lakes and can't find anything wrong there, so we don't know what's going on," Blaustein tells me one chilly Oregon summer day in his office in Corvallis. He is a stocky man with thick black hair shot with threads of silver, a thick black mustache, and a just-as-thick New York accent. He is wearing blue jeans and a windbreaker advertising the 1991 U.S. Tennis Open. The two rooms that make up his office are packed with overflowing filing cabinets, bookcases, and desks.

Blaustein is scrappy and boisterous. He loves practical jokes and good gags. A poster on one wall of his office displays a toad hanging upside down in a martini glass with an olive. "One for the Toad," reads the caption. As a scientist, he is noted more for his work in the lab than his studies in the field. He often keeps the progress of his research projects as close to the vest as a poker player in a winner-take-all game.

In some ways, Blaustein seems the exact opposite of Marc Hayes. Generally reserved, Hayes thrives on fieldwork and has the patience to do it with the same degree of precision other scientists apply at their lab bench. Despite these differences—or perhaps because of them—Hayes and Blaustein hit it off when they first met at the Irvine conference. Both were anxious to keep working on the declining-amphibian issue, and after the meeting was over and they returned to their respective cities, they continued to exchange phone calls and letters.

As Hayes became convinced that it was time to investigate a possible UV-B link to the high-mountain frog declines in the western United States, he turned to Blaustein and shared the data he had found. At first Blaustein was skeptical, so Hayes found and shared more data. In one five-page letter, five months after the Irvine meeting, Hayes ran through the findings step by step. Then he sketched out a field experiment that would involve watching egg and tadpole development in a series of filtered and unfiltered boxes containing eggs and tadpoles in their natural settings. The filtered boxes would block out all UV-B light, and the unfiltered boxes would leave the eggs exposed as they naturally would be.

"This is a real juicy experiment—we are talking *Science*-level paper," Hayes wrote, referring to the prestigious scientific journal that is to scientists what *The New Yorker* is to writers. "Please consider it carefully. I would be enthusiastic about coordinating its execution, if you agree."

Hayes enclosed with the letter a packet of papers about UV-B. It proved to be convincing. Soon Blaustein was talking about how to get funding for exploring the UV-B question.

By 1991 the federal government was budgeting about $12 billion a year for basic research. About 90 percent of that money went to nondefense research. When that 90 percent was distributed, ecosystem and ecological research took a backseat to biological research geared toward human health issues.

The National Science Foundation, which is directly funded by Congress each year, is the country's primary agency for nonmilitary, nonmedical basic research. In 1991 its budget was more than $1.5 billion, of which about $40 million was earmarked for general ecosystem and ecology research. Competition for funding from the agency is stiff. But Blaustein figured the agency was his best chance to get the kind of money he estimated he needed for a good study.

After talking to other scientists at OSU, Blaustein decided the best approach to NSF would be a proposal for a project that would bring in scientists from other disciplines to look at various angles of the possible UV-B link to amphibian declines. He asked Hayes to draft the field part of the grant proposal. If the money came through, they agreed, Blaustein would hire Hayes as a part-time consultant to do the field experiments. Blaustein also invited two other OSU scientists, John Hays and Frank Moore, to share coinvestigator status on the proposal with Blaustein. John Hays, a molecular geneticist, would conduct lab work to see how different frogs were able to repair UV-B damage at the cellular level. Moore, an endocrinologist with vast experience studying the way hormones affected the central nervous systems of newts, agreed to investigate how UV-B increases might affect adult frogs and toads and the levels of hormones they created during stress.

Blaustein believed that the more multidisciplinary the study was, the better chance it had at NSF. Funding agencies want the most information they can get for their dollar. The broader ecological and environmental research questions have more luck getting funding than does a single-focus proposal that might, for instance, offer to find basic natural-history information about a single species of frog. Ironically, a lack of that basic information is what a lot of scientists have found is the greatest stumbling block to understanding whether and why certain amphibian species have declined. Without basic information, the scientists can't answer some of the complex questions or offer ways to remedy problems.

Blaustein's reading of funding agencies proved to be right on target. The grant application was in the mail in the fall of 1990, and by the following spring he received word that the NSF was sending money. The agency would grant $272,000 to the trio.

When you consider what an average person could do with $272,000, it sounds like a lot of money. It's enough to pay cash for a house in a decent neighborhood in Southern California, or to buy two or three houses in a decent neighborhood in Portland, Oregon. It is about twelve times as much as a schoolteacher earns in a year in Mississippi, and about seventeen times as much as the average person earns in a year in South Dakota.

But scientific research doesn't come cheap. In molecular biology, for instance, where scientists spend their days trying to decipher how cells and their genes work, $272,000 would buy one or two essential machines. There would be no money left over for the lab in which to house the machines, or for the salary of the scientist who works there. By comparison, Blaustein and company's project proposal was a deal: a two-to-three-year bargain that promised to begin to answer a question about UV-B exposure that could have broad implications for other life on Earth, including human life.

The funding would keep the team on a shoestring budget because not all of the $272,000 actually would go to the scientists. About 40 percent would be eaten up by the scientists' parent institution, Oregon State University, to cover what are commonly called indirect costs. These include building and maintaining labs and administering grant funds. That left about $160,000 to be split among three labs to fund research over at least two years and, in some cases, three. The money would have to buy equipment and pay employees, usually graduate students and technicians. "You don't have that much in the end," says Moore. A single graduate student working in Moore's lab for a year, for example, can cost about $20,000, which includes the cost of paying the student's tuition and health insurance.

When Blaustein won the NSF grant, word of it spread quickly through the relatively small world of biologists working on amphibian declines. It was the first significant money anyone had received since the Irvine meeting, a year earlier. And though they weren't directly involved in the grant, that meeting's organizers and leading participants embraced the award as their own triumph. It was a sign that someone had listened to the meeting's warning and the subsequent flood of media attention to frog declines.

As soon as Hayes heard that Blaustein had won the NSF funding, he began planning his own move west. First, though, he flew back and forth between Miami and Oregon three times to set up a test run of the field experiment.

Nothing seemed to go right during those trips. The frogs and toads weren't breeding during their usual times. The weather had been playing havoc with the snowmelt and breeding cycles. The plastic boxes Hayes had designed weren't working as they were supposed to. There apparently wasn't enough air circulation in the boxes when they were covered. "We were getting more mortality in the controls than in experimental subjects," Hayes recalls. "With that type of experiment you try to figure out as much ahead of time as possible. It's science, though, and it's not unusual to have a trial that doesn't work." Also, he had clashes with other researchers at OSU. There were disagreements about field methods, disagreements about work habits, disagreements about computer availability. Hayes saw places where things could be done better. He dismissed the disagreements as minor, but apparently the others didn't.

In September 1991, Hayes finally packed his belongings in Miami into a U-Haul truck and drove nearly nonstop across the country to Corvallis. He figured he would be ready within a week or two to concentrate on fixing the plastic boxes before the next breeding season arrived. After he settled into an apartment, he tried to talk with Blaustein about how to fix the boxes. He set up meetings, and Blaustein either wouldn't show up or would cancel meetings to attend to something else, Hayes says. Blaustein, Hayes recalls bitterly, didn't want to be bothered. "It was supposed to be a cooperative project where we sat down and went through the steps together. Andy was treating it more like, 'I don't want to be bothered. I just want results.' " In mid-November, Hayes received a note from Blaustein that essentially told him he was booted from the project.

Blaustein doesn't like to talk about his experience with Hayes. As I bring it up, he becomes visibly edgy. Firing Hayes was something he didn't like doing, he says. "There [were] a lot of things involved. It was a very political situation. . . . He's a very strong personality." Blaustein's students, his department head, and some of his colleagues were complaining that Hayes was too bossy. And, Blaustein adds, the apparatus Hayes devised didn't work and needed redesigning.

Hayes was depressed and angry at first about the outcome of his work with Blaustein. But soon he developed a network of contacts within state and federal agencies in Oregon, and began collecting contracts to survey and study certain declining amphibians in the state. He moved from Corvallis to Portland and picked up part-time teaching jobs at local college campuses. He met and fell in love with Jill Mellen, the director of research at Portland's Washington Park Zoo. Life went on.

Meanwhile, Blaustein and his students continued the fieldwork. Blaustein and the work were featured in a frog-decline story in *Smithsonian* magazine the following spring, and it was discussed a few months later in *The New York Times* magazine. Later he was featured on a network morning show. His UV experiment is mentioned now whenever frog declines are discussed. The UV work brought Blaustein a measure of fame that kinship studies never had. And it all happened even before he had results.

The Oregon UV-B study asks three main questions: Does UV-B cause stress in frogs? Can a frog's cells repair damage that UV-B exposure may cause? Do frog eggs developing at high mountain locations in Oregon show notable damage caused by UV-B? Each of the three scientists took charge of researching one of the questions.

Frank Moore, the endocrinologist, took the first question. Amphibians have very simple brains, and certain behavioral responses—courting, for instance—seem to be especially sensitive to the ups and downs of hormones. Some hormones increase as an animal is stressed. Stress has some known effects on amphibians that could affect population sizes: Frogs won't reproduce under stress, and stressed amphibians are more susceptible to disease. Moore hypothesized that UV-B could stress adult frogs, and that that stress could be gauged by measuring hormone levels.

To test his hypothesis, Moore selected three types of frog subjects. One was the African clawed frog, the laboratory white rat of amphibians. Another was the Pacific tree frog, a common western native that wasn't showing any unexplained declines. The third was the declining Cascade frog.

Moore set up a test container in his lab, over which hung a light that emitted about ten times the normal outdoor level of UV-B. Part of the container was covered by a filter that blocked the UV-B. The frogs were placed in the container one at a time so that they could get exposed to UV-B, which, presumably, would increase their stressor hormone. However, each of the frogs quickly took cover behind the filter. This surprised Moore. The UV-B light didn't emit heat, so he could eliminate the possibility that the frogs were avoiding the light to avoid a higher temperature. Clearly, Moore concluded, the frogs were avoiding the light to avoid the UV-B. This meant that the frogs could actually detect UV-B. More important, by detecting it, they were able to keep themselves out of a potentially stressful situation.

This discovery illustrates the unpredictability of science, and shows why scientists often have to be flexible in their thinking to respond to this unpredictability. Moore had to reshape his original question. Whether adult amphibians exposed to extraordinary levels of UV-B were stressed became irrelevant as long as it appeared that the animals could detect and avoid the UV-B. Now the question became whether the frogs in the wild could also detect and avoid UV-B. If they did, then researchers could be fairly certain that adult frogs were not being stressed from overexposure to high levels of UV-B.

Moore and his student researchers took frogs to a mountain lake and reproduced the lab setup. Again, frogs of three species were placed in containers that were half covered by filters. This time, though, the only light source was the sun and the only UV-B was that emitted by the sun. As in the lab experiment, most of the frogs hopped for cover under the filter. However, the Cascade frogs seemed to prefer the unfiltered light. In fact, they basked in it.

To reduce stress during transport, Moore had placed the Cascade frogs in a cold refrigerator before carrying them to the mountain.

By the time they reached the outdoor experiment, the frogs were still cool. This, Moore figured, might be one reason the frogs preferred the UV-B. They were trying to warm themselves, just as they might on a spring or summer morning after a long, cold night. But the unfiltered side of the container was no warmer than the filtered side. The Cascade frogs may have been drawn to the UV-B because they associated it with warmth.

Moore doesn't know what the UV-B level was at the mountain lake the day he conducted the outdoor experiment. It may have been normal, it may have been higher than normal, but it was certainly much lower than the tenfold lab exposure. For the purposes of this experiment, though, the exact level of UV-B is irrelevant. What matters is that the frogs responded. "The bottom line is that they could detect UV-B," Moore explains. And while some frogs chose to avoid it, the Cascade frogs chose to stay in it. If normal or slightly elevated UV-B stresses adult frogs, Moore's Cascade frogs displayed behavior that suggested they could become victims.

The next step would be for researchers to try to determine whether stress hormone levels increased in the adult Cascade frogs as they basked in the UV-B in the outdoor experiment. However, by the time Moore finished the outdoor work, he had run out of research money. So the stress hormone questions still await answers.

John Hays, a molecular geneticist who has done work on the effects of UV on plants, tackled the second big question of the three-part project. Within each animal cell, where UV-B does its damage to DNA, there are enzymes that can work to repair the damage. Hays's job was to figure out whether frog cells had enough of the repair enzymes to repair UV-B damage. To do this, he put his research assistant, Pete Hoffman, to work with the eggs from African clawed frogs, Cascade frogs, western toads, Pacific tree frogs, and a newt and a salamander. In a lab filled with glassware and machinery, Hoffman ran each batch of eggs through a complicated recipe to create a protein extract. Then he added bacterial DNA that had been damaged by UV, and watched with instruments and computers as the repair enzyme in the protein mix went to work to fix the DNA's damage.

The process can be described in just a few sentences now, but it took Hoffman about a month and a half of work to come up with the right recipe and techniques for the experiment, even before he began to watch the repair enzyme do its job. The effort proved worthwhile, though, and Hoffman and Hays found three interesting things.

First, the repair activity was higher in the eggs of the wild frogs and toads than in the eggs of newts and salamanders. This is significant because the frogs and toads lay their eggs in sunlight while the newts and salamanders lay theirs under rocks or wrapped in leaves. The toad and frog eggs "were prepared to deal with more UV damage, if you will," Hays says. "This is what you would intuitively expect." The best of the frog eggs were thirty times more able to repair themselves than the worst of the salamander eggs.

Second, because he had already done much work on the African clawed frog, Hays decided to test their eggs for repairability as well. The clawed-frog eggs he used were from lab-raised animals that came from a long line of lab-raised animals that had never been exposed to sunlight. The eggs proved to have the least repairability of any of the amphibians tested. This prompted Hays to consider another idea.

"Maybe the frogs sense the amount of light in their environment, and that turns on the enzyme. If yeast and plants are exposed to ultraviolet light, among other things, the levels of [repair enzyme] go up," he explains. "What I'm suggesting is that it's possible that exposure of the frogs to even normal sunlight triggers the additional synthesis of this repair enzyme to deal with that sunlight, and that would be very exciting." It would suggest that the cells of frogs and other amphibians might be able to change or adjust their ability to repair UV damage. But finding the answer to this, Hays notes, is another experiment.

Finally, Hays and Hoffman found that of all the frogs they looked at, the Pacific tree frog produced the highest levels of repair enzyme activity. "Interestingly, it is the one of the three [wild frogs tested] that is not in decline. That's consistent with this notion that UV might have something to do with [declines], but it's far, far, far, far, far, *far* from being conclusive," Hays says. "But if we had the opposite result, then that would have certainly been a strike against UV theory."

Blaustein and his students have handled the third question of the study. This has required conducting field experiments to test whether the sun's UV-B is damaging the eggs and tadpoles of Cascade frogs and western toads in their natural mountain environment. The researchers also included eggs and tadpoles of Pacific tree frogs as a comparison species.

The field-test design is fairly straightforward. First, the scientists wanted to create an environment that was the same as the amphibians' breeding lakes and ponds in every way except that it was protected from natural predators. Then they wanted to create within these environments two different levels of UV-B exposure: (a) total exposure to UV-B emitted by the sun, and (b) no exposure to UV-B. To do this, the researchers sank plastic boxes into outdoor ponds and lakes where the frogs and toads had just laid eggs. The boxes were flooded with water. Then the scientists placed fresh eggs from each of the species into the boxes.

Next, the scientists placed over some of the boxes a coated piece of plastic filter that eliminated exposure to UV-B. They left a second series of boxes uncovered, so the eggs in it had full exposure to UV-B. They covered a third series with a clear piece of plastic similar to the coated plastic UV-B filter; the clear plastic provided no UV-B protection, however. Instead, it served as a control to make sure that if any changes occurred in the coated plastic box, they had nothing to do with the plastic's presence.

The idea driving this experiment was the proposition that if UV-B was causing amphibian declines, the declines would be taking place during the animals' early development. Therefore the eggs or the tadpoles in the unfiltered boxes would show signs of death or deformity, while those in the filtered boxes would show no such signs.

Like Hayes the year before, Blaustein encountered a slew of unexpected problems during the first full year of the field experiments in 1992. Oregon was still plagued by a drought that year, and winter snow levels, temperatures, and snowmelt times continued to be unpredictable. Frog and toad breeding times were unpredictable as well. The western toads bred two months earlier than normal. At one site they bred two weeks earlier than ever before recorded, and at another site they didn't breed at all. When the Cascade frogs bred, the equipment was still being used for all the early toad breedings, and the researchers didn't have enough equipment to do the frog experiments.

The next year, the experiments went more smoothly. The researchers began the fieldwork in March with enough equipment, and breeding was on schedule. The only glitch occurred when some boxes containing tadpoles in a lake were temporarily left unattended. "We're not sure if it was vandalism or a big storm, but let's put it this way: Every single one of our cages . . . [was] broken and all the tadpoles just happened to be gone," Blaustein complained. "This is in a very small lake in a very isolated area, but there are people that go up there because this is a wilderness area that people hike into."

By midsummer, the field experiments were finished and Blaustein began analyzing the data. Only one year, 1993, provided a complete set of field results for all three frogs. Scientists are typically reluctant to draw conclusions from a single year's worth of data.

There is always the risk that one year's data reflects an anomaly and not a true trend. It is usually better to have data from several years. However, the results from the 1993 fieldwork were so dramatic and compelling, particularly when coupled with John Hays's lab findings, that Blaustein decided to go ahead and publish them immediately.

On the last day of February in 1994, almost exactly four years after scientists raised the alarm about declining amphibians, Blaustein and Hays published a paper in the prestigious *Proceedings of the National Academy of Science* that would make frogs front-page news again. The summer fieldwork showed that about one-fourth of the Cascade frog and western toad eggs died when they were not shielded from UV-B radiation. At the same time, virtually no unshielded Pacific tree frog eggs died. The results were consistent with the earlier results from Hays's lab that showed that Pacific tree frog cells have a greater ability to repair from UV-B damage than do cells from either the Cascade frog or the western toad.

"It means that natural levels of UV are killing frog eggs in the field, and that these natural levels are increasing every year and we've got a problem here," Blaustein said at the end of a day spent fielding phone calls from the press about the new findings. "The big picture is that it's not just amphibians that are getting hit. There's probably some plant life, some invertebrates, and even fish."

Blaustein's results have raised new sets of questions. What levels of UV-B were hitting the frogs in the natural environment in the Cascade Mountains? Why did three-fourths of the frog eggs survive? Are frogs and their eggs in other high mountain areas suffering from UV-B as well? Does the UV-B alone kill them or does it simply make them susceptible to other stresses, such as fungus infections and increased water acidity? It will take more research in Oregon and elsewhere to begin to answer these questions.

Science is much like masonry in that it is a slow and steady process of adding bricks to other bricks until there is one solid entity in the form of an answer or theory. This early UV-B work is a brick in the complex answer to why frogs are declining. It may also be an important warning that ozone thinning is a more serious threat today than anyone could have imagined.

7

Whither Weather?

Martha Crump spent most of 1990 working in Argentina, but her mind was in Monteverde, Costa Rica. She was hoping Monteverde's famous golden toads would finally reemerge and breed again. It had been three years since she had become the last person known to witness the toads' spring breeding fling. She hoped this year she could be one of the first to witness their return.

Crump still had a few hundred dollars left from the National Geographic Society grant she had won two years earlier to study the toads' breeding habits. She decided to use that money to hire Wolf Guindon to check the toad sites in Monteverde for one more season. So, that April and May, when the dry season began to merge into the rainy season, and the potholes and basins on the Costa Rican forest floor began to fill with water, Guindon hiked regularly into the forest in search of golden toads.

Meanwhile, Crump waited in Argentina for word. She was prepared to drop her work on a moment's notice and fly to Costa Rica if he found breeding toads. But the call she wanted never came. The toads didn't reappear in 1990, just as they hadn't in 1988 or 1989. Three years running, the toads went without breeding, and as the years passed, the odds were growing that they would never reemerge.

Crump left Argentina at the end of summer to resume teaching at the University of Florida in Gainesville. One of her first tasks upon returning to the campus was to finish a paper describing the golden toad's disappearance and speculating on the causes. Meanwhile, another scientist in Monteverde, J. Alan Pounds, was working on the same problem. At first independently, and later together, they would suggest that a weather change had been a key factor in the decline of Monteverde's amphibian populations. Their suggestions would become pieces of a growing body of evidence that one of the toughest environmental and science issues of the late twentieth century—global climate change—might affect amphibian declines.

Pounds had been a graduate student of Crump's at the University of Florida in the early 1980s. It was through her that he was first introduced to Monteverde's amphibians and the sometimes aggravating unpredictability of tropical field research on frogs. But even before he worked with Crump, disappearing and declining frogs had helped shape his scientific career.

It began one humid summer in the late 1970s, when he started to do a master's-degree thesis on green tree frogs. "I had my study area all set up. It was this lake in southern Louisiana; it was a beautiful place, lots of green tree frogs," he recalls, with an accent that hints of his Arkansas roots. "It was kind of a cypress lake habitat. I was using a canoe to go in there, and I noticed that the water looked lower. Then, after a couple of days, it was so low I couldn't even get in there. All I could do was stand on the bank and look at this mud. There was still some water, way out in the middle of the lake, but you couldn't get out to it."

Pounds couldn't figure out what was happening. Then he learned that workmen were busy draining the lake, pulling the habitat right out from under the frogs. The St. Martin Parish governing body had decided to drain and dredge the lake to make it deeper, and to clear out some of the cypress and snags to create a better place for recreational boating and fishing. So much for the frogs. Discouraged, Pounds ended up studying lizards at another site that was, at least for the moment, safe from the whims of politicians.

A few years later, in 1982, Pounds had a second chance to study frogs while he was a doctoral student working under Crump. This time his target creatures were harlequin frogs, *Atelopus varius,* that lived along the headwaters of the Rio Lagarto near Monteverde. He arrived from Florida in early summer and planned to do a population ecology study by focusing on the peculiar breeding habits of the harlequins.

Harlequins are bright yellow-and-black frogs whose extremely toxic skin contains the same nerve-damaging chemical found in Japanese puffer fish. Male harlequin frogs are notorious for their combative, territorial behavior during breeding season. They drive away any competing wooers by physical intimidation. They roll on top of competitors and sort of squash them until the competitor decides to leave. Then, once the winning male has found a suitable female, he mounts her and wraps his arms around her abdomen and hangs on until she lays eggs. This mating behavior, called amplexus, can last an exhausting week or more.

Harlequins were everywhere at the Rio Lagarto study site that summer. The stream there was rocky and steep, broken by small waterfalls that stirred up a mist that kept the streamside boulders moist. The harlequins, slow-moving and placid when they weren't battling competitors, sat on the moistened rocks or hid in crevices between the rocks. The males, particularly, sat in the open, guarding territory and waiting for a female to dare to emerge from a hiding place. Pounds was sure that he would be able to gather valuable information about their breeding habits and so he watched and waited for the breeding to begin. But it did not happen that year. The harlequins simply skipped the chance to repopulate for one season. Once again, Pounds's plans to do a major project with frogs were dashed. By November, anxious to find a subject for his doctoral dissertation, he turned his attention back to lizards.

If Pounds had followed the normal path for a young scientist, as soon as he finished the lizard dissertation, he would have hustled off to some entry-level teaching and research position at an American college or university. But as his contemporaries sent news about their new jobs, Pounds felt discouraged. The work sounded uninteresting compared with what he had been doing in the tropics. And from those who had settled outside the Sun Belt, the dark and cold winters sounded horrible. Pounds liked Costa Rica and Monteverde too much to leave. He liked living close to the forest, and there was still plenty he wanted to study in the tropics.

Instead of moving back to the states, then, Pounds stayed and made a modest living combining work from the Monteverde Cloud Forest Preserve with other research projects. And that was where he was in early 1990, when George Gorman, who was overseeing Stanford University's Center for Conservation Biology research program in Costa Rica, asked Pounds to look into the golden toad disappearance. Ultimately the research would provide about $15,000 in funding over two years. The money would come from the Stanford center, the philanthropic MacArthur Foundation, and the Brookfield Zoo. Declining frogs once again were shaping Pounds's career.

Pounds had never studied the golden toad, and he had seen it in the wild only a few times. But like virtually everyone else living and working in Monteverde, he knew it was one of the area's most famous attractions. For years the preserve had kept a live golden toad on display in a terrarium. Each year the captive toad was released and replaced with a newly captured animal. The system had worked fine until the mid-1980s, when the captive animals inexplicably stopped surviving in their glass homes. The first golden toad Pounds had ever seen was one of the captives. Now that the toads in the wild had apparently disappeared, Pounds was more intrigued than ever by the animal. Explaining its disappearance would be a challenging problem that would require a combination of science and detective work.

In the spring of 1990, Pounds and an assistant began routinely hiking into the forest to check on old golden toad sites. Wolf Guindon was doing the same, although the two parties never encountered each other on the trail. However, each team came up with the same result: nothing. By the end of May it was clear that 1990 would not be the year the toads returned to Monteverde.

Pounds looked for more than just golden toads that year. He hunted for harlequin frogs and for those in the genus *Eleutherodactylus* as well. Oddly, like the golden toads, the Rio Lagarto population of harlequins had disappeared after the 1987 breeding season. Likewise, various species of *Eleutherodactylus* were scarce. Before 1987 it was difficult to walk a few steps within the forest without seeing one.

Pounds also looked for a number of species of glass frogs. Marc Hayes had spent parts of several years from 1979 to 1983 studying parental care among a population of glass frogs that lived along a stream that ran beside Monteverde's famous cheese plant. In the case of amphibians, parental care generally means any care a parent amphibian gives to its offspring beyond simply fertilizing an egg. Usually this care is meant to increase the egg's or tadpole's chances of survival. In amphibians, parental care is demonstrated in a variety of ways. Some frogs, for instance, build foamy nests or dig burrows to protect eggs while they develop. Others carry developing eggs or tadpoles on their backs or in pouches. Some amphibians simply stand guard over the eggs, while others actively make sure the eggs they are guarding are also moist enough or warm enough.

Hayes looked specifically at how the males of a certain species of glass frog, *Centrolenella fleischmanni,* help care for their young. Once the female frog lays her eggs on a leaf, she abandons the site. The male, however, stays close to the leaf and periodically returns to the clutch of eggs to urinate on them, to keep them moist. After about twenty-five days, pink to red tadpoles hatch from the eggs and drop into the stream or onto the stream bank, where they wiggle and flop their way into the stream. At that point the father's work is done.

Pounds checked Hayes's old study site. The *fleishmanni* and other populations of glass frogs along the stream were noticeably smaller than they had once been. In October 1992, Hayes revisited his old study site and estimated there had been a tenfold decline in the glass frogs since his previous visit, almost a decade earlier.

By the end of his 1990 survey, Pounds was convinced that the amphibian declines and disappearances that had begun after the 1987 breeding season still plagued Monteverde's forests. His mission, then, became an intellectual search for a logical and workable hypothesis for determining what had happened to the frogs.

A hypothesis is a hypothetical answer. For scientists, the questions shape the hypotheses, and the hypotheses shape the experiments. An experiment's purpose is to test the hypothesis. A hypothesis signals what work has to be done, what information needs to be gathered. It can take as much work to create a viable hypothesis as to test the hypothesis. Usually scientists require more than one question and many small hypotheses to lead them to a complete and single answer or theory to explain significant events.

Alan Pounds spent the last half of 1990 looking for data to shape the questions and a strong hypothesis to guide the amphibian-decline work in Monteverde. "I was devoting a lot of energy to racking my brain, trying to figure out what was going on," he tells me two years later, as he finishes off a bottle of Coca-Cola in his home built in a clearing in the forest. Heavy rain drums brutally on the rooftop, and Pounds raises his voice to be heard above it. "I pretty much discarded all possible hypotheses at one point and then started over," he says, amused now at his old frustration. Nothing seemed to fit, and every possible decline culprit had a logical alibi.

Pounds had begun his search with a general hypothesis that an event or combination of events had hurt the adult amphibians. The Monteverde amphibians weren't gone because offspring hadn't been generated or hadn't survived; they were gone because the adults had suddenly declined or disappeared within a single year. His focus became 1987, the last time many of the adults were seen. His driving question: What happened in 1987 to make the population collapse?

First Pounds considered weather. It was possible, he thought, that there might have been some dramatic change—a drought, a heat wave, or a cold snap—that could have killed the harlequin and golden toad adults and weakened the other populations. There was a precedent for strange frog behavior during extreme weather changes. The summer he had watched the harlequin frogs fail to breed was in the middle of the 1982–83 El Niño.

The El Niño was originally viewed as a simple seasonal warming of the Pacific Ocean waters off the coast of Peru. The warming would typically begin around Christmastime—thus the locals called the event El Niño, in reference to the Christ Child. The events were relatively mild, and came as ocean currents carried warm water south from the equatorial tropics.

Scientists' interest in the El Niño grew in the 1960s, when they realized, from looking at historical weather data, that these events had varying degrees of strength and could have more than a local impact. Today, scientists reserve the term El Niño for major ocean-warming events in the Pacific that occur every two to six years and have global impact. These events appear to occur in conjunction with atmospheric changes. The trade winds that normally blow with enough force to keep a giant pool of warm water in place in the western Pacific slow down for some reason, allowing the water to bleed into the eastern Pacific. Why these winds become slow when they do is uncertain. But their slowdown and the movement of the warm water trigger a suite of other events.

El Niños change normal weather patterns, introducing unsea-sonable droughts in some places and prompting increased storms in others. They can disrupt the natural ecology on land and in the ocean. During a particularly strong El Niño, the cold currents that typically run through the southern Pacific can be overpowered by the warm waters. The first victims of these warm waters are the organisms that live in the upper layer of ocean, at depths still reached by sunlight. These include plankton, a group of microscopic plant and animal organisms that are the main food source for many marine animals. In the past, El Niños have—with a domino effect—wiped out plankton colonies, the ocean fisheries that depend on them, and the seabird populations that live off the fish.

During the 1982–83 El Niño, Pounds noticed that there was little runoff water. Although the Rio Lagarto continued to flow, its flow was slower and lower. It was being fed mostly by underground springs, and as the groundwater was drained, the forest floor became obviously drier. Pounds and Crump collected data that year that showed that the harlequins that normally dispersed along the riverbank to catch the splashes from the river were clumping together on the bank in tighter colonies near waterfalls as the shoreline wet zones diminished. The frogs, which, oddly, do not like to sit directly in a stream or pond, were depending on the waterfall spray to keep them moist. One of the outcomes of this clumping, the two scientists later reported, was that the harlequins became more susceptible to attack by a parasitic fly that patrols waterfall areas.

"Naturally, when the Rio Lagarto population later declined [in 1987], I thought about a fall in stream flow and groundwater as one hypothesis, but soon discarded it," Pounds says. Why? Because the 1982–83 year had been unusually dry, and the El Niño that year was one of the harshest on record to that date. "There was a moderate El Niño (in terms of the thermal signal in the Pacific) in 1986–87, but if the 1982–83 event hadn't done in the population, how could a moderate event in 1986–87 make a difference? Besides, streams in the area had never dried up completely."

Also, there just didn't seem to be enough weather data available to do a good analysis. "There were only twenty years of rainfall data [for Monteverde], a mere drop in the bucket on an evolutionary time scale," he later observed.

Pounds decided early on that he could confidently eliminate increased UV-B exposure as a hypothesis worth pursuing to explain the Monteverde declines. The tropical amphibians are typically shaded by the jungle. Golden toads, especially, rarely felt sunlight directly on their skin.

Habitat destruction through deforestation was another cause Pounds considered. During the last two decades, tropical forests around the world have been logged at an astounding rate. Enough tropical forest to fill the entire state of Washington was destroyed in 1990 alone, according to one estimate. By that year, the world's rain forests covered about 6 to 7 percent of the Earth's land surface, only half of their original area. Biologists believe that at least half of the world's plants, animals, and insects, which they estimate total anywhere from 5 million to 30 million different species, are harbored within the tropical forests. As the trees fall, so too do the numbers of creatures that can be supported by the rain forests.

Costa Rica's forests were vigorously logged and cleared between 1970 and 1989. Researchers figure that 2.1 million acres, or 28 percent, of the country's forests were destroyed. Most of the area was converted to land for grazing cattle or growing crops. Evidence of deforestation is clear in Monteverde and the surrounding communities. The cheese plant, established decades ago, is now a significant business, and dairy farming is a mainstay of the local economy. Pastures dot the roadsides and valleys where forests once thrived. However, the Monteverde Cloud Forest Preserve and other local conservation efforts have protected significant habitats, including the golden toad's. So Pounds decided he could eliminate deforestation or other obvious habitat destruction from the list of possible culprits.

That left air and water pollutants on Pounds's list of causes to consider. The protected nature of the area's watershed, as well as the ephemeral nature of the toad's breeding ponds, argued against water pollution. The air in the area also seemed generally clean.

Pounds was stumped. There was only one way to get out of this seemingly impossible situation, and that was to start over. He began, again, with weather. This time he decided to take a more careful look. He hadn't been in Costa Rica in 1986–87; he had been in the United States, finishing his doctoral dissertation and then doing postdoctoral research at Harvard University. He knew that year had been marked as an El Niño year, but he had been under the impression, from his first look at the 1987 weather data for Monteverde, that the event had been fairly mild. But then he learned from a scientist at Costa Rica's meteorological institute that the 1986–87 El Niño had cut stream flows so much that a hydro-electric plant north of Monteverde had been forced to shut down temporarily.

As Pounds began to reexamine the weather data for 1986 and 1987, he decided to try a different approach. He would attempt to think like a frog and look at the world and its weather patterns the way a frog would. "It occurred to me that if groundwater is impor-tant in the water economy of amphibians, the severity of a dry season, the probability of moisture stress, depends on more than the weather at the time," he explains. It depends also on how well the rains of a previous wet season recharged groundwater, how quickly the transition from a wet to a dry season occurs, how much evapo-ration occurs during the dry season, and how quickly the rains replenish the lost moisture after the dry season.

It also occurred to Pounds that the human calendar was "a pretty meaningless way to look at weather data. It didn't really mean any-thing to an amphibian," he says. "So I asked what would make sense to me as the most logical way to analyze data." He decided to define a weather year not by months or by traditional seasons, but by cycles or seasons that were based on the amount of rain and cloud mist that fell over an area. In Monteverde, that meant the weather year would include a late wet season (July–October); a transition into dry season (November–December); a dry season (January–April); and a post-dry or early wet season, also called a recovery season (May–June).

While he was defining the new seasons and the weather calendar, Pounds didn't look at any specific year's rainfall data, so that the data wouldn't bias the way he set up the new seasons. Then, after he had programmed the cycles into his computer, he began plugging in two decades of rainfall data for Monteverde. A pattern immediately jumped out. The 1986–87 weather cycle showed abnormally low rainfall during each of the four seasons, and it was the only year of the twenty that showed that pattern. Even though the golden toads had bred in April and May of 1987, that season had been drier than normal.

Pounds got on the phone to George Gorman and told him he was seeing some interesting patterns. He didn't know what to make of them yet, but a hypothesis involving the weather in 1986–87 was percolating.

Meanwhile, back in Florida, Marty Crump and Frank Hensley, the graduate student who had worked with Crump in Monteverde in 1989, began analyzing the data collected from four golden toad breeding seasons, including three in which the toads did not breed. Since the toads had bred in 1987, they began their search with the general hypothesis that the year was a normal breeding year and that something had made it impossible for the toads to breed in the subsequent years of 1988 through 1990. Their main question: What was different about the years after 1987 that discouraged the toads from emerging and breeding?

Their approach contrasted with Pounds's in two ways. First, they focused on a single creature, the golden toad, while Pounds considered in greater detail a number of amphibians that declined after 1987. Second, Crump had hiked up to the Brillante ridge many days in 1987 and had felt the cold and wet as she huddled over the pools watching the toads. She knew the pools had been full when the toads laid their eggs. It was hard to imagine that anyone could consider that season an abnormal one, certainly not a dry one. So it seemed logical to Crump and Hensley to look at the subsequent years when the toads didn't emerge as the problem years. Meanwhile, Pounds believed the key lay in looking at what might have been wrong during 1987, when, as his second analysis showed, there were unusual weather patterns. Either approach had its pros and cons. The two approaches, though, illustrate just how differently scientists can see one issue.

The data that Crump and Hensley had available for their analysis was more limited than Crump thought ideal. For example, they didn't have pool water samples from 1987 to compare with pool water from subsequent years. And for 1988, when she figured the toads' absence was just a single-season anomaly, Crump collected less information on the pools than she did in 1989, when she began to believe something was wrong. Still, despite its limits, the information that Crump and Hensley did have revealed some interesting patterns.

In 1987 and 1989 they had measured the depths and temperatures of the water in the breeding pools. They had rainfall data for all the years. That data came from a rain gauge in the backyard of a local resident who lives a couple of miles from the toad breeding site. They also had pool water samples they collected in 1989 at the breeding site. Finally, Kenneth Clark, a scientist at Monteverde who had been studying the chemical content of cloud precipitation over the Monteverde Cloud Forest, also had cloud water samples for 1988 and 1989.

Clark analyzed the pool water and cloud water samples for acidity and found no evidence of unusual levels. Thus the researchers could eliminate acidity as a reason the toads didn't breed in 1988–90.

That left Crump and Hensley to analyze the other rainfall and pool data. As Crump knew from firsthand observation, in 1987 the pools had been full enough for breeding several weeks earlier than in subsequent years. Also, the water temperatures during the 1987 breeding season had been several degrees cooler than the water temperatures recorded after the pools filled in 1989. Finally, the transition from the dry to the wet season that coincides with the breeding season had been more abrupt in 1988 and 1989 than in 1987. Based on these findings, Crump, Hensley, and Clark concluded in a paper they drafted that either of two hypotheses could explain why the toads hadn't emerged from their underground hiding places to breed in the three years after 1987.

One hypothesis held that breeding conditions just hadn't been right. The trio suggested that if the toads had laid their eggs under the 1988–90 weather conditions, when the pools had formed later and faster than in 1987, "additional heavy rains could cause the pools to overflow, and presumably the eggs or tadpoles would be swept out of the pools onto the forest floor. A subsequent day without rain would dry the substrate, and the tadpoles would be left stranded. Thus the toads may have a narrow window of time between dry season and wet season when their offspring can avoid both desiccation and being washed from the pools."

If this hypothesis was true, the trio suggested, then the toads might simply be hiding in their underground retreats, waiting for better conditions to return. And if they were hiding in their retreats, the toads would be aging. By the time the better conditions returned, the toads might have died or might have been too old to reproduce. "The unpredictable environment might select for long life span, but only future monitoring will allow determination of whether the population has been reduced to such a low level that it cannot recover," the researchers wrote.

A second possible hypothesis, they suggested, was that some catastrophic mass mortality of the toads had occurred after the 1987 breeding season. That other amphibians also declined or disappeared at the same time in Monteverde supported this idea, they noted. But what could have caused such a mass death? Changes in precipitation patterns and temperatures might have been a factor, the researchers said. "The monthly rainfall data for 1987–90 are often below the thirty-one-year averages and we did measure warmer water temperatures in 1989 than during the last year the toads reproduced. Whether these climatic factors are responsible for the decline of the golden toad (and possibly other anurans in the region) is, however, still a matter of speculation," they concluded.

Pounds phoned Crump after she returned to Florida in late 1990 and asked if she would like to collaborate with him on a paper speculating about the amphibian declines. By then, Crump, Hensley, and Clark were already well into their own paper, so she declined. Instead, Pounds and Crump agreed to do a short piece documenting the harlequin frog's disappearance along the Rio Lagarto. Crump promised to send him harlequin data that she had collected in 1987.

Pounds reluctantly put aside his amphibian–decline research and waited for the harlequin data. When it arrived in the mail, it included even more information than he had anticipated. Crump had commented on water levels in the Rio Lagarto, and had noted how many frogs, male and female, there were at different plots along the stream bank. The data were "like from outer space," Pounds recalls, because the ratio of males to females on the stream bank was dramatically different from the ratio Crump and Pounds had seen in previous years.

"It fit this idea that something was terribly wrong," he says. "Females stay hidden more than males, so if the females all emerge from their crevices at once, it causes the sex ratio to change." Apparently the water levels in the crevices had declined so much that the females had been forced to emerge to sit on the banks and collect moisture from the waterfall spray. This fit into a hypothesis Pounds had been developing that a combination of decreased ground-level and underground moisture, plus temperature changes, all brought on by the 1986–87 El Niño, had stressed the amphibians in Monteverde. That stress had made the creatures vulnerable to some factor or combination of factors that killed many of the adult amphibians before the 1988 breeding season, he speculated. Pounds didn't know what those factors could be, but he did know that stress made amphibians susceptible to bacterial infections (such as red-leg disease), parasites, viruses, and, possibly, airborne or waterborne pollutants.

San Jose, the capital city of Costa Rica, has a population of about 300,000, and half of them seem always to be crowding the city's narrow downtown streets and sidewalks, hurrying to work, shopping, tending shop, or generally hanging out. The downtown is small enough to cover on foot, but it is as vibrant and full of life and chaos as the downtown districts of other cities many times its size. For some reason, shoe stores are particularly abundant in downtown San Jose. So, too, are late-model Japanese-made automobiles, American expatriates in search of cheap real-estate deals with big returns, and tourists. For anyone visiting Costa Rica, including scientists beginning a research stint, San Jose is the first and last stop, a meeting place only a crowded, bumpy, four-hour bus ride from Monteverde.

In February 1991, almost precisely one year after the Irvine meeting, a dozen scientists gathered in San Jose. They called themselves the Working Group on Declining Amphibian Populations in Lower Central America, and included Pounds, Crump, George Gorman, Dave Wake, and Jay Savage. The group hoped to plot a strategy for studying—and getting funding to study—amphibian declines in various parts of Costa Rica and Panama. If the scientists succeeded, Wake believed the group's strategy could become a prototype for other groups of scientists working with the new Declining Amphibian Populations Task Force.

Scientists rarely work in a vacuum. Stories of scientists racing to be the first with a discovery are legion. Yet even as they race, they are almost constantly looking for comments and criticism from trusted colleagues. They float ideas, piece by piece, and rely on their colleagues to find the holes they might not see themselves. Then they patch the holes and float the idea some more. Eventually they will have a paper that they send out to a journal, where more colleagues are solicited for comments and criticism. If those colleagues deem the paper valid and valuable, the journal will publish it.

As scientists see it, this kind of constant review helps prevent bogus research from making its way into the scientific literature. It also helps keep scientists from making embarrassing mistakes in print. By the time a paper passes through the informal and formal reviews, ideas that might seem weird, irrational, or illogical have been smoothed or dumped, and grammar and syntax have been corrected.

Pounds figured the San Jose meeting was a good time to float some of his developing ideas about the causes of Monteverde's amphibian decline. When the meeting agenda turned to a discussion of Monteverde, he briefly presented his research concluding that weather, particularly an El Niño event, might have played a critical role. The other scientists at the meeting, including Crump, were enthusiastic about his findings, Pounds later recalls. He left San Jose feeling encouraged and excited.

After a few days he called Crump in Florida again. He wanted to do a paper about the declines of the Monteverde amphibians, and wanted to use her harlequin frog data. He needed her permission to use the data, and he wanted her collaboration. Would she reconsider joining him on a paper, he asked. Her own paper was already on track to be published, but she was intrigued by Pounds's analysis and said yes. Within weeks, Pounds had begun a working rough draft.

As the work progressed, Crump became Pounds's most demanding critic. When she was in Monteverde in 1987 during the toad breeding, the weather was miserably wet. But Pounds's analysis of weather data, with his abandonment of the standard calendar, showed that the weather that season had been drier than normal.

"He had to pound it into me and say, 'Marty, don't think about the condition when you were there, just look at these numbers,' " she recalls.

Pounds had to employ creative detective work to get some of the critical data to strengthen his case that the weather in 1986–87 had been abnormal. For instance, he knew that if the ground-moisture levels were lower than normal, they would be reflected in stream flows. But no scientists had been routinely measuring stream flow during that time. The best information he had came from Crump's notes about the Rio Lagarto, but they didn't include hard numbers. Pounds knew that the Instituto Costarricense de Electricidad, Costa Rica's electric company, relied in part on power from waterfalls and rivers to run generators in some parts of the country. So he decided to ask the ICE what information it might have. The inquiry opened a treasure chest. The electric company had collected hydrological data in two sites that were close enough to Monteverde to be relevant. The data confirmed that stream flows and ground moisture in the Costa Rican forests had dropped during the 1986–87 El Niño.

By mid-1992, two years after Pounds had started his search for clues, he and Crump completed their paper. It offered a different twist on the weather-as-culprit idea that Crump had explored with Hensley and Clark. In the new paper, Pounds and Crump concluded that the 1986–87 weather, with its four-season cycle of lower-than-usual moisture, was probably a significant factor in the amphibian declines. They also suggest that climate alone was unlikely to have been the only culprit. Instead, they say, the odd weather probably worked in combination with other factors to wipe out many adult amphibians.

What were those other factors? Pounds suggests that one may have been microparasites, which include bacteria, viruses, and parasitic insects. As the weather dried and forced the amphibians to clump together in smaller spots of moisture, it became more likely for microparasites to pass among the creatures. Also, as the amphibians suffered through the drier weather and accompanying higher ground-level temperatures, their bodies were facing unusual stress that might have made them more vulnerable to microparasites.

Another factor may have been contaminant chemicals that would have blown into the area with mist and cloud water. During March and April, a visible haze reaches Monteverde. A temperature inversion combines with winds to draw up from the lowlands particles of eroded agricultural soil and smoke from fires set to burn agricultural waste. Pounds found that other scientists had discovered that the cloud water they collected during a recent March and April in Monteverde contained abnormally high amounts of nitrates and phosphates, two chemicals often found in agricultural fertilizers. The existence of those chemicals probably doesn't explain why amphibians declined in the cloud forest, Pounds and Crump said, but the high amounts showed that it was possible for contaminants to blow from other places into Monteverde with the cloud water. Cloud and rain water might contain other toxic chemicals that scientists haven't yet detected. The researchers speculate that one source of such long-range contamination could be the "massive and indiscriminate use of pesticides" typical in Costa Rican farming.

Over the years there have been scattered reports, published and unpublished, by scientists who have stumbled across amphibians in the wild that appeared to have been poisoned by pesticides. There have also been some studies in laboratories on how certain common pesticides—such as DDT—and common pesticide ingredients affect amphibians. Not surprisingly, effects vary depending on concentration, method of exposure, and the life stage at which the amphibian is exposed. A number of pesticides are able to maim or kill. But in general there isn't much research on amphibians and pesticides. The U.S. Environmental Protection Agency, for instance, which is responsible for registering all pesticides before they can be used in the United States, doesn't include effects on amphibians among its routine test requirements. If it comes to EPA's attention that a pesticide is having some detrimental effect on amphibians in the wild, then the agency can require new tests to include them.

EPA's lack of routine inclusion of amphibians is typical of the historic attitude toward amphibians by many regulatory and wildlife management agencies. I recently asked a National Park Service official about whether that agency considers the impact on amphibians when it prepares to use herbicides on Park Service property to get rid of nonnative, invasive plants. The official thought for a moment and then noted that none of the herbicides we were discussing was used in water. It did not immediately occur to the official—just as it does not occur to most people—that the majority of amphibians spend most of their lives on land, where they might be in the path of various pesticides.

Each year, farmers and gardeners in the United States buy more than one billion pounds of pesticides to spray on everything from weeds to aphids. The rest of the world's consumers buy another 3.4 billion pounds. In the United States, where pesticide use is monitored more closely than in most parts of the world, more than half the states have shown some pesticide contamination in groundwater. One can only imagine how much pesticide contamination there might be of soil, streams, and groundwater in other countries—such as Costa Rica—where pesticides are used with less care and without monitoring. Based on his own observations, Australian amphibian scientist Michael Tyler suspects that one common American-made herbicide may be endangering Australian frogs because there are no precautions on the product's Australian label to warn against using it in wetlands and swamps. The American label contains such warnings, but U.S. labeling laws typically don't carry across international lines. Neither, apparently, do manufacturers' consciences.

Nobody knows whether pesticides are among the compounds that blow or have blown into Monteverde. If they are, they could

work in a variety of ways to disturb the normal amphibian populations. During dry periods there would be less precipitation to dilute
the pesticides, and the chemicals could become concentrated in the
soil. As the moisture continued to decrease, the chemical concentration could increase. Amphibians, such as the golden toad, rely
on soil moisture for much of the year. They could be susceptible to
absorbing unhealthy levels of the chemicals as their skins absorb the
soil moisture.

Pounds's and Crump's hypotheses that a weather change seriously
affected Monteverde's amphibians adds another facet to scientists'
discussions about global warming and its impact on life on Earth.
Other scientists in the past have speculated that weather either
prompted or stimulated some amphibian declines in the 1980s. For
instance, when scientists working at a research station in southeastern Brazil noticed dramatic declines and some extinctions of amphibians in the early 1980s, they speculated that unusually heavy
frosts in 1979 were to blame. Scientists working at the Savannah
River Ecology Lab in South Carolina blamed certain temporary
population fluctuations of amphibians in that area during the late
1980s on local drought. The drought caused ponds to dry before
tadpoles developed into baby frogs and salamanders.

The effects of a seven-year drought may also have contributed to
Cascade frog and western toad declines in Oregon's Cascade
Range during the late 1980s. Deanna Olson, a U.S. Forest Service
biologist who has studied amphibians in the Cascades since the
early 1980s, decided in 1992 to look at how Cascade frogs used
natural corridors to travel between the seasonal ponds they used for
breeding. The natural corridors are typically small streams and
springs. Usually, in the spring and fall, when it is rainy, the corridors are wet, and by late summer they are dry. But in 1992, many
of the corridors Olson checked had already dried by early summer,
a byproduct of the drought. Also, some seasonal ponds dried out

and lake edges receded as early as April and May that year, leaving frog and toad egg masses, as well as tadpoles, high and dry.

Amphibians have survived millions of years of weather changes, including ice ages, and adapted to the changes well enough to bring them to the late twentieth century. It seems impossible, then, that a few years of drought or a day or two of freezing would be significant enough to cause permanent decline and extinction. However, as scientists have increasingly begun to believe, the world's climate is being forced by human activity to change at a faster-than-natural rate. And that change may come too fast for many animals to adapt.

The first warning of a human-induced climate change came as early as 1896. In that year, the Swedish geochemist Svante Arrhenius determined that massive burning of fossil fuels to run industry was increasing the amount of carbon dioxide in the atmosphere enough to raise the Earth's temperature. In retrospect, Arrhenius's observation didn't garner the kind of public attention or action it deserved. It wasn't until 1988, when NASA climatologist James Hansen testified before a U.S. Senate Committee, that concern about global warming took hold. Global warming was real, he told the senators, and it had begun to change the Earth's climate.

Today, many scientists agree with Hansen's assessment that global warming is real. The main cause is believed to be, as Arrhenius's earlier work suggested, increased emissions of what today are called greenhouse gases. These include carbon dioxide, methane, ammonia, and a list of others. Under normal conditions, such gases make up less than 2 percent of the Earth's atmosphere. But since industrialization, the balance in the atmosphere has been shifted as activities ranging from burning fossil fuels to cutting down forests have added more of these gases. For instance, researchers estimate that human activity has caused carbon dioxide in the atmosphere to increase by about 25 percent, and methane by 100 percent, within the last two hundred years.

These increases in greenhouse gases have had the effect of adding another layer to the atmospheric blanket that naturally covers and helps keep the Earth warm. The amount of heat the blanket traps has climbed, and so has the Earth's average temperature. And as the years progress and people continue to add to the greenhouse gases, temperatures are expected to go even higher. How high is open to debate, but some scientists say that by the mid-twenty-first century, the average temperature could increase by another 2 to 9 degrees Fahrenheit.

What effect might these temperature increases have? That's open to debate as well. But some changes that may occur include a rise in global sea level, changing storm patterns, more or harsher El Niño events, and a general shift in climate ranges and species habitats. With these possibilities in mind, some scientists speculate that the amphibian declines and disappearances in places like Monteverde just might be pieces of biological evidence that global climate change is already having serious effects.

One of those scientists is Richard Wyman. The simple fact of global warming alone may not be the worst threat that climate change poses for amphibians, he believes. The biggest threat may come from what he calls "indirect effects and synergistic interactions" that occur in the face of the climate change. These effects and interactions would include combinations of events like those that Pounds hypothesizes may have occurred at Monteverde. One example would be the ground-level moisture deficit that may have combined with microparasites to wipe out the harlequin frogs. And that combination might not have come about without the climate change of El Niño.

Wyman has seen other evidence in his own research of possible interactions that could occur with climate change to hurt amphibians. An ecologist, Wyman directs the Edmund Niles Huyck Preserve in Rensselaerville, New York, about twenty-five miles southwest of Albany. The privately sponsored preserve covers about two thousand acres and is surrounded by another seven thousand acres of mostly rural land. On this preserve there are woods, grasslands, and open space for biologists who want to study whole organisms—insects, birds, amphibians, mammals, plants—and natural systems. In a typical year, more than seventy scientists spend some time at the preserve, researching everything from how leaf litter decomposes to how spiders behave.

Wyman began his research career working on fish evolution. At the Huyck Preserve he set up an aquatic lab that allowed him to do research during the snowy, cold winters. During the summers he worked on amphibians because he likes them and it gave him a chance to be outside. Then, in the late 1980s, he became increasingly bothered by what he saw happening to amphibians in the area. Leopard frogs that had been longtime residents of the preserve dropped in numbers to almost nothing. In his first seven years at the preserve, Wyman heard what sounded like leopard frogs calling only in 1991, his sixth year there. Other amphibians on the preserve seemed to be dropping in number as well. Scientists and amateur naturalists have been collecting data on the preserve's amphibians as far back as the late 1930s. At one time there were at least seventeen different species found there. Now Wyman figures two or three of those species no longer exist at the preserve, and several others are found only in smaller numbers.

In light of these declines and his continuing concern about global climate change, Wyman decided in 1988 to change his research direction. "I drained my fish tanks, resigned an editorship from the journal *Fisheries Research,* stopped attending fishy meetings, and put away all the manuscripts on fish that were in preparation or being rewritten following peer-review comments. So now I study and write about amphibians year-round," he says. ". . . I want to do something to help save some of these magnificent creatures for my children's children."

Most of Wyman's amphibian research has focused on redback salamanders, a lungless creature that spends its life on land. When it reproduces, it relies entirely on the moisture of the forest floor to keep its own skin and its eggs wet. The mother digs a chamber under a log or rock, lays a clutch of eggs—usually no more than nine at a time—then wraps her body around the eggs to keep them moist until they hatch. As its name suggests, the redback salamander usually has a red stripe running from its head down the length of its back. It is one of the most abundant amphibians in the northeastern United States, and, based on forest-floor surveys, Wyman estimates there are as many as 17 billion in New York State alone.

In the early 1980s, Wyman began looking at how acid rain affects redback salamanders. Acid rain is a catchall term for an assortment of acidic precipitation types, including snow, fog, and dry precipitation. It is one of the environmental plagues of industrialization, and is formed when sulfur dioxide and nitrogen oxides mix with other gases and water droplets in the atmosphere to create sulfuric and nitric acid. The typical sources of sulfur dioxide and nitrogen dioxides are machines that burn fossil fuels such as coal and oil—from automobiles to factory boilers.

As they have done with so many other pollution problems, scientists noted the existence of acid rain in the late nineteenth century. But intense public reaction and public policies addressing the issue didn't follow until the 1970s and 1980s. By then, though, significant damage had been done. Acid rain is particularly insidious because it often falls hundreds of miles from the pollution source, so that even pristine regions suffer from urban pollution. It is responsible for killing trees and damaging forests in Sweden, Canada, Germany, Central Europe, and the northeastern United States, among other places. It burns tree leaves and needles and destroys root systems. It pollutes soil and water, increasing acidity levels as it simultaneously increases toxic metal levels.

By the mid-1980s, scientists had produced a significant collection of studies on the effects of water acidity on amphibian eggs. Those studies show that amphibian eggs and tadpoles are sensitive to changes in pond or stream acidity, and that tolerance for acidity varies among species. At intolerable levels, the acidity essentially drains sodium from tadpoles and eggs while at the same time it blocks sodium intake. At some levels, acidity will outright kill certain tadpoles. At other levels the damage is more subtle, causing stunted growth or slowed development.

Scientists had done almost no research, though, on the affects of acidity on adult amphibians, particularly terrestrial amphibians. This research gap was especially noticeable because most amphibians spend a good part of their adult life on land, and have constant contact with the soil. The soils in northeastern U.S. forests are fairly acidic to begin with, and appear to have become more so from acid rain. In some northeastern forests, the soil is even more acidic than the water in the ponds and streams.

Wyman began to fill this research deficit on adult amphibians in the early 1980s by looking at soil acidity and redback salamanders. With another scientist, Dianne S. Hawksley-Lescault, he established field and laboratory studies. First, for the field studies, the scientists selected two large sites in forests in Delaware County in south-central New York. Then they divided the sites into an imaginary grid of meter-square plots. Twice a year for five years they counted the numbers and types of salamanders living in a randomly selected group of the plots. They also measured a list of physical characteristics in each of the plots, including soil moisture and soil acidity.

In the lab, the scientists determined what soil acidity level the salamanders preferred, by letting salamanders wander among soils of varying acidities. The acidity levels corresponded with levels that were known to exist in soils at various sites in Delaware County. The scientists noted which soils the salamanders avoided and which they preferred over three separate twenty-four-hour periods. Finally the researchers conducted a series of experiments that exposed salamanders to specific acidity levels under different conditions and then noted the effects those levels had on the animals.

Acidity is measured on a scale that runs from 0 to 14. Each point stands for a pH value that reflects the number of hydrogen ions in a concentration, and corresponds with acidity. On the scale, 7 is neutral. Pure water is 7, and human blood is about 7. Anything less than 7 is acidic, anything greater than 7 is basic or alkaline. Lemon juice has a pH of about 2, vinegar has a pH of about 3, and tomatoes have a pH of about 4. Normal rainwater has a pH of 5.6. Rain with a lower pH than that is considered acid rain. The pH scale is logarithmic, which means that below the number 7, each point represents an acid concentration ten times greater than the next higher point. For instance, vinegar, at pH 3, is ten times more acidic than a tomato with pH 4.

In lab tests, Wyman found that almost all of the redback sala-manders preferred to live on soils where the pH was above 4.5. Half preferred to live on soils where the pH was above 6. In other words, given the choice, the salamanders avoided highly acidic soils. The lab tests also showed that when the soil pH dipped to some point between 4 and 3, salamanders began to die after living on the soil for periods of several months. At pH 2, salamanders died after living on the soil for less than a week. Wyman also found that growth rates were stunted at lower pH levels.

In the field, Wyman found that there were few salamanders liv-ing on soils with pH below 3.8. More than one-fourth of the plots in the areas he studied had soil pHs that were lower than that, too acidic for the redback salamanders. When Wyman later analyzed data he had collected about amphibian distributions in five forests in south-central New York, he found that eleven of seventeen am-phibian species seemed to be influenced by soil acidity. Not sur-prisingly, the eleven were found on less acidic soils. Most were on soils that were above pH 4.

Wyman's findings suggest that amphibians can detect whether a soil is too acidic. They also suggest that as soil becomes more acidic, the habitat available for many amphibians decreases. Just as acid rain has made some ponds and lakes uninhabitable for amphibians, acidic soil can make the forest floor uninhabitable as well. Increased

acidity is a habitat destroyer, more subtle than a bulldozer but, over ⨯
time, just as damaging.

This realization alone is disturbing when you consider how much forest land has been hit by acid rain. Estimates increase each year as more data is collected, but generally at least one-fifth of Europe's forests and broad swaths of forests in the northeastern United States and Canada show acid rain damage. The realization becomes even more alarming when the effects of climate change are added in. One effect would be drought, which causes soils to dry. That drying, Wyman says, removes the soil moisture and intensifies its acidity.

Climate-change models "project that droughts may occur more frequently and with greater intensity in the greenhouse world," Wyman wrote in an essay in the book *Global Climate Change and Life on Earth*. "The combination of dryness and increased soil acidity might eliminate from large areas of North America many amphibians that would not be eliminated by one factor alone. Amphibians may also be affected before the forest would show other major adverse effects."

A few years ago, Wyman did a phone survey of herpetologists he knows in the Northeast, in which he asked them about their impressions of the status of amphibians in the region. There are approximately thirty-one species of salamanders and fifteen species of frogs in the Northeast. He ended up hearing about eighteen salamanders from these herpetologists, who rated twelve as uncommon, rare, declining, or threatened. Of the twelve frogs he heard about, eight were rated uncommon, rare, declining, or threatened. "There are a number of provisos about this sort of data," Wyman notes. "First, this is anecdotal. Second, I called up asking about declining amphibians, so it's likely that what would come into peoples' minds would be those sorts of things. Third, at any particular time, somewhere in the species' range, it is likely to be rare, uncommon, or declining because animals don't occur equally everywhere. They occur most densely . . . where the conditions are most appropriate for them, but as you get away from there, they get less and less dense."

But most revealing about the data, anecdotal though it was, were the reasons the herpetologists gave for the apparent low numbers or declines. The most common reasons given were acidity, drought, and the fact that the populations were at the edge of their range.

Amphibian species, like many animals, usually have specific ranges where they can be found. That range can span a few miles, as in the case of the golden toad, or thousands of miles, as in the case of leopard frogs. Plant, food, and climate conditions in the middle of a range are typically ideal, and populations are dense. At the edge of a range, such conditions are usually less clearly defined and a species' populations are usually less dense.

Climate-change theorists say that if carbon dioxide emissions double in the next thirty to fifty years, the world's climate could effectively move north from the equator by five hundred to one thousand kilometers, the equivalent of three hundred to six hundred miles. If an animal population is now in the middle of a large range, a movement of climatic regions by several hundred miles probably wouldn't have any effect on the population. However, at the edge of a range, a climatic movement could significantly alter the local ecosystem, changing everything from the weather to the plant and animal life. Plant and animal populations now living on the edges of their ranges would be most vulnerable to climate change and begin to show the effects of the change first, Wyman says. That kind of vulnerability is what scientists are seeing in some amphibian declines. Some are occurring fastest and most noticeably at the edge of ranges. "So again," he says, "we have this feeling that it may be related to changing climatic conditions."

Alan Pounds continued to look for golden toads in 1992 and again in 1993. Again the rains came, the pools formed, but no toads appeared. Every once in a while someone—a visitor who has been out hiking in the hills above Monteverde, or a worker at the reserve—will report seeing a golden toad. Sometimes they even bring back what they believe to be a golden toad as proof. The proof invariably ends up being some other colorful amphibian.

As I chatted with Pounds in his Monteverde home in the late summer of 1992, he broke off our conversation momentarily and retreated to another room. He returned carrying a lunchbox-size plastic container. In it sat a frog about the size of a peach and the color of an apricot. If I had been walking in the surrounding forest and seen this creature, I know my heart would have stopped dead. I would have believed I had just stumbled across one of the last golden toads. And I would have been wrong.

The frog in the box was a member of the genus *Eleutherodactylus*. Its skin was not as brilliant as the golden's and it was larger than a golden toad. Also, it had distinct tympanums or eardrums, two circular skin patches on each side of the head, something that golden toads lack. A friend of Pounds's found the frog in a nearby valley. He thought it looked like the kind of creature someone would mistake for a golden toad, so he brought it back to Pounds and jokingly presented it to him as such. Pounds named it Sapo, the Spanish word for toad.

Will humans ever again see a true golden toad? Or is the famous creature really gone forever?

Scientists are cautious about making final statements about anything. Exactly when something can be called extinct is an issue they debate. Some scientists say that it is premature to declare something extinct until it has not been seen for a period equivalent to the creature's entire life span. Nobody knows for sure how long a golden toad can live. Based on what scientists know about other toads its size, a golden could live for ten or twelve years, according to Martha Crump. So, considering that the last adult toad was seen in the late 1980s, it won't be until the late 1990s that scientists can say with almost complete confidence that the animal is gone.

Crump, for one, isn't going to jump the gun. Now living in Northern Arizona, she remains prepared to take the first flight to

Costa Rica upon any word that the toads have returned. "I refuse to say they've gone extinct just because I'm hoping that they're not," she told me in the fall of 1992. "But," she added, "based on scientific evidence, it's starting to look more and more discouraging, I have to admit."

8

· · · · · · · · · · · · · · · · · · · ·

Unnatural Disasters

The first time I visit Sam Sweet's office in the summer of 1992, I think maybe I have walked into a large storage closet recently struck by one of those irritating earthquakes that occasionally rattle California. Papers are all over the room. I do mean *all over*. Stacks, piles, mountains. Some are even taped to the wall. One, a list of questions Sweet wants to answer about amphibians and reptiles that inhabit—or used to inhabit—the mountain and coastal regions around Santa Barbara, California, was taped up more than a decade earlier. A two-foot-high pile on top of a file cabinet contains recent manuscript submissions to the *Journal of Herpetology,* which Sweet is about to give up editing after more than eight years. He can hardly wait to finish his last issue and get more time to do his own research. The other overflowing stacks and piles contain some of that research.

Sweet is sitting at the back of the room, a very tall man with a bushy black and gray beard and long black hair pulled back into a ponytail. The ponytail doesn't whisper Hollywood chic, it yells fashion rebel. He is wearing blue jeans and boots. He could be mistaken for a biker, except that there is no Harley in sight. The only machine here is the manual typewriter he is huddled over as he taps out what sounds like a two-finger hunt-and-peck speeded up.

Cigarette smoke hangs in the room. Sweet is a chain-smoker, and as I interview him over the next four hours he almost always has a cigarette lit. He dumps the ashes into a clay ashtray that resembles a heap of dog poop. It was a gift from a friend who worked in a ceramics shop and hated his smoking.

Sweet is a professor at the University of California at Santa Barbara. He calls himself a herpetologist. I have noticed that many people who are trained in graduate school in herpetology, and continue to work with amphibians later, call themselves something else. Some describe themselves as evolutionary biologists—scientists who study how organisms evolved over time. Others are ecologists—scientists who study how organisms and their environment interact. Still others call themselves herpetologists only when they are among other herpetologists, and call themselves ecologists when they are among ecologists and other scientists. Herpetology, one scientist explained to me, has connotations of narrowness among scientists. As naturalists, who observe, have gone out of style and experimentalists, who manipulate, have gained the upper hand in science, sciences that focus on whole organisms, such as herpetology, have sunk in status. Sweet does both ecology and evolutionary biology, so perhaps it is a sign of his individualism that he hangs on to the herpetologist label when he could so easily adopt something with more status.

I have come to see Sweet to hear about the arroyo toad, *Bufo microscaphus californicus,* a creature whose habitat has declined about as rapidly as the toad itself. Sweet has been studying the toad for more than a decade, and in recent years he has become its most vocal and angry advocate. Habitat destruction has shrunk the animal's historic range by about 75 percent in the last half-century. It could once be found within a band of territory that ran the length of coastal Southern California and into northwestern Baja. Now it can be found only in isolated spots within that range. About half of the arroyo toad populations are located along a handful of streams within a portion of Los Padres National Forest that spreads from Ventura County across Santa Barbara County.

That forest, established in 1938, covers almost 2 million acres, of which about 1.74 million acres are actually owned by the U.S. Forest Service. The rest of the land is privately held, surrounded on all sides by the Forest Service property. Five hundred miles of streams weave through the entire forest. Arroyo toads are scattered along fewer than fifty of those miles. Sweet figured in 1992 that the Los Padres populations included about 350 adult toads, as many of the squat, round animals as could fill two or three water buckets. The toads have probably occupied this part of California for twelve thousand years, surviving ice ages, fires, and floods galore. Now their biggest test is to survive the Forest Service.

If the shrinking populations of arroyo toads have anything working in their favor, it is that they have managed to escape two of the most easy-to-identify habitat problems bothering forest amphibians around the world. These are cattle grazing and logging. Sometimes the two go hand in hand, and sometimes they spring up separately. Either way, they work to wipe out frogs and their cousins.

I used to believe that one of the most serene scenes imaginable was the view of a contented herd of spotted cows grazing on a rolling hillside or a mountain meadow. But that was before I learned about frogs and started listening to herpetologists lament cattle's impact.

Cows are big, clumsy, heavy-footed creatures with seemingly insatiable appetites for anything green. Exactly how much impact cows have on any particular area varies with the habitat. Scientists are still trying to learn how best to measure those impacts and how long they last. But there is no doubt that these animals can, within only a few weeks, make big changes in an area's ecosystem.

Scientists who study range management have found that cows can significantly change a riparian habitat. They pound a stream bank flat, break overhanging banks, and compact surrounding soil so that it can hardly absorb rainwater. This can change the way a stream flows, the amount of silt that builds up or is carried away, and the type of plants that can survive on a stream's banks. These changes can cause water temperature increases and enhance bacteria growth. When cows graze on the wall of plants along a stream, simply by nibbling on the tender shoots they love so much, they can slowly destroy the plants' ability to regenerate themselves. One study found that shrub production was thirteen times greater in an ungrazed area than in an overgrazed area.

Exactly how cattle grazing affects all the wildlife on grazed land is not certain. Most published studies on those effects have focused on birds. None has looked specifically at the impacts on amphibians. In at least some studies, however, the impact on birds has been linked to destruction of habitats shared by amphibians. One study found that there were five to seven times more birds nesting in riparian habitat that had not been grazed in forty years than in riparian habitat that had recently been open to cattle grazing. If the riparian habitat had been damaged that much for birds, then the damage probably had some effect on frogs as well.

Even without formal studies, though, many herpetologists are convinced from their routine field observations that cattle grazing is a serious amphibian killer. David Lamar Martin, a graduate student who has studied Yosemite toads in the Sierra Nevada, blames cattle for weakening some of the last significant toad populations there. Martin figures that on one meadow complex in Stanislaus National Forest, north of Yosemite National Park, cattle have been killing about half of the toad's offspring each year in two of the toad's largest known wild populations.

On one occasion in 1991, Martin witnessed—and photographed—a cattle rancher driving his herd right through a spot on a meadow creek occupied by about two hundred toadlets. In their wake, the cows left thirty dead baby toads. That rancher's family has been grazing cattle on that land for nearly one hundred years, most of it by permit from the U.S. Forest Service. Martin figures that the toads haven't been totally wiped out by now because in the past the meadow populations could be regularly recolonized by Yosemite toads moving in from other areas. Now, though, the other populations are mostly gone. Martin worries that the toads in the Stanislaus meadows are doomed unless the cattle are removed or the Forest Service takes strong measures to protect the toads. So far, though, any help is slow in coming. The agency began considering how to accommodate grazing and protect toad habitat in the meadow complex at a 1991 meeting that included environmentalists, cattle ranchers, and Martin. By the summer of 1993 the agency was still working on a plan, but had taken no action to protect the toads in the meantime.

In the United States, two agencies manage most public grazing lands: the Bureau of Land Management and the U.S. Forest Service. Together these agencies allow grazing on about 270 million acres, an area bigger than California, Arizona, and Nevada combined. Both agencies are required to make sure the grazing doesn't irreparably damage the public lands. But two federal studies by the General Accounting Office in the early 1990s concluded that both fell far short of meeting that requirement. The main reason given: staff shortages.

The U.S. government has long encouraged grazing on these public lands by charging low fees for the right to graze. Those fees don't come close to meeting the real costs of monitoring and protecting the public lands—and their native plants and animals. Yet each time Congress faces the option of raising grazing fees, that body balks. Cattle ranchers who use public lands remain a powerful lobby, even though they represent a minority of the country's cattle ranchers, and their animals represent less than 8 percent of the cattle produced in this country. The ranchers who use public lands have managed to maintain what amounts to a special grazing subsidy at the expense of the ecosystem.

In many developing nations, contemporary cattle grazing has

gone hand in hand with massive logging. About 50 million acres of forest in Latin America have been destroyed to make room for pastureland since 1970, according to the Worldwatch Institute. The impact on forest amphibians by such deforestation is devastating and obvious.

Martha Crump saw an example of that impact firsthand in the spring of 1993, when she returned to a study site in Ecuador where she had worked as a graduate student about fifteen years earlier. "It was so neat to get in there," Crump says. "It was depressing too." A military base in the area had grown to about five times its former size in the intervening years, and most of the forest had been chopped down to make room for the changes. There were still many amphibians, but not the variety of species that Crump used to find there. Certain species of tree frogs and toads that were both hardy and not completely dependent on forest cover and clear water were abundant in roadside ditches. But the more exotic and colorful species that needed forest were gone. Biological diversity had collapsed.

In the United States, in a handful of studies, biologists have tried to identify exactly how logging affects amphibians by comparing logged and unlogged areas. In one study in western Oregon, biologists Paul Stephen Corn and R. Bruce Bury looked at the abundance of three salamander species and one frog species in streams in uncut forests and forests that had been logged within fourteen to forty years of their study.

"Species richness was highest in streams in uncut forests," the scientists concluded in a 1989 paper about their study. "Eleven streams in uncut forests contained all four species, and only two of these streams had fewer than three species present. Eleven streams in logged stands had one or no species present, and only one contained all four species. Density and biomass of all four species were significantly greater in streams in uncut forests."

In past studies, researchers have concluded that logging has some benefits for big game such as deer and elk (especially if you discount the loss of hiding and living space). It opens up the forest canopy, increases plant diversity—at least temporarily—and can increase the number of plants available for food for large mammals. However, in a study published in 1983, Bury looked at the effects of clear-cutting on amphibians in redwood forests in Northern California and found that they suffered from the cutting, even years after the logging had occurred.

To do his study, Bury marked off eight plots in the redwood forests. Half had been logged within six to fourteen years of the study; the others had never been logged. Then teams of from two to five people searched for and counted all the amphibians they could find in each of the plots. They turned over logs, and raked leaf litter to find everything they could. The search was more productive on the unlogged plots. There were more salamanders and frogs and a greater variety of species on the old-growth plots than on the logged plots, even though more than a decade had passed since cutting had occurred on some of the logged plots. Bury's results suggest that logging has a long-term effect on amphibians in redwood forests. "Apparently, opening of the canopy favors a few species to the detriment of the majority of forest-dependent species," he concluded.

Logging harms amphibians in both obvious and subtle ways. Obvious harm comes from taking out the trees and plants that provide shade and hiding places for the animals. Land and water temperatures change. Rains slough off soil once held in place by the forest into nearby streams and ponds, increasing silt loads and changing the water habitat. More subtle harm comes from the way logging turns a solid body of forest into a checkerboard of fragments. Such fragmentation can cut one amphibian population off from another by removing a forest or stream pathway between the populations. An apparently healthy population in one section of forest can become vulnerable to natural events, such as a fire or flood, with no chance of being recolonized later by outside populations in another part of the forest. Today, in the United States, only about 5 percent of the old-growth forests still stand, and many of those stand like isolated islands separated from each other.

Common sense would suggest that the Los Padres National Forest's arroyo toad populations would be fairly safe from danger, compared with other amphibians scattered in other forests. The Los Padres doesn't have enough trees for logging. Cattle grazing is the only significant commercial use of this forest, but that grazing is conducted far from the toad's current homes. Most of the Los Padres is still largely undeveloped, and almost half is designated as wilderness. It even includes the last two creeks in Southern California that haven't been overrun by nonnative fish or other introduced creatures, including bullfrogs.

Nevertheless, the toad has barely been protected from extinction in this forest. Various interests—miners, motorcyclists, campers, and even Forest Service employees—vie with the toad for use of its shrinking streamside habitat. And when the toad's survival requirements have conflicted with the Forest Service's goals for public recreation in the Los Padres, the toad has often lost. With the exception of a few of the agency's own biologists, the Forest Service in this forest has been one of the greatest stumbling blocks to stopping the toad's decline. In some cases the agency has been the creature's worst enemy.

There is little or no mystery in the arroyo toad's decline throughout California. Urbanization and habitat destruction, including the diversion and damming of streams, can account for most of the arroyo toad declines, just as they can account for the declines of many other amphibian populations around the world. But stopping the steady slide, as Sweet has learned, can become nearly a full-time job of persuading the uncaring to care.

Sweet would prefer to study the arroyo toad without fanfare, he says. But he has had to step out of the standard role of academic scientist into the role of conservation activist, pushing and prodding the Forest Service and other government agencies to do what's needed to protect the toad. Such a role change is one that an increasing number of biologists around the world feel forced to take as they watch the creatures they study—from beetles to pandas—disappear.

"Doing something about arroyo toads is a huge problem," Sweet says. "It requires . . . big changes in how some of these public lands are managed. It's tough."

If you look at an arroyo toad in a field guide, you're not likely to be impressed. But the illustrations don't do this animal justice. The word *cute,* trite as it is, aptly applies to this toad. An adult measures no more than about three inches from nose to tush. Its body is typically round and soft. Its smooth belly is a pale, creamy white, its bumpy back is mottled black on a background of cream or tan. Its legs seem unusually pudgy, and its gold eyes have horizontal pupils that give it a look that suggests sleepiness. Unlike the more common western toad, which usually moves itself by walking, the arroyo toad hops exclusively. But it isn't a jumpy animal. It will sit still and passive in a hand's loose grip, patiently waiting as though it hopes that it will be released if it simply acts polite and pleasant. When a male arroyo calls, its voice comes out as a long trill that sounds more like the song of an insect than an amphibian. When it otherwise speaks, which it will do if it has been held too long and wants to be released, it does so with a quiet, birdlike chirp.

Sweet became interested in the little toad shortly after he arrived to take up a research and teaching position at UC Santa Barbara in 1977. At that time almost nothing had been written and little was known about the area's reptiles and amphibians. The campus's museum collection of amphibians and reptiles was small and, as Sweet recalls, inadequate for teaching and research purposes. He immediately set out to learn as much as he could about what was living in the mountains and valleys around Santa Barbara, and to build up the museum's collection. He would hike into the mountains every chance he could get, collecting animals and data, learning the local geography and ecosystems. Within less than an hour's drive from the seaside campus, he could be in the backcountry, finding amphibians and reptiles he had never seen before.

The more Sweet learned, the more curious he became about some trends he was seeing. Some animals were harder than others to discover, harder than others to track. One of those was the arroyo toad. He would visit a place that seemed to be perfect arroyo toad habitat—a broad stream with a rocky bottom and sandy beaches—and expect to find toads easily. Instead, he would often find nothing. The more he looked, the more questions he had. "Are they rare because they are uncommon, or do I just not know how to look for them?" Sweet recalls thinking. "Some afternoon you just get it in your head that, shit, I just don't know much about this critter." In 1981 he typed a list of thirty unresolved questions about the amphibians and reptiles in the area, and then taped it to his office wall, where it still hangs. One question asks where the arroyo toads are.

Now, after more than a decade of visits—sometimes weekly—in spring, summer, and fall to the toad's Los Padres hangouts, Sweet knows where they are and that they've declined in number. He also confidently concludes that the toad's greatest curse is its choice of home and lifestyle. They share too many tastes in common with humans.

"Arroyo toads are people," Sweet says. "They like to live exactly where the Forest Service likes to put campgrounds, because they like high, sandy terraces of oak and cottonwood trees by the stream. You can fly over Los Padres and drop a smoke flare on every one of those [terraces] and you'd find you had dropped a smoke flare on someone's tent, courtesy of the Forest Service.

"They lay their eggs right at the peak of trout-fishing season, when people are wandering up and down the creeks right along the edge and stomp on [the eggs]. When they metamorphose, the juveniles spend two or three months—July, August, and September—on the beach. The openest, flattest, sandiest beaches along these streams where there are pools—which is, of course, where everybody else wants to go and set their lawn chairs and play Frisbee or soccer.

"They love to sit on roads," he continues. "A road, to a toad, is just everything they've ever wanted because they have a clear field of view, all the bugs they want, no grass or stickers. It's just perfect. And oftentimes the road stays warmer in the evening than the sand if there's a heat wave. So when Ralph the bozo comes and drives around the campground at nine o'clock looking for a campsite, can't find one, then drives out, in the process he's run over ten toads."

Campers, campsites, and clumsy trout fishermen are just part of the arroyo toad's problem, though. The animal chronically suffers from what Sweet playfully calls ICP: Idiotic Clutch Placement. The toads, Sweet complains, have a tendency to lay their eggs in the shallow part of a creek, where water depth is no more than one-half inch, at a time when the creek is drying at a rate of an inch or more a day. Anything that lays four thousand to five thousand eggs at a pop, as the arroyo toad does, expects to lose a lot of eggs anyway; otherwise it would probably be laying fewer to begin with. But actually placing the eggs in such unsuitable spots seems, well, idiotic. In 1991, Sweet spent part of the breeding period along one stream moving seventy egg clutches to deeper water. At other times he has dug narrow channels in streams to divert water so it will continue to bathe nearly stranded, idiotically placed clutches.

The female toad lays the clutches in two long, thin threads of black, beadlike eggs. Placed end to end, the strings from a single toad can stretch about twenty-four feet. It takes about five days for the poppyseed-size eggs to hatch into tiny tadpoles, and then another two to two and a half months for tadpoles to develop into nickel-size toadlets. All this development occurs from late spring to midsummer, the time of year when creeks and streams are in a drying mode. A lot can happen in that two and a half months, and often does.

Off-road vehicle fanatics, the bane of hikers and anyone else who goes to the wilderness to get away from road traffic, are allowed to ride their two-, three-, and four-wheel vehicles in national forests on roads and certain marked trails. In the Los Padres, riders ignore posted signs warning against riding off trails often enough to become one of the top hazards facing the forest's arroyo toads. They power their machines through creeks and streams, creating havoc. The renegade vehicles stir up creek-bottom silt, which buries and smothers toad eggs. Their wheels crush egg clutches and decapitate tadpoles, leaving nothing behind but carnage and tire tracks. As the ORVs weave along the wide creek banks, they pack the sand and crush young toadlets, which spend their early weeks buried there.

Fences and gates are not much more effective than signs in keeping the worst ORV renegades on the trails and out of the water. Thick metal gates have been torched open by ORV riders who apparently didn't think their right to trash public wild lands should be hindered. In 1992, barbed-wire fences erected at the behest of Sweet and a sympathetic Forest Service biologist to keep riders out of creeks during toad breeding were ignored as riders either broke through or went around them—leaving their tire tracks in the sand like some kind of in-your-face profanity.

Weekend gold miners legally working their streambed claims are another hazard to the toads. A few wiped out nearly a whole year's worth of egg clutches on one Los Padres creek during a single Memorial Day weekend in 1991. The miners come armed with portable suction dredging machines that vacuum up creek silt, check it for treasures, and then spit the silt out again. The silt moved downstream along Upper Piru Creek before it settled and buried toad eggs and tadpoles. The dredging and subsequent silt settlement wiped out five miles of toad habitat, Sweet figures. "For years, the forest biologist had been pushing for closing all streams to suction dredging," Sweet notes.

According to that forest biologist, Maeton Freel, the agency's ability to close even the stream sections that contain toad breeding spots has been hampered by the 1872 Mining Act. That act gives miners nearly free rein on federal lands that might hold minable minerals. Any efforts to reform the 120-year-old law have been squelched in Congress. The best the Forest Service biologists have been able to do to protect the toad from the miners so far, according to Freel, has been to persuade the state's Department of Fish and Game (which, through a web of laws and regulations, has some jurisdiction) to prohibit suction dredging on critical creeks from May to September, when the toads are breeding. Unfortunately for the Upper Piru Creek toads, the state agency didn't establish that new prohibition until after the Memorial Day massacre.

In mid-1992, the Forest Service decided to begin a formal environmental assessment of mining's impact on the Los Padres streams. In 1993 the Forest Service decided not to accept any of about one hundred applications for permits to mine in the Los Padres until the agency had completed that study. Mining groups and clubs, made up mostly of recreational miners, indicated to the Forest Service that they resent the restrictions and will likely challenge them in court.

After the Memorial Day fiasco, there were still a few pools with eggs and tadpoles upstream from where the dredging occurred. But on the July Fourth weekend, Sweet says, those toad offspring were wiped out by ORV riders who cut a fence between the riding trail and the stream and drove their machines through the water.

Enter any U.S. Forest Service–managed forest and you're likely to see a sign bearing the motto "Land of Many Uses." Over the years, demands on the forest and its uses have increased from various groups—from loggers to miners to campers to ORV riders to cattle ranchers to environmentalists. Since the agency was created in 1905, a list of laws has defined and redefined the purpose of the

U.S. Forest Service and the 156 forests it oversees. The basic thrust of the current laws requires that the Forest Service balance the recreational and commercial demands on forests with the need to preserve the forests' wildlife and biological diversity.

Critics, including some Forest Service staff, have contended for years that the agency has ignored the wildlife and favored the commercial and recreational users. A 1992 report by the U.S. Congress's Office of Technology Assessment concluded that Forest Service's existing management plans for forests "focus on producing timber and other physical annual outputs. . . . Outputs from the national forest are clearly important, but sustaining the ecological health of national forests is paramount." The report found a number of reasons for the agency's emphasis on what the forest can produce at the expense of its ecosystem's health. One of those is the agency's dominance by foresters, people trained in the business of cultivating and cutting down trees, who "typically emphasize use of the resources." Foresters are less dominant today than they were ten or twenty years ago, but they "still account for more than 50 percent of professionals and for more than 75 percent of the technicians employed by the Forest Service," according to the OTA.

The way to get ahead in the agency, even if you aren't a forester, some agency insiders say, has been to think like a forester and view the forest as something to be used, not let alone. Biologists have been a smaller but growing element in the agency. The biologists' primary purpose is to make sure the forests' biology is not irreparably sacrificed to accommodate commercial and recreational uses. Not surprisingly, biologists who follow their mandate have frequently come into conflict with the agency's forester mentality.

In the last two decades, pressure has increased on forest managers around the world to protect biological diversity. In 1990 the Forest Service and the White House, then occupied by George Bush, began feeling the pressure of increased public concern about worldwide deforestation and loss of wildlife and wildlife habitat. The agency introduced an initiative it called "New Perspectives."

The initiative, according to the agency, would incorporate newer views of land and resources that would emphasize a better balance between ecosystem protection and economic demands on the forest. The "New Perspectives" initiative might be viewed as a declaration by the agency's Washington, D.C., leaders that it would care about and work hard to protect creatures like arroyo toads and their diminishing habitats. If that's so, the message apparently was sent by carrier pigeon, because it has yet to make it to many key agency players in the field.

A day after my interview with Sam Sweet in his office, I met him again to join him on a field trip to the hills above Santa Barbara. He is in a good mood when I find him, having received word that he has won an important round of a dragging dispute with the U.S. Forest Service's Mount Pinos District ranger about how to protect the arroyo toad from ORV riders.

The Mount Pinos District is one of five administrative units that make up the Los Padres National Forest. Forest Service districts are typically run like fiefdoms headed by a ranger, and the rangers report to a supervisor who oversees the whole forest. District rangers, according to current and former agency staffers, can be either benevolent or bullying. But in either case they hold a great amount of influence and power over the land in their charge, and to get anything done in the forest usually means getting the district ranger's support.

The Mount Pinos District sits in the northeast corner of Ventura County, near a state-owned ORV park whose trails reach into the Los Padres. At one point in the forest, one of those trails crosses Piru Creek, a home for arroyo toads. As the Forest Service made plans to repair parts of the trail in late 1991, the agency's district officials insisted on placing the creek crossing at a spot within ten feet of an arroyo toad breeding pool. The district ranger supported the plan, as did local ORV organizations. But the plan went against the advice of the agency's own hydrologist, the U.S. Fish and

Wildlife Service, and Sam Sweet. So Sweet and two environmental groups filed administrative appeals with the Forest Service.

On this day, Sweet has learned that the district ranger has decided to reconsider his decision. (A few months later, Forest Service officials and Sweet agree to a compromise that places the crossing much farther upstream from the breeding site.) The Mount Pinos District has been particularly resistant to doing anything to protect the toads until now, Sweet says, so he finds this small victory especially satisfying. As we bound down the stairway from his office, though, it is hard to tell whether Sweet is happier about the win or about getting released from his desk for an afternoon and a long night of toad hunting. A colleague greets him and asks how he is. Better with each step that takes him farther from his office phone, he tells her.

We climb into his dusty yellow Toyota Land Cruiser. It is ten years old, and when Sweet bought it used, it had hardly been driven. Now it has more than 143,000 miles on it, most of that accrued just in the mountains around Santa Barbara. Inside, the vehicle is stripped down to the bare essentials. This is not a yuppified four-wheel-drive car meant to spend most of its time on city streets. The ride is bumpy and the engine is loud. As we drive, Sweet has to raise his voice to be heard above the roar.

Before we get very far, Sweet pulls into a McDonald's. He orders two cheeseburgers, which he places into a cooler in the back of the Land Cruiser. He'll eat them for dinner later. He developed a taste for cold cheeseburgers as an undergraduate at Cornell University. At spring break, he and a few friends would pile into a car, drive to the nearest hamburger joint, buy about a dozen burgers each, and then drive nonstop to Florida, where they would spend the week tramping through swamps to catch amphibians and reptiles. They would ration the cheeseburgers en route south to avoid losing time on travel that they could spend in the field.

Within half an hour we are within the Santa Barbara District of the Los Padres, preparing to leave the comfort of paved roads. We drive farther into it on a rocky, rugged, and winding dirt road that seems at times to hang in the air above deep canyons. It takes us about ninety minutes to go just fifteen miles on this road. The scenery along the way is never the sort of lush, tree-packed view normally associated with anything called a forest; this country is too dry for that. Here there are sycamores along streams, and oaks scattered throughout. But mostly there are grasses and bushes and chaparral. As we move deeper into the outback, the geology changes enough to make the plantlife even more sparse. This is where the string of mountains called the Coast Ranges, which extends from just south of the Oregon border, ends and the Transverse Ranges, which stretches east to form the northern border of the Los Angeles basin, begins. About one hundred miles south and 150 miles east of here begins the Peninsular Ranges, the state's southernmost mountain range, which forms the eastern edge of the L.A. basin and stretches south into Mexico.

Our destination is Mono Creek. This creek and neighboring Indian Creek combined stretch only about twenty miles, but they stand out from the rest of Southern California's fresh waters. There are no nonnative fish and no bullfrogs living in these streams. They are the only two creeks in Southern California that can make that claim, Sweet says.

In some ecosystems, fish and amphibians coexist successfully. Usually the coexistence coincides with a mutual distaste for each other. The local amphibian species' eggs may taste bitter to the local fish species, or vice versa. But in other ecosystems, introduced fish, including native fish that have simply been transferred to a fishless stream, have been suspected of contributing to amphibian declines in many parts of the western United States. The intruder fish can make a quick lunch of amphibian eggs and tadpoles. Within a few years they can wipe out a lake or stream's entire amphibian population. Andrew Blaustein also has found evidence that hatchery-grown stocked fish may introduce a fungus that he has identified as responsible for killing western toad eggs in several Oregon lakes.

Peter Moyle, a biologist at the University of California at Davis, who has studied nonnative fish in California, has estimated that fifty of the 133 different species of fish in the state are nonnative. Some of these newcomers are the descendants of fish planted in the state's streams and lakes more than a century ago. The planting began after the completion of the transcontinental railway in 1869, according to Moyle. The railroad made it easy for state and federal fish commissions to import exotic fishes from the East Coast and release them into California's streams and lakes. These early introductions were done mostly to improve sportfishing. The state's new residents were convinced that the fish from the East were superior to the native fish. That perception may have been true in some locations, Moyle has written, because natural habitats were being disturbed by the new settlers, and the introduced fish seemed to thrive in streams and lakes that had been changed, while the native fish diminished.

For about a decade after the railroad was built, fish planting was intense. Then, according to Moyle, it continued on a smaller scale until the 1950s, when both authorized and unauthorized planting of fish within California soared—as did the state's human population. Some of the authorized fish planting has included fish used for insect control, such as mosquito fish. Unfortunately, the pest control fish often dine on amphibian offspring. Even now, state and federal agencies continue to plant trout and other fish in streams and lakes throughout the West to control pests and keep recreational fishermen happy.

The impact of all this fish planting is multiplied with time, as the fish gradually expand their range by swimming through networks of streams or by getting washed to other waters during heavy storms. In the Sierra Nevada, for instance, high mountain lakes and streams were virtually free of fish until planting began in the 1800s.

Today, about 60 percent of the range's three thousand lakes have fish. David Bradford, who has studied mountain yellow-legged frogs in the Sierra, has determined that before fish stocking began, frogs may have been present in most of the range's lakes and streams. Now, where there are fish, there rarely are mountain yellow-leggeds.

In some cases, exotic fish have been transported through the California Aqueduct, the giant system of concrete and pipe that carries water from Northern California to Southern California. Sweet says that parts of Piru Creek in the Los Padres National Forest now contain seventeen introduced fish species, most of which came through a circuitous network that links the creek to the aqueduct. In those fish-infested parts of the creek, the native amphibians are barely hanging on. Their hold is made weaker by periodic increases in water releases at an upstream dam by the California Department of Water Resources, the agency that oversees the state water system. The releases have the same effect as opening a faucet from a drip to a full flow. The water tumbles down rapidly, tearing up plants and the creekbed and washing out tadpoles and toadlets. A dam poised to release heavy flows with the turn of a dial is, Sweet says, "like having a cocked, loaded gun pointed at the ecosystem."

That there are no nonnative creatures in Mono and Indian creeks may be the single most important reason these waters are still home to several native amphibian species, including California red-legged frogs and arroyo toads. Here the toads must dodge the garter snakes and moles that like to dine on them, but the only introduced species that threatens to stomp them out faster than they can regenerate their populations here is the *Homo sapiens,* whose appetite for creeks, streams, and their riparian habitat seems insatiable.

"Southern California has done a better job than any other society at destroying a regional ecosystem," Sweet says about riparian habitats, the belts of trees and shrubs that border creeks and streams and are essential living space for much wildlife during long, dry summers. "Our rivers have been seen as eyesores—dry most of the year—or annoying threats," he continues. They've been dammed, diverted, and drained to feed agriculture and the burgeoning human population. Of the ten major river systems in the region's Transverse and Peninsular mountain ranges, six have been dammed to the headwaters. Dammed or not, most of the area's streams have been used and abused for recreation and reduced to fragments of their natural selves. "It's like taking a body and leaving only a few fingertips," Sweet concludes about the current status of the ten river systems. "We are in a position in Southern California to essentially write off the riparian ecosystem." And as goes that ecosystem, so go the amphibians who depend upon it.

Californians aren't alone in their ability to harm the aquatic ecosystem, though. In the two hundred years following the American Revolution, Americans destroyed half of the lower forty-eight states' wetlands—the mudflats, swamps, marshes, and bogs that are breeding and feeding grounds for vast numbers of amphibians, birds, and fish. They are equally tough on streams and rivers. One federal agency estimated in 1989 that 41 percent of the nation's year-round streams had been harmed by "siltation, bank erosion, and channelization."

On this day at Mono Creek, Sweet wants to count and identify toads that are one year old and older. The goal is part of a systematic study of the creek's arroyo toad population that Sweet began a few months earlier. A key to understanding population dynamics is recruitment. A "recruit," in this case, is a toadlet that has somehow survived the vulnerable egg and tadpole stages and, by the next breeding season, still has its limbs and body intact. Sweet hopes the study will help him understand how much recruitment is normal for arroyo toads in a relatively undisturbed setting, and how many of those recruits make it to adulthood and reproduce. The study should give Sweet a lot of basic information about the arroyo toad that until now has been unknown. It might also shed some light on what prevents the arroyo toads from having enough recruitment to keep their populations from growing very much. Sweet suspects that the killdeer, a native bird that lives along Mono Creek, might be so aggressively feeding on arroyo toads that recruitment on the creek is kept low. In recent years, drought has probably also taken a toll. Anything Sweet learns about the toad population dynamics could be useful in helping the Forest Service manage the habitat for this little animal that nobody except Sweet knows much about.

By the time Sweet swings his Land Cruiser into a roadside clearing near Mono Creek, it is five-thirty in the afternoon. It has taken us about two hours to get to this spot. "This sort of distance is the only thing that's keeping these populations around," Sweet tells me. "Otherwise the creek would be full of floating Pampers." I think at first that he is joking, but he is dead serious. In other creeks in the Los Padres, particularly ones near campgrounds, Sweet routinely sees rolled-up and discarded disposable diapers in the water. His ambition, he says, is to witness a person actually in the act of diaper tossing. "I swear if I catch one, I'm going to force them to eat it."

It will be 2:00 A.M. before we leave the creek. The portion that Sweet will monitor tonight is only about two and a half miles long, but we will hike four times that distance, tracing and retracing our steps, stopping whenever a toad appears to identify it, measure it, and record its location. After just a few months on this study, Sweet has learned from his regular hikes along the creek that the toads move around more than he suspected. Some toads move more than two miles from one sighting to the next.

Sweet packs a few essentials for the hike: a stubby pencil and an index card for writing down data, equipment for marking toads, a couple of cans of soda, and a pillowcase to hold the sodas and equipment. Then he pulls from a box a leather holster that he straps around his waist. He removes a .44 Magnum revolver from the box and loads five bullets into it, leaving the chamber under the hammer empty for safety's sake. He places the gun in the holster. Standing there against the backdrop of dry mountains, with his bushy dark beard and dressed in blue jeans and a khaki shirt and cap, Sweet looks like a young, tall Fidel Castro preparing for guerrilla warfare.

I have heard stories about early biologists who collected frogs by shooting them from a distance. I think of those stories as I watch Sweet load the gun. Then he explains that he carries the weapon for his own protection. An eccentric loner with a fondness for guns has taken refuge in a nearby canyon. Some hard-core drinkers from town often party in the area also. And, he explains later, some people who don't want their weekend pastime of riding fast motorcycles through creeks to be hindered by toads see Sweet as their nemesis. He has only had to pull the gun once, when a motorcyclist threatened to run Sweet and his wife down while they were checking on toads in another part of the Los Padres. He didn't have to fire, though. Waving the gun was enough to encourage the rider to reconsider.

We walk a long while up the road without seeing any toads. Usually arroyo toads don't emerge from their hiding places—a sandy beach or bank they've dug into—until after dark. While we walk, Sweet smokes and, like a willing nature guide, talks about the sights along the way.

"There's a snake trail," he says, pointing to a pencil-thin curved line in the dusty road. I jump instinctively. I've never made full peace with snakes and their tendency to appear from nowhere and shock. "Toad poop," he notes later. This time he points to a dark plug no bigger than a cigarette ash. He prods it with his boot toe. It falls apart easily. It is full of ant heads. In the summer, ants are arroyo toads' favorite food.

At a spot where the creek crosses the road, a barbed-wire fence spans the creek, blocking access to it from the road. A second fence runs parallel to the first, a few feet upstream. Nancy Sandburg, the Forest Service biologist in the Santa Barbara District, installed the upstream fence at the beginning of the breeding season to discourage people, particularly ORV riders, from driving through the breeding grounds. She made the agency hold off opening the road in the spring for two weeks until the fence was in. Then, later, she installed the second fence when she discovered that the toads were breeding closer to the road than she'd realized. The fence hasn't been entirely effective. At one end, the barbed wire has been spread wide apart and ORV tire tracks run through the sandy beach beyond it.

Farther up the road, a line of wooden barriers with signs warn visitors not to bring motor vehicles there after dark. Sandburg put the barriers up after Sweet discovered five squashed toads on the road. Over the Fourth of July weekend, Sandburg feared that holiday celebrants would ignore the barriers and signs, so she camped out on the road to make sure no toads were killed.

Sandburg, a soft-spoken blonde with steely blue eyes, is the only person in the Forest Service's Santa Barbara District who has actively tried to protect the toads, Sweet says. She and a few others like her in the Los Padres help Sweet resist the temptation to write the agency off as all evil and no good when it comes to amphibian protection. "The Forest Service is not an entity," he says. It is an organization made up of people, and "there are extremely good people, good people, so-so people, and buffoons." Sandburg is a top-notch biologist, Sweet says, who regularly challenges her district's administrators' general lack of enthusiasm for protecting the toad and other wildlife. "How she's managed to avoid getting fired until now, I don't know."

Sandburg knows why she has retained her job, she tells me a few months later over lunch. She has done nothing but what her role as biologist requires her to do: tell the truth and work hard to satisfy the agency's mandate to protect the forest's natural resources. Still, she admits that the going hasn't been easy in the agency, particularly in the Santa Barbara District. When she wanted to apply to the agency's regional office in San Francisco for a grant to fund riparian habitat studies that included protection measures for the Mono

Creek arroyo toads, some of her bosses discouraged her. She took vacation time to write the funding proposal, and ended up winning a $160,000 grant. One official in the Los Padres National Forest supervisor's office tried to prevent Sandburg from submitting with the grant application a videotape of Sweet giving a public lecture about the toad and riparian habitats. He dismissed Sweet as some kind of radical conservationist. Sandburg calls Sweet "the best friend this forest has."

Sweet and I leave the main road and walk up the creek. For the rest of the evening I will never know quite where I am, as we weave back and forth across the creek, occasionally leaving it to take a shortcut through the dry land to another pool farther upstream. Early on, we stop momentarily as Sweet notes the size of a stand of sycamores. When he returns to his office, he will use the information to change the details on a map of the creek. "Anybody that does any fieldwork has got to love maps," he told me earlier, in his office. "You don't know anything without a good map."

Sweet makes his own maps by hand, without the aid of any fancy computer programs. His maps are elegant line drawings that are both simple and detailed. Mono Creek is a lazy, wavy line that thickens here and there into various widths representing deeper, broader pools. Dashed and dotted rivulets branch off occasionally.

On a standard Forest Service map of the Los Padres, Mono Creek appears as a barely visible wavy blue line. Crossing and bordering the line in spots is a dotted black line. A similar dotted line passes through and beside the creek on Sweet's map as well. On both maps it represents Ogilvy Ranch Road, a seasonal dirt road that increasingly appears to be one of the greatest avoidable threats to arroyo toad survival on this creek.

The Ogilvy Ranch Road leads from a campground downstream of where we are to a privately owned ranch a few miles upstream. Along its path, the road passes through several oak terraces where some adult arroyo toads live, and then the road crosses the creek itself sixteen times as it winds its way to the ranch. Ten of those crossings run through or near toad breeding pools.

For many years each winter, as Mono Creek filled from the season's rains, its power destroyed the road crossings. Then each spring, after the rains finished and the creek diminished to a gentle flow, the Forest Service routinely sent crews out to regrade and rebuild the dirt road. The Forest Service is required to provide and maintain access to the outside world from private properties surrounded by the forest. Yet, even though there was already another road on higher ground leading to the ranch, the agency continued to fulfill the ranch owner's requests to use its equipment and money to rebuild the Ogilvy Ranch Road through Mono Creek, because the creek route was faster than the other one.

This annual roadbuilding seemed like lunacy to Sweet. The road construction killed toads as bulldozers slammed through breeding ponds at the peak breeding season and then pushed around huge quantities of sand, some of which contained hiding toads. After the road was built, toads were squashed by people driving on it at night. As long as the annual roadwork continued, especially at the height of breeding season, Sweet would never be able to do a decent study on the population dynamics of the Mono Creek toads. Sandburg understood Sweet's concern, and through conversations and meetings with district administrators, the two biologists worked out a verbal agreement with the Forest Service. The agency would not rebuild the road in the spring or summer of 1992, the arroyo toad breeding season. If the agency did decide to rebuild by the time autumn rolled around, Sweet understood, he would be consulted.

The agreement satisfied Sweet, and as we take our first hike of the evening up the creek, Sweet points out a sandy bank that in another year would have been bulldozed. As he talks, he spots two baby toads on the bank. Each is about the size of a quarter, and they blend in with the sand almost perfectly. Sweet reaches down to examine them, and as he does so, I catch the sudden movement of grass out of the corner of my eye. I look closer, and there is nothing but an indentation in the sand, shaped like the top of a miniature dormant volcano. Sweet recognizes it as the path of a hiding toad, and he begins to dig with his hands in the sand, swiftly but carefully. In a second he has an adult toad, a paunchy thing a little larger than an Oreo. Greeting it gently—"Hi. How are you?"—he holds it in his left hand while he kills his cigarette and then rinses his right hand in the creek to rid it of nicotine remnants. Nicotine kills toads, he explains.

He examines the toad for any sign that he has caught it before. Marking a toad or frog so that it can be identified again in the future is essential for most long-term studies of the animals. The rationale is that without marking them, a researcher can't follow their growth or movement over a period of months or years. And if you can't follow their growth or movement, you can't know very basic information about them that could be essential in understanding them or even in protecting them and their habitat. The actual marking, though, is no easy task. Biologists are constantly trying to figure the best way to do it without hurting or burdening the animal. Birds can be marked with leg bands, bears can be marked with ear tags or even tracked with radio collars. Snakes can be marked by cutting a few scales in a specific pattern. It's like cutting a fingernail that never grows, and for year after year the mark remains visible. Frogs and toads, though, don't have scales, and a band around their legs could easily get tangled in the debris they encounter daily.

During the early years of his graduate work, Marc Hayes tried using a system of small beaded metal chains locked around their lower abdomens to mark some red-legged frogs he was studying. He discovered very quickly that the few animals he marked were developing skin abrasions from the chains, so he spent an evening recatching them and removing the chains. Eventually he tried a more common method of marking by clipping toes in a specific pattern unique to each frog in the study area. One frog, for instance, would be marked by clipping the third toe on its right hind foot to distinguish it from another frog which was marked by clipping its second toe on the right hind foot. The thumbs are never clipped, since males use these during mating to hang on to their female companions. And no more than one toe is clipped on any single foot.

Anuran skin heals quickly, and losing a toe or two doesn't seem to slow a frog or toad down, at least not when they are released from the clipping ordeal. But the method isn't perfect. If there are no more than a few hundred animals in a site, the toe-clipping method works okay. But, in a long-term study of a large population, the number of creatures that are marked can eventually outnumber the number of toe sequences available.

Sweet also has struggled to come up with a good marking method for the arroyo toads. He has rejected toe clipping. "I don't feel like doing that. They have those fingers because they use them," he says. He has rejected branding with numbers. "They need their skin. I wouldn't feel so good about having a set of numbers burned across *my* stomach." For a while he used a thread of colored beads tied around the toads' waists, but that method didn't last long because the threads wore out and broke.

Now Sweet uses a high-tech marking method more commonly used by biologists to mark mammals. He cuts a very small V-shaped notch in the skin on the back of a toad. Then he inserts an electronic device called a passive integrated transponder, or PIT, tag into the notch. The notch heals shut and the tag is held permanently in place under the skin.

The PIT tag is about the diameter of the lead of a standard pencil, and less than a half-inch long. It is a thin glass tube that carries a microchip, a wire coil, and a tuning capacitor. The tag has been programmed at the factory to transmit a unique identification number once it is activated by a low-frequency radio signal. Sweet uses a machine that is about the size of a hand-held hair dryer to emit that signal and electronically "read" a PIT tag's identification code. He waves the reader over a toad's back, and if it is tagged, a series of numbers appears on a small screen on the reader.

One of the drawbacks of the new marking method is the cost. The reader is fairly delicate and costs about $1,200. Each tag costs about five dollars. Marking a few hundred toads can get expensive.

We don't see another toad until after dark. Then, using a miner's headlamp, Sweet begins to pick up the characteristic eyeshine with regularity. Arroyo toad eyes glow under the light's shine like pink marbles. As we walk down a dirt path during our second sweep of the creek, Sweet's light finds the shine about ten yards ahead. Sweet picks up his pace. At the last minute the toad reacts to Sweet's approach and begins to hop toward a bush.

Sweet gives his common toad greeting. "Hi, how are you?" The toad keeps moving. "Nooooo," Sweet coos as he lifts the animal off the ground. The toad barely moves as Sweet inspects it for signs of a PIT tag. He doesn't find any. "You're new." He measures it. "Fifty-two millimeters. You're small." He takes a PIT tag and scissors from his shirt pocket and does the V-notch cut. When he has finished, he places the toad gently on the ground. It sits still for a moment and then, surprisingly slowly, hops away.

For the rest of the evening, Sweet repeats the routine dozens of times. By the time we return to the Land Cruiser, it is 2:00 A.M. A thermometer on the dashboard says it is sixty-five degrees, but soaked socks and wet hiking boots make it feel much colder. The mountains around us loom like gentle, dark giants. The only sounds are of insects chirping and buzzing. Sweet unloads his gun and puts away the marking equipment. Then he rolls the Land Cruiser back up the route we came in on along the bumpy road. As we leave, big, warty western toads are perched here and there along the sides of the road. They stand like sentries guarding this rare territory and bidding us farewell.

. . .

Four months later, on November 16, 1992, a Forest Service work crew began a three-day job, grading and rebuilding part of the Ogilvy Ranch Road. The job included bulldozing tons of dirt and sand from the creek banks and pushing it into the bed of Mono Creek. After three days' work, the road was three miles long and crossed the creek at least fourteen times. Nobody in the Santa Barbara District office—neither the resources manager who ordered the work nor the district ranger who oversees the entire district—informed Nancy Sandburg, the district's biologist, that the work was being done.

They knew that the road had not been constructed earlier in the year to protect breeding toads. Sweet had told them that the creek and its sandy banks were sensitive habitat, that the arroyo toad lived there. They knew that Sweet was conducting a long-term study of the toads. They knew the toad was being considered for listing on the federal endangered species list. Under the circumstances, they should have known that to build the road without some kind of environmental review would be unwise and possibly illegal. They should have known that if they had informed Sandburg about the road construction plans, she would have put the kibosh on them.

On November 20, one of the engineers on the work crew happened to ask Sandburg a technical question about the roadbuilding. It was the first she had heard of the project, and she was furious. She stopped any additional work on the road immediately. Then she joined the small but growing ranks of Forest Service whistleblowers. She called Sweet to let him know what had happened. The news was devastating, and Sweet drove out to Mono Creek to examine the grading.

In the aftermath of the roadbuilding, it was difficult to ferret out why the district's administrators had ordered the road rebuilt in the first place. At one point it appeared that it had been built to allow quick access to the Ogilvy Ranch—even though rains would wash it out within weeks. At another time it appeared that only a few crossings were to be graded, to allow easy access to a backcountry location where a small weather station was to be installed. In this scenario, the bulldozer operators misunderstood their instructions and rebuilt the entire road. Whatever the reason, the damage was done.

By November 22, Sweet had prepared a ten-page, single-spaced report on the damage to the creek and the arroyo toad populations. "My principal concern is that by this action the USFS has killed a significant proportion of young-of-the-year arroyo toads on Mono Creek. If this is so, there may be cause for concern about the viability of this population. Arroyo toads did not breed on Mono Creek in 1989 or 1990 owing to low water levels, and in 1991 there were no more than 36 young toads produced," he wrote. "The 1992 season produced upwards of 200 young toads; this success is viewed as critical, since the 1992 breeding population of adults consisted of large (=old) animals, and there had been no recruitment for at least three years." Sweet figured that as many as three-fourths of those two hundred young were probably killed by the bulldozing. Some adults were probably also killed.

"Whatever the mortality figure is (and this cannot be learned directly), the road project has also rendered a major focus of the research I have been conducting invalid," he continued. "This project was not simply done without the agreed-upon consultation. It was clearly a major undertaking in an extensive riparian area well known to the USFS to have very sensitive populations of endangered species." Noting that the project was done without any formal assessment of its environmental impact, Sweet concluded that it was "in short illegal, and in my view criminal."

About a week later, representatives of the U.S. Fish and Wildlife Service, which is responsible for protecting endangered wildlife, and the Army Corps of Engineers, which is partly responsible for regulating wetlands and other onshore waters, toured Mono Creek to inspect the damage. Sam Sweet and several Forest Service staff members, not including Sandburg, were also on the tour.

As the group walked along Mono Creek, the Corps of Engineers representative said little and took copious notes. The Forest Service crew, Sweet recalled, chattered jovially, commenting that the damage was slight, that the grading wasn't such a big deal. As the walk finished, though, the Corps of Engineers member solemnly informed the Forest Service officials that the agency had violated a list of regulations by not applying for a permit from his agency before grading began. Those concerns were reiterated in a follow-up letter that was, in effect, like a slap on the wrist. Later, a letter from the Fish and Wildlife Service to David Dahl, the Los Padres National Forest supervisor, would lay out a list of other state and federal regulations the road construction violated. But because none of the animals harmed had been formally listed on the endangered species list (in the case of the arroyo toad, because of Fish and Wildlife Service foot-dragging), the Fish and Wildlife Service had no real power to go after the Forest Service.

Forest Service officials who attended the tour seemed unmoved by the creek damage evaluation done by the Corps, the Fish and Wildlife Service, or Sam Sweet. According to the minutes of a Los Padres National Forest staff meeting a few days after the tour, the Forest Service officials concluded that "all maintenance was done appropriately, and effect was 'light on the land.' Some mortality of juvenile arroyo toads may have occurred."

In June 1993, Dahl, the forest supervisor, told me that the grading incident seemed to be the result of a communication gap. He was organizing a multiagency investigation of the incident—a full seven months after it had happened and also after an environmental law firm began taking legal action in response to the incident. Questions of accountability and punishment still hadn't been resolved. Dahl provided only vague answers to my inquiries about who had ordered the bulldozing and why. But, he assured me, before any grading was ever done again on Ogilvy Ranch Road and through Mono Creek, his agency "would do an intense review" to make sure no toads would be harmed. "Obviously," he said, "we would not open it if it threatened the toad."

Forest Service officials in Washington, D.C., routinely contend that the agency is reforming and is becoming more sensitive to the needs of the ecosystem in the lands they manage. Yet, as various Forest Service biologists have asserted, it doesn't matter what the agency heads in D.C. say; the real power to affect a forest and its resources resides at the district level, with the district rangers and their lieutenants. And at that level, the old-school insensitivity to ecosystem management and wildlife preservation still dominates in many forests. In the Los Padres National Forest, and in many other forests around the country, a more accurate motto for the agency's millions of acres would be "Land of Many Abuses."

9

. . . .

A Place for Frogs

Mark Jennings, Marc Hayes, and a few volunteers stand on a dirt road beside their caravan of trucks and vans, packing into picnic coolers about thirty-five plastic bags, each bag containing a live California red-legged. The frogs come from deep pools in a spring-fed creek a few hundred yards away. These are particularly rare red-leggeds, part of the last-known red-legged population in Southern California south of the Los Padres National Forest.

That these frogs have survived while every other red-legged population in the region has disappeared is probably the result of an isolated location and simple good luck. These red-leggeds live atop a plateau that was once part of a cattle ranch. But the plateau is now included in 3,100 acres owned and protected by The Nature Conservancy as an ecological reserve. Smooth, rolling grasslands dotted with mature oaks dominate this land. A strip of riparian habitat, rich with pools, reeds, and sycamores, lies just inside one border of the reserve and sustains these frogs.

Hayes and Jennings have been returning to this reserve each year since 1989 to mark, measure, and weigh the red-leggeds. They will continue to visit this spot and its frogs for many years to come. The researchers hope to collect from these animals some of the long-term basic information about red-legged population dynamics that could help preserve these and other frogs around the state.

Typically the scientists would mark, measure, and weigh each frog at streamside and return it immediately to its home. But Hayes and Jennings plan to return to the same ponds to catch more frogs this evening. To avoid catching the same frogs twice, they decide to hold the frogs they have collected this afternoon—mostly first-year juveniles—until the next morning. And so they are arranging and checking frog bags when a slender, tanned man in purple shorts jogs down the dirt road toward them.

This reserve is closed to most trucks and cars by a gate secured by a chain and lock. But it is open to pedestrians, and it is not unusual to see visitors hiking or jogging along the plateau's trails. So the man attracts no attention until he slows and asks Jennings what he has in the bags.

"Critters," Jennings responds pleasantly, anticipating the kind of gentle conversation that usually occurs when he encounters curious passersby in the field. Why, the man asks. Because he is studying them, Jennings answers. The man begins to pelt Jennings with a hail of questions: Why don't you leave the animals where they are? What right do you have taking them away? Leave them in the pond, he demands.

Jennings is stunned. Then, with the tone of a teacher guiding a student, he explains that the frogs will be returned to the pond. But the jogger isn't satisfied. "Why do you even do that? Why do you guys come in and mess with them? Why do I have to park out there and you get to park in here and mess with the animals?"

I am standing next to Hayes, and I see his jaw clench as he begins to breathe heavily. The jogger is yelling at Jennings, who watches the man benignly, waiting for a break in the argument. One of the volunteers tries to convince the man that the study will help the frogs. Suddenly Hayes moves closer to the jogger. "Listen," he demands as he points his finger at the man. Then Hayes explains again that the frogs will be returned.

The jogger is wound up and in no mood to listen. "I think you guys are wrong," he insists. "You should just let the frogs alone. You guys are just milking the system." He begins to jog away but turns for one parting shot. Leave the frogs here alone, he shouts. Go to the Amazon to study. "Why mess up the frogs here?"

The group quietly watches the jogger until he is out of sight. Everywhere you go and study creatures, you disturb them, Hayes sighs. That is the trade-off for understanding them.

The jogger's choice of targets for venting concern about the plateau's frogs was an ironic one. By the time of his encounter with Hayes and Jennings in 1992, the two researchers had become the California red-leggeds' most important champions.

Shortly after publication of biologist George Schaller's book about efforts to save the diminishing panda population in China, Schaller gave voice to a growing sentiment among scientists who study wildlife. "Research is fun and it's easy. But no scientist can afford just to study," he told *The New York Times* in a brief interview. "There's a moral obligation to do more for conservation. If you only study, you might get to write a beautiful obituary but you're not helping to perpetuate the species."

The group of scientists who joined in Irvine in 1990 to notify the world about the declining amphibian problem did so believing something needed to be done, that time was running out for some frogs, toads, salamanders, newts, and caecilians. Also, they knew that a variety of environmental problems were smoldering around the world, and examining amphibian declines provided a focus for examining the impacts of those problems. They believed that science and scientists could be tools to get something done. For most of those involved in the issue, being a useful tool has meant doing the normal stuff of science: conducting research, collecting data, doing experiments, writing papers.

In the fall of 1991, Jennings and Hayes decided they needed to do more than scientific work to save amphibians. They knew the

California red-legged needed protection. Its best chance for protection, they figured, was to get it included on the federal list of endangered species under the Endangered Species Act. But to get it on the list, someone had to nominate the frog. The Fish and Wildlife Service could nominate it, but years could pass before the paperwork finished winding its way through the understaffed agency's hierarchy. Outside parties could also nominate the frog. An outside nomination would likely result in a listing sooner, because the act gave the agency specific, swift deadlines by which it had to make a decision on outside nominations.

Nominating an animal involves more than just submitting a species' name. The nominator has to provide a detailed account of the evidence that the animal needs protection. That evidence must be backed by published and unpublished scientific research. The Fish and Wildlife Service has been known to reject deserving animals because a nomination was poorly compiled and unconvincing.

Jennings and Hayes knew that getting involved in the nominating process would be time-consuming. They already had many projects sitting on hold while they finished their statewide survey of amphibians and reptiles. They weren't anxious to put even that survey on hold to compose a nomination. At the same time, though, they were worried that a delay of several years could be disastrous for some California red-legged populations. So, after a few months of discussion and writing, "the two Marcks" completed a nomination for the California red-legged frog and submitted it to the Fish and Wildlife Service in January 1992. It was more than eight single-spaced pages long, not including its maps and bibliography of supporting scientific literature.

"Evidence for the disappearance of the California red-legged frog is most consistent with four types of human interference . . . : (1) loss of habitat; (2) fragmentation of habitat to produce deleterious area and demographic effects; (3) overexploitation; and (4) the spread of exotic (introduced) species," Jennings and Hayes wrote in the nomination. "A fifth major class of human interference, pollution, may have contributed; and a sixth, climate change, has a significant possibility of detrimentally affecting this taxon in the near future. . . .

"The California red-legged frog . . . is estimated to have disappeared from over 99 percent of the inland and southern California localities within its historic range and at least 75 percent of all localities within its entire historic range," the two concluded. "Many of the factors believed responsible for the extirpation of [the red-legged] from localities within its historic range still affect the large majority of populations that remain, and future conditions are anticipated to become even less favorable for this taxon."

The Endangered Species Act has been under attack almost since the day it was adopted into law, in 1973. The act relies primarily on biological evidence to determine whether an animal is eligible for listing as either threatened or endangered. Depending on the level of its listing, any activity that would hurt the listed animal—from destroying habitat to owning or selling the animal—is prohibited. The act's principal critics are developers, logging companies, utilities, and other commercial interests who complain that complying with the act costs too much money, time, and jobs. The Secretary of the Interior can, in fact, waive the act for a species if it is causing "undue economic hardship."

In reality, the act has been neither as damaging as its critics claim nor as effective as its supporters would like. Few development projects have been stopped. Logging has continued in most forests, despite the presence of declining species. Many animals that deserve listing have died without notice.

The act has rarely been backed up with the kind of government funding and other support that would be required to implement it fully. The Fish and Wildlife Service has never had as many staff members as it needed to compile and process the complex nominations as quickly as the law requires, or to put into effect programs to help endangered animals recover from their precarious situations.

During the 1980s, under the antienvironment White House regimes of Ronald Reagan and George Bush, government support for the endangered species program dipped to an all-time low.

A 1990 audit by the U.S. Department of the Interior's Inspector General found that six hundred candidates that the Fish and Wildlife Service deemed eligible for listing had not been listed. In addition, the service had identified another three thousand species that it suspected of being eligible, but on which it still had taken no action. "During the last ten years," the audit said, "at least thirty-four animal and plant species have been determined to be extinct without ever having received full benefit of the act's protection, and those species currently known to merit protection, as well as those candidate species eventually determined to need protection, are similarly in jeopardy of extinction."

When Jennings and Hayes decided to nominate the California red-legged for listing, they expected the process to move fairly quickly. They knew their nomination package was strong and backed by solid research. Jennings, who was in California and routinely in contact with the U.S. Fish and Wildlife Service offices, took on the task of being primary contact on the nomination. He was afraid the application would get lost in the paperwork maze if he didn't keep tabs on it.

Even then, though, things moved more slowly than he expected. The act requires the Fish and Wildlife Service to decide within ninety days whether there is enough information to consider listing a nominated animal. It took the agency more than nine months to make its decision. The act also requires the agency then to decide within one year of the nomination whether to list an animal. Less than a month before that one-year deadline was up, Jennings got a call from a harried Fish and Wildlife Service biologist who had just been given the job of reviewing the application.

Jennings and Hayes had attached the red-legged nomination to a nomination for listing of the western pond turtle, which shared the same riparian habitat. The turtle's nomination, cosponsored by another scientist, was riddled with problems and had helped slow the red-legged paperwork, Jennings learned. Now the two had been separated, and the red-legged was getting closer attention. And the agency biologist needed copies of all the papers about the red-legged that were referred to in the nomination. Could Jennings help? For the next two days, Jennings stood in a photocopy shop, putting a boxload of papers together. "My feeling is that if I propose something, I'm going all the way," he said later. "If you want the animal listed, you have to be available to provide the data and stand by it."

Meanwhile, Jennings and Sam Sweet decided to join forces to get the arroyo toad listed. The toad had earlier gotten entangled in an internal Fish and Wildlife Service dispute that centered on the interpretation of part of the Endangered Species Act. As a result, the service's own nomination of the toad hit a dead end. Sweet and Jennings decided to avoid more wasted time by nominating the toad themselves.

Finally, as the Fish and Wildlife Service missed deadlines to act on each of the nominations, the Environmental Defense Center, an environmental law firm in Santa Barbara, got into the picture. The firm notified the agency that it intended to sue unless the agency hurried up and made its decisions on the animals. The threat of a lawsuit has become a common tactic to push the Fish and Wildlife Service to respond to listing nominations. The sad truth, as one of the agency's biologists told me, is that the agency is so swamped that it chooses which Endangered Species Act nominations to respond to first based on which ones have lawsuits attached.

Late in July 1993, I got a phone call from a very cheerful Jennings. He had just heard that the Fish and Wildlife Service had published in the *Federal Register* its intention to list the California red-legged frog. "That means that the major hurdle is over," Jennings explained. The notice didn't say whether the frog would be listed as threatened or endangered—two levels that carry different legal weight—but Jennings didn't mind. Either way, the California red-legged would become the first North American frog on the federal endangered species list. "The goal was to get it listed. What was critical was to get it listed so they keep from sliding into oblivion."

But already he was anticipating opposition to the listing. It could result in more protection of riparian habitat, the bushy streamside ecosystem that is disappearing about as fast as the red-legged. Right away, two proposed State Water Project dams that Jennings said would "blow out" red-legged populations on the "last good streams" in the hills on the west side of the San Joaquin Valley could be affected by the listing.

Three years earlier, when I'd first joined Jennings on a field trip to see California red-leggeds, he had been decidedly pessimistic about their future. Now, finally, he has reason to be optimistic. "Does it help the frog survive into the future?" he asks rhetorically. "Oh, yes it does!"

In August 1993, the Fish and Wildlife Service announced that it intended to list the arroyo toad as endangered, and was seeking public comment. Jennings was batting a thousand. Sweet anticipated there would be opposition to that listing also, and he wouldn't rest easy until the agency made its final decision, which would take at least a year. However, the announcement alone would have benefits for the toad.

U.S. Forest Service policy requires that as soon as the Fish and Wildlife Service says it intends to list an animal, that animal is to be treated in national forests as though it were already listed. Now the managers of the Los Padres National Forest would have added incentive to stop building roads through arroyo toad habitat and operating campgrounds beside arroyo toad breeding grounds. The toad's numbers had already shown signs of improving in that forest in 1993, when California's seven-year-long drought ended. Reproduction was high, and Sweet figured that the number of adult toads in the entire forest could be up to one thousand. With the

Fish and Wildlife Service announcement, the toad's chances for long-term survival suddenly looked much better.

When someone sounds an alarm, there is always the risk that later it will be discovered that it was unneeded, that there was no real danger, but only the appearance of danger. After the Irvine meeting, some scientists worried that the warnings of amphibian decline were premature or exaggerated. These included scientists who were working on the problem themselves.

One researcher fairly new to the decline issue, who found himself suddenly plunged into it almost full-time, asked me more than once, over the three years in which I followed the story, whether other scientists still believed there was a decline. He thought there was, but clearly he was concerned that he might end up hanging out there on his own, sounding an alarm that nobody else believed anymore.

The issue has been made even more difficult because not all amphibians are in obvious decline. A few species are even notable for continuing to do well in regions where other species have disappeared. Pacific tree frogs, for instance, are doing fine in areas that no longer have California red-leggeds or arroyo toads. Rough-skinned newts are abundant throughout western Oregon, even where western toads and various native ranids are missing. If these odd survivors have anything in common, it is that they are less specialized in their habitat requirements. They don't need a specific type of bromeliad or a certain kind of rare stream bank to survive. Sometimes they don't even need clean water.

Scientists still do not know the exact magnitude of the amphibian decline, and that's one of their greatest frustrations. About eight months after the Irvine meeting, a group of scientists decided to try to gauge the scale of the decline by establishing a network of researchers concerned about the issue. The group's creator was George Rabb, director of the Chicago Zoological Society's Brookfield Zoo and a leader in international wildlife conservation efforts. Rabb's idea was to form a task force that would keep the amphibian-decline issue in the public eye while at the same time bringing scientists together to address the main questions of the declines: Which species were declining, and where? Why were they declining? What could be done to stop the process? The Declining Amphibian Populations Task Force would have a life of three years and be funded by a mix of grants and private donations.

Rabb's vision for the task force was a big order. He recruited Dave Wake to the chair while it got organized, and they hired Jim Vial, a veteran herpetologist, to run DAPTF from its office in Corvallis, Oregon. Wake and then Vial recruited another ninety scientists around the world to voluntarily head committees of other amphibian specialists. Ideally, these working groups would feed information about local amphibian declines to Vial, and they would help initiate local studies.

By the summer of 1993, however, as DAPTF approached its three-year deadline, it was clear that meeting the organization's main goal would be impossible within its original time frame. As scientists have tried to pinpoint the decline's magnitude, they have discovered they are hindered by a lack of basic information about many species. It is obvious that certain species are in decline. But to move beyond anecdote and come up with hard numbers for many species requires knowing more about life habits and population dynamics than scientists do. Even where they are confident that there is a decline and have some hard numbers—as they do for certain species in the western United States—scientists often don't have enough basic information about the species and their relationship to the environment to identify the reasons for the declines. The situation is comparable to cancer researchers trying to identify cures for the disease without knowing anything about basic cell biology.

Despite the frustrations, continuing amphibian absences bolster the validity of scientists' 1990 alarm. Once-abundant boreal toads that began dwindling in the early 1970s in the Colorado Rockies still can hardly be found throughout that region. The golden toad and the harlequin frog populations that disappeared in the late 1980s still haven't returned in Costa Rica's Monteverde Cloud Forest Preserve, despite a return to normal weather patterns. Scientists continue to complain that they can't find certain species of the genus *Atelopus* in the Andes. Worldwide, there have been no signs of significant rebounding by dozens of amphibian species that scientists at the Irvine meeting had noted anecdotally were in decline.

For certain high-mountain species, the causes remain especially elusive. Is UV-B radiation weakening frog immune systems in the western United States? Is global climate change introducing such stress—through drought especially—that some isolated populations, and populations on the edges of their ranges, are being driven into extinction? Answers thorough enough to satisfy precision-oriented scientists aren't likely to be found for years. But for many other threatened amphibian species, the cause is well known: habitat destruction, both obvious and subtle. That cause puts these animals in the same boat as other declining wildlife worldwide, from songbirds to elephants.

Human population growth is behind much of the habitat destruction. There are more than five and a half billion people in the world today. That number rises by about 90 million each year. As the number of people increases, the world's available land and resources shrink.

Humans alter and destroy wetlands and forests and streams of every variety—from California to Calcutta—at a rate almost too fast to count. The Harvard biologist E. O. Wilson has estimated that tropical forest destruction alone causes the extinction of about 17,500 species of plants, animals, and insects each year. Assuming the entire world has about 10 million species, Wilson has concluded that about one out of every one thousand species goes extinct each year. Plants and creatures, including amphibians, are disappearing even before scientists have had a chance to discover and describe them. As long as that remains true, the amphibian scientists can feel confident their alarm wasn't premature. Indeed, it may have been too late for many amphibian species.

The amphibian declines, perhaps more than those of other animals, show just how vast and deep is the impact of even subtle habitat destruction. Many of the most notable amphibian declines have occurred in areas that people believed they had protected from environmental assault. This suggests that *pristine* is rarely still an accurate descriptive term for any wild area, even for protected national parks and preserves. They prove that building a fence around a swath of forest does not automatically protect it and its creatures from the environment beyond the forest. If nonnative fish are stocked in streams leading into the forest, if clouds polluted by acid or pesticides continue to roll over the forest, or if upstream dams change the waterflow through it, the creatures inside will be affected.

Blair Hedges, a scientist who studies amphibians of the West Indies, witnessed just how inaccurate the word *pristine* has become one evening when he was working in a so-called virgin forest. He was climbing among the trees, trying to record the calls of local frogs, when a very large and very clumsy black rat fell from the tree canopy and landed on Hedges's head. It was, to say the least, a frightening experience. "Fortunately it didn't bite me," he recalls. What was most notable about the rat was that it didn't belong in that forest. It, like so many other mammals in the West Indies, was first carried by boat to the islands decades ago—most likely as a stowaway. As Hedges learned through experience, the rat has expanded its territory even farther than most realized.

At the Irvine meeting, several scientists suggested one way in which amphibians differ significantly from other declining and disappearing animals. They referred to amphibians as possible bioindicators, living markers that flag serious environmental change. They told journalists that amphibians' physical characteristics could make them vulnerable to a variety of environmental assaults that might have less impact on other animals. Their skin is hairless, which puts them in immediate contact with the atmosphere and sunlight. Their skin is also permeable, and gases, particularly oxygen, flow through it readily. Amphibians typically spend part of their lives in a wet environment and part on land, so they have twice the possibility of assault as an exclusively aquatic or terrestrial creature. Because their eggs are typically jelly-coated, their embryos are less protected from the elements than are most vertebrate embryos. Declining amphibians, they said, are like miners' canaries, early warnings of impending disaster. But this time the disaster was occurring worldwide, not just in a deep mine.

It was an enticing image that journalists—including this one—readily embraced. Coal miners once carried caged canaries into their underground workplaces because the birds would respond early to dangerous gas leaks. The minute a canary keeled over, the miners knew it was time to evacuate without delay. By linking the frog to this classic story, scientists not only captured journalists' and their readers' attention, but managed to elevate the lowly frog's status from simple hairless creature to benevolent and important herald. Intentionally or not, it was great marketing.

However, scientists who have kicked around the world of endangered animals for some time have been skeptical of the frog-as-early-warning idea. "When things start going into decline, it's a pretty late warning, not an early warning," the prominent tropical biologist John Terborgh complained impatiently during a phone conversation a few weeks after the Irvine meeting.

To be a useful bioindicator, from a scientist's point of view, an organism has to be able to do more than simply die. One scientific committee convened by the National Research Council to identify forest biological markers of air-pollution stress concluded that any biological marker or indicator had to be *measurable*. Declining and disappearing amphibians would be bioindicators under this definition if a scientist could measure some part of their physiology or chemistry to get a reading of exactly how much of what environmental pollutant was causing the problem. For instance, frogs would be a bioindicator if scientists could look at a population of sick frogs in a pond and tell through measurements that a specific pollutant at a specific level was making them ill. That ability doesn't exist now.

In the past, other groups of scientists have tried to attach bioindicator status to their organism of interest and failed. One group was lichenologists, researchers who study lichen. Lichen is the flat, plantlike growth commonly found on rocks, bark, or the forest floor. It actually comprises two organisms, a fungus and usually an algae, that work together to grow and survive. The fungus relies on the ability of the algae to absorb nutrients from sunlight to feed the organism, while the algae relies on the fungus's durable form to give the organism structure.

Lichens are particularly sensitive to air pollutants, and when lichenologists discovered that lichens disappeared in the presence of sulfur dioxide, a common pollutant, they dubbed their organism a powerful bioindicator. However, as they looked more closely at their study subjects, they found that lichens couldn't be used to measure pollution or say anything about the pollution's impacts on the rest of the environment.

"They don't tell us anything at all about the real ecological impacts the pollutants have had, just that lichens have disappeared," says William Winner, an Oregon State University botanist who followed the lichen work and was an early board member of the Declining Amphibian Populations Task Force. "When a lichen population starts to disappear or show a pattern of distress, people have used that data to launch full-scale studies that lead to installing [sulfur dioxide] monitors so that over the course of five years or so you have a record of SO_2. In addition to that, they have studies of other plants to see how they are faring. But lichen in and of itself cannot tell anything about pollution except where to put new studies."

A number of studies have been done on different organisms to find bioindicators, and so far, Winner says, the general conclusion has been that there is no good single bioindicator. For now, then, frogs and other amphibians aren't true bioindicators—as scientists define the term—of a degraded environment. If they are like other troubled organisms, they will never be true, single bioindicators of environmental disaster. They are simply the latest creature that humans have recognized as suffering from human insensitivity to earth's environment. They are simply another of our victims.

Why should anyone care about frogs and other amphibians? Why do they matter?

I have asked many scientists variations of these questions. Frequently, I have heard in response versions of the ecologist Paul Ehrlich's famous rivet theory. This concept is based upon the idea that if you remove too many rivets from an airplane, it will eventually fall apart and the whole thing will fall from the sky. The airplane becomes a metaphor for the ecosystem. The frog, some scientists tell me, is like a rivet. Take one away, and things may still run smoothly. Take a few more, and the plane will rattle feverishly. Take some more, and eventually the whole ecosystem, including everything that relies upon it as prey and predator, will collapse. All the wetlands, all the forests, all the marshy meadows and seasonal backyard ponds will become like that patch of forest in Australia's Conondale Mountains where the gastric brooding frog once lived. They will become silent.

Sam Sweet is less inclined to spout rivet theories. If the arroyo toad disappears, it won't mean the end of the ecosystem, he says. The local biological diversity will be less rich, but some sort of system will still exist. "Is it the end of life? No," he grumbles as I follow him on his toad-marking rounds one evening. "It's not even the end of nature."

So why does saving toads from extinction matter? Because, Sweet says, breaking into mountain-man colloquial, "it ain't none of our business to be fooling around with Mother Nature to that extent. Who told you that you could wipe out Carolina parakeets or passenger pigeons?" He pauses to point out a big western toad in the distance, sitting on a leafy path among oak trees. "I guess I feel there's a lot of cheek involved, a lot of presumption," he continues. "Where is the logic for wiping out whole species just for the hell of it?"

But what if you have to change the landscape—the flow of a river, say—to help sustain human life, I ask. In that case, the arroyo toad just happens to be a victim of the choice to dam a river to feed the water needs of a burgeoning human population. Isn't that logical? "I reject the idea that some species have got to die so some fatheads can wash their cars and water their lawns," he snaps. "Most of the development out here is predicated on having more water than we do."

Sweet has a point. Many of the declines are caused by human choices. Bad choices, from an environmental point of view. The lawn or the toad? But sometimes the choices are more compelling. In Haiti, only about one percent of the island's original forest still stands, and it is quickly being chopped away. The reason? Primarily to turn the wood into charcoal for fuel. There are more efficient fuels that would do less damage to the last remaining ecosystem there. But there is no money to buy that fuel. So extreme poverty pushes Haitians to destroy their only forest and its resident amphibians. How do you tell a Haitian to starve instead of making charcoal? How do you persuade an Indonesian, in a country where wages are low and good work scarce, to stop collecting frogs to sell for pennies to exporters who then sell them to restaurants abroad?

The trick, I suppose, is to make the easy choices first. It's easy to stop using pesticides in backyard gardens. It's easy to stop riding motorcycles through creeks. It's easy to build furniture with plantation-grown pine instead of old-growth fir or redwood. It's easy, especially for the educated and affluent, to use birth control and stop contributing to the world's overpopulation—but it's not so easy to persuade many, including even the stereotypical thirty-something environmentally aware professional, to be a living example of that sacrifice.

But without making the right, tough choices, or without finding a way to make the toughest choices possible if not easy, we will likely end up with a world that has fewer forests, fewer streams, fewer frogs. What will we miss? For one thing, sounds that now, in many parts of the world, we take for granted. This spring, after the first good rainy winter in seven years, tree frogs croaked in my backyard. I don't know where they came from, but they were a joy to hear. Now, even as summer beats down and the frogs have gone into hiding again, I can listen to a mockingbird outside my office window that includes a tree frog's croak in its repertoire.

I remember looking for tadpoles in a canyon stream when I was a child. The chances are strong that if you were born before 1960, you remember seeing tadpoles in the wild when you were a child too. You may remember taking some home or getting some in a classroom at school and watching them develop over a few weeks into froglets. I still know creeks where I can find tadpoles. But I know a lot where they don't appear anymore, too, and I wonder how long it will be before few children anywhere, and no children in California, will still be able to see native frogs in a pond in the wild. Or how long will it be before the only poison-dart frogs are those living behind glass in zoos and private collections?

Why do frogs matter?

In 1906, Mary C. Dickerson wrote what remains a classic book about frogs. Dickerson's career was devoted to studying and educating others about the natural world, and she accomplished this by serving in a number of roles, including that of curator of herpetology at the American Museum of Natural History in New York. At the museum, she gave young scientists their first real jobs in herpetology before they went on to become leaders in the discipline. For many years, Dickerson's *The Frog Book* was the major field guide to North American frogs and toads. But it is much more than a field guide. It is a book full of prose that reads like poetry and makes it hard not to appreciate frogs and the part they play in nature's rhythm. They may or may not be essential, but Dickerson makes a strong argument that life's essence would be diminished without them.

> *And so, in pond and marsh, the contest goes on, as it always has in past ages. Each day the life of the individual [frog] is given to maintain the life of the species, and the balance of life among the races is kept, although the scales may tip somewhat now in one direction and now in another. Very definite and very emphatic is our admiration for the individual. Each represents high specialization along a given line of development, and seems perfected to the minutest detail in its fitness for its life. Each is so invisible in its environment that it seems wonderful that an enemy ever finds it at all. Each is supplied with the power of extremely rapid movement. However, certain characteristics may be of the greatest advantage to a given individual, but of the greatest danger to that individual when the same powers are possessed also by an enemy. Thus the rapid flight of a bird or insect is counteracted to its disadvantage by the invisibility and rapid movement of the frog, and these characteristics of the frog are offset fatally for him by the same characteristics and the power of stealthy approach in the snake.*
>
> *So life goes on, and gladsome but arduous days are passed by the denizens of the pond.*

I follow Marc Hayes one July day in 1992 to a bog tucked among two-hundred-year-old mountain hemlocks and pines in Oregon's Cascade Mountains. It is here that I see what Dickerson was talking about. And it is here that I understand why frogs matter and why that mattering is—as Mark Jennings has tried to tell me in so many ways, so many times—sometimes easier to feel than to explain.

The bog sits about five thousand feet above sea level, in an area of national forest that has been placed off limits to logging, for this summer at least, to protect the spotted owls that nest here. The Forest Service has designated the bog itself an ecological research area, closed to much of the kind of recreational activity that would probably have destroyed it long ago. There are no boats allowed, and no motors that would break the background music of insects buzzing and birds calling.

The bog is hidden from the road where we park by a steep slope and a broad screen of trees. So my first view of it comes as we emerge from the shelter of trees. The word *bog* conjures up images of murky water and shadowy figures in my mind, so I did not expect what I was to see. In the distance is a view of the tops of a pair of snow-covered mountains called Diamond Peaks. Closer in, there are pines and tall, slender hemlocks. Then there is the bog itself, a mix of large puddles surrounded by a wetland covered with shin-high bushes that resemble blueberry plants but aren't. Islands between the puddles on parts of the bog hold taller bushes and some spindly trees. The whole bog stretches about half a mile. As we approach it, our boots make powerful sucking sounds each time we pull our legs out of the wet earth.

The bog is teeming with life. Neon-blue mayflies dart about in the air. Red-winged blackbirds fly by. A spotted owl hoots. (I know it is a spotted owl only because we are accompanied by a Forest Service biologist who has worked with the bird and recognizes its call.) Hayes points to a hopping creature. "Toad behind you," he tells me.

Then, as we draw closer, we see young frogs hop from the bushes and into the bog's muddy patches and deep pools. They are dark and spotted, and the adults, like northern red-legged frogs, have a blush of red on their legs. But they are not red-leggeds; these are spotted frogs, *Rana pretiosa*. Historical records show that this species once lived in at least twenty-three locations in western Oregon, on the Klamath and Willamette river systems. Hayes has checked twenty-two of those twenty-three locations, and so far only this bog still has spotted frogs. And here they are abundant. There are both adults and juveniles, and within minutes, Hayes is up to his thighs in water, reaching for a frog hiding in a cover of reeds.

For the next seven hours, as morning passes into midday and then late afternoon, Hayes continues catching frogs, marking, weighing and measuring, then returning them to the spot where they were caught. Dan Heath, a former zookeeper, helps him. I mostly watch until I find it too difficult to resist the urge to touch one of these tiny creatures. I reach toward a juvenile that hops from a bush as I pass. It has landed in a shallow pool of water, just out of reach. I move closer, it hops farther away. I move, it hops. Finally, I move just fast enough and clap my hand over it before it hops again. It feels cool and soft against my fingertips, and when I lift it, it kicks its legs to try to break free. I talk to it. It doesn't respond. It is an animal and I am a human. It believes, I am sure, that I am a predator and it is prey. I know that in some sense it is right. I have disturbed its peace, and I carry it to Hayes to mark, weigh, and measure before I return it to its spot in the bog. I want it to survive, perhaps as much as it wants to survive. As I place it back in the shallow pool, I worry a bit while it sits still, adjusting to the water, before it bounces into hiding again.

Clouds gather in the sky as the day progresses. A grouse demonstrates its plungerlike call. A heron screams and rises from a distant bank and flies away. A woodpecker knocks a tree in the forest. A mallard swims to within feet of where Hayes works. The clouds continue to gather, and then, in the distance, lightning flashes. The lightning moves closer, and large raindrops begin to fall on us and the bog. The frogs continue to hop from the bushes into the ponds. Hayes continues to catch and weigh them. The rain falls harder and a thread of smoke on a distant hill, where a tree has been struck by the lightning, moves up into the sky. The frogs keep hopping.

It is quiet and still and noisy and chaotic at once. It is peaceful and turbulent. It is full of life, this bog, and these frogs are part of that life. This, I realize, is the way it is supposed to be. This is why frogs matter.

BIBLIOGRAPHY

Books

Adler, Kraig, ed. *Contributions to the History of Herpetology*. Oxford, Ohio: Society for the Study of Amphibians and Reptiles, 1989.

Behler, John L., and F. Wayne King. *The Audubon Society Field Guide to North American Reptiles and Amphibians*. New York: Alfred A. Knopf, 1979.

Brown, Lester R., et al. *State of the World 1984, State of the World 1988, State of the World 1989, State of the World 1990, State of the World 1991, State of the World 1992, State of the World 1993*. New York: W. W. Norton.

Brown, Lester R., Hal Kane, and Ed Ayres. *Vital Signs 1993*. New York: W. W. Norton, 1993.

Cochran, Doris M. *Living Amphibians of the World*. Garden City, New York: Doubleday, 1961.

Committee on Biologic Markers of Air Pollution Damage in Trees. *Biologic Markers of Air-Pollution Stress and Damage in Forests*. Washington, D.C.: National Academy Press, 1989.

Committee on Restoration of Aquatic Ecosystems. *Restoration of Aquatic Ecosystems: Science, Technology, and Public Policy*. Washington, D.C.: National Academy Press, 1991.

Commoner, Barry. *Making Peace With the Planet*. New York: Pantheon Books, 1990.

Conant, Roger, and Joseph T. Collins. *A Field Guide to Reptiles and Amphibians: Eastern and Central North America,* 3rd ed. The Peterson Field Guide Series. Boston: Houghton Mifflin, 1991.

Cope, E. D. *The Batrachia of North America.* 1889. Reprint, Ashton, Maryland: Eric Lundberg, 1963.

Daniel, Joseph E., et al., eds. *1993 Earth Journal—Environmental Almanac and Resource Directory.* Boulder, Colorado: Buzzworm Books, 1993.

DeGraaff, Robert M. *The Book of the Toad.* Rochester, Vermont: Park Street Press, 1991.

Dickerson, Mary C. *The Frog Book.* 1906. Reprint, New York: Dover Publications, 1969.

Duellman, William E., and Linda Trueb. *Biology of Amphibians.* New York: McGraw-Hill, 1986.

Dumas, Alexandre. *Alexandre Dumas' Dictionary of Cuisine.* Edited, abridged and translated by Louis Colman from *Le Grand Dictionnaire de Cuisine.* New York: Simon and Schuster, 1958.

Eldredge, Niles. *The Miner's Canary: Unraveling the Mysteries of Extinction.* New York: Prentice Hall, 1991.

Fay, James S., and Stephanie W. Fay, eds. *California Almanac,* 5th ed. Santa Barbara, California: Pacific Data Resources, 1991.

Fitzgerald, Sarah. *International Wildlife Trade: Whose Business Is It?* Washington, D.C.: World Wildlife Fund, 1989.

Frazer, Deryk. *Reptiles and Amphibians in Britain.* Collins New Naturalist Series. London: Bloomsbury Books, 1989.

Grinnell, Joseph. *Joseph Grinnell's Philosophy of Nature: Selected Writings of a Western Naturalist.* Berkeley: University of California Press, 1943.

————, and Tracy Irwin Storer. *Animal Life in the Yosemite*. Berkeley: University of California Press, 1924.

Harris, Larry D. *The Fragmented Forest: Island Biogeography Theory and the Preservation of Biotic Diversity*. Chicago: University of Chicago Press, 1984.

Intersociety Working Group. *AAAS Report XV: Research and Development FY 1991*. Washington, D.C.: American Association for the Advancement of Science, 1990.

————. *AAAS Report XVII: Research and Development FY 1993*. Washington, D.C.: American Association for the Advancement of Science, 1992.

Lewis, Stephanie. *Cane Toads: An Unnatural History*. New York: Dolphin/Doubleday, 1989.

Mattison, Chris. *Frogs and Toads of the World*. 1987. Reprint, New York: Facts on File, 1989.

McNelly, Jeffrey A., et al. *Conserving the World's Biological Diversity*. Gland, Switzerland, and Washington, D.C.: IUCN, WRI, CI, WWF-US, World Bank, 1990.

McWilliams, Carey. *California: The Great Exception*. 1949. Reprint, Salt Lake City: Peregrine Smith, 1976.

Muscatine, Doris. *Old San Francisco: The Biography of a City from Early Days to the Earthquake*. New York: Putnam, 1975.

Nussbaum, Ronald A., Edmund D. Brodie, Jr., and Robert M. Storm. *Amphibians & Reptiles of the Pacific Northwest*. Moscow, Idaho: University of Idaho Press, 1983.

Palmer, Tim, ed. *California's Threatened Environment: Restoring the Dream*. Washington, D.C.: Island Press, 1993.

Pyrom, Jay. *Frogs and Toads: A Complete Introduction*. Neptune City, New Jersey: T.F.H. Publications, 1987.

Raup, David M. *Extinction: Bad Genes or Bad Luck?* New York: W. W. Norton, 1991.

Raven, Peter H., and George B. Johnson. *Biology,* 3rd ed. St. Louis: Mosby-Year Book, 1992.

Reisner, Marc. *Cadillac Desert: The American West and Its Disappearing Water.* New York: Viking Penguin, 1986.

————. *Game Wars: The Undercover Pursuit of Wildlife Poachers.* New York: Viking Penguin, 1991.

Ribuoli, Patrizia, and Marina Robbiani. *Frogs: Art, Legend, History.* The Bulfinch Library of Collectibles, edited by Giorgio Coppin. Boston: Little Brown, 1991.

Roan, Sharon L. *Ozone Crisis: The 15 Year Evolution of a Sudden Global Emergency.* New York: John Wiley & Sons, 1990.

Schneider, Stephen H. *Global Warming.* San Francisco: Sierra Club Books, 1989.

Schoenherr, Allan A. *A Natural History of California.* Berkeley: University of California Press, 1992.

Sergeev, B. F. *The World of Amphibians.* Revised edition, Moscow, Russia: Mir Publications, 1986.

Smith, Janet, ed. *Mark Twain on Man and Beast.* Westport, Connecticut: Lawrence Hill, 1972.

Stebbins, Robert C. *A Field Guide to Western Reptiles and Amphibians.* The Peterson Field Guide Series. Boston: Houghton Mifflin, 1985.

————. *California Amphibians and Reptiles.* Berkeley: University of California Press, 1972.

Steger, Will, and Jon Bowermaster. *A Citizen's Guide to Environmental Action.* New York: Alfred A. Knopf, 1990.

Stern, Paul C., Oran R. Young, and Daniel Druckman, eds. *Global Environmental Change: Understanding the Human Dimensions.* Washington, D.C.: National Academy Press, 1992.

Tyler, Michael J. *Australian Frogs.* Ringwood, Victoria, Australia: Viking O'Neil, 1989.

U.S. Congress, Office of Technology Assessment. *Forest Service Planning: Accommodating Uses, Producing Outputs, and Sustaining Ecosystems.* Washington, D.C.: U.S. Government Printing Office, 1992.

Western, David, and Mary Pearl, eds. *Conservation for the Twenty-first Century.* New York: Oxford University Press, 1989.

Wilson, E. O., ed. *Biodiversity.* Washington, D.C.: National Academy Press, 1988.

Wilson, Larry David, and Louis Porras. *The Ecological Impact of Man on the South Florida Herpetofauna.* Lawrence, Kansas: University of Kansas, 1983.

World Resources Institute. *The 1992 Information Please Environmental Almanac.* Boston: Houghton Mifflin, 1992.

Wyman, Richard, ed. *Global Climate Change and Life on Earth.* New York: Routledge, Chapman and Hall, 1991.

Pamphlets, Booklets, and Special Publications

Adler, Kraig. *A Brief History of Herpetology in North America Before 1900.* Oxford, Ohio: Society for the Study of Amphibians and Reptiles, 1979.

American Society of Ichthyologists and Herpetologists (ASIH), The Herpetologists League (HL), and Society for the Study of Amphibians and Reptiles (SSAR). *Guidelines for Use of Live Amphibians and Reptiles in Field Research.* 1987.

Aspelin, Arnold L., Arthur H. Grube, and Robert Toria. *Pesticides Industry Sales and Usage, 1990 and 1991 Market Estimates.* Washington, D.C.: Environmental Protection Agency, 1992.

Bury, R. Bruce. "Habitat Relationships and Ecological Importance of Amphibians and Reptiles." In *Streamside Management: Riparian Wildlife and Forestry Interactions,* edited by K. J. Raedeke. University of Washington, Institute of Forest Resources, Contribution No. 59, 1988.

―――, et al. *Conservation of the Amphibia of the United States: A Review.* Resource Publication 134. Washington, D.C.: United States Department of the Interior, Fish and Wildlife Service, 1980.

―――, and Paul Stephen Corn. "Douglas-fir Forests in the Oregon and Washington Cascades: Abundance of Terrestrial Herpetofauna Related to Stand Age and Moisture." In *Management of Amphibians, Reptiles, and Small Mammals in North America: Proceedings of the Symposium, July 19–21, 1988,* edited by R. C. Szaro, K. E. Severson, and D. R. Patton. USDA Forest Service General Technical Report, RM-166.

―――, and Jill A. Whelan. *Ecology and Management of the Bullfrog.* Resource Publication 155. Washington, D.C.: United States Department of the Interior, Fish and Wildlife Service, 1984.

Check, G. *How to Make Money Collecting Biological Specimens.* Tomahawk, Wisconsin: The Real Outdoors Co., 1992.

Corn, Paul Stephen, R. Bruce Bury, and Thomas A. Spies. "Douglas-fir Forests in the Cascade Mountains of Oregon and

Washington: Is the Abundance of Small Mammals Related to Stand Age and Moisture?" In *Management of Amphibians, Reptiles, and Small Mammals in North America: Proceedings of the Symposium, July 19–21, 1988,* edited by R. C. Szaro, K. E. Severson, and D. R. Patton. USDA Forest Service General Technical Report RM-166.

Corn, Paul Stephen, William Stolzenburg, and R. Bruce Bury. *Acid Precipitation Studies in Colorado and Wyoming: Interim Report of Surveys of Montane Amphibians and Water Chemistry.* Biological Report 80 (40.26). Air Pollution and Acid Rain Report No. 26. Washington, D.C.: U.S. Department of the Interior, Fish and Wildlife Service, 1989.

De Vosjoli, Philippe. *The General Care and Maintenance of Horned Frogs.* The Herpetocultural Library. Lakeside, California: Advanced Vivarium Systems, 1989.

———. *The General Care and Maintenance of White's Tree Frogs and White-lipped Tree Frogs.* The Herpetocultural Library. Lakeside, California: Advanced Vivarium Systems, 1990.

Froglog: Newsletter of the IUCN/SSC Task Force on Declining Amphibians. Nos. 1–6.

Guerrero, Peter F. *Pesticides: 30 Years Since Silent Spring—Many Long-standing Concerns Remain.* Washington, D.C.: U.S. General Accounting Office, GAO/RCED-92-77.

Hayes, Marc Philip. *A Study of Clutch Attendance in the Neotropical Frog* Centrolenella Fleischmanni *(Anura: Centrolenidae).* Unpublished dissertation, University of Miami, 1991.

———, and Mark R. Jennings. "Habitat Correlates of Distribution of the California Red-legged Frog *(Rana aurora draytonii)* and the Foothill Yellow-legged Frog *(Rana boylii):* Implications for Management." In *Management of Amphibians, Reptiles, and*

Small Mammals in North America: Proceedings of the Symposium, July 19–21, 1988, edited by R. C. Szaro, K. E. Severson, and D. R. Patton. USDA Forest Service General Technical Report, RM-166.

————, J. Alan Pounds, and Walter W. Timmerman. *An Annotated List and Guide to the Amphibians and Reptiles of Monteverde, Costa Rica.* Herpetological Circular No. 17. Oxford, Ohio: Society for the Study of Amphibians and Reptiles.

Hedges, S. Blair, and Richard Thomas. "The Importance of Systematic Research in the Conservation of Amphibian and Reptile Populations." In *Status y Distribución de los Reptiles y Anfibios de la Región de Puerto Rico,* edited by J. A. Moreno. Puerto Rico: Departamento de Recursos Naturales de Puerto Rico, Publicación Científica Miscelanea No. 1, 1991.

Jennings, Mark R., and Marc P. Hayes. *Amphibian and Reptile Species of Special Concern in California.* Report to the California Department of Fish and Game, Inland Fisheries Division, 1993.

Sweet, Samuel S. *Initial Report on the Ecology and Status of the Arroyo Toad* (Bufo microscaphus californicus) *on the Los Padres National Forest of Southern California, with Management Recommendations.* Goleta, California: Contract Report to USDA, Forest Service, Los Padres National Forest, 1991.

U.S. General Accounting Office. *Global Warming: Emission Reductions Possible as Scientific Uncertainties Are Resolved.* Washington, D.C.: U.S. General Accounting Office, GAO/RCED-90-58.

————. *Public Land Management: Attention to Wildlife Is Limited.* Washington, D.C.: U.S. General Accounting Office, GAO/RCED-91-64, 1991.

————. *Rangeland Management: Forest Service Not Performing Needed Monitoring of Grazing Allotments.* Washington, D.C.: U.S. General Accounting Office, GAO/RCED-91-148, 1991.

————. *Rangeland Management: Interior's Monitoring Has Fallen Short of Agency Requirements.* Washington, D.C.: U.S. General Accounting Office, GAO/RCED-92-51, 1992.

————. *Rangeland Management: Profile of the Bureau of Land Management's Grazing Allotments and Permits.* Washington, D.C.: U.S. General Accounting Office, GAO/RCED-92-213FS, 1992.

UNEP Environmental Effects Panel. *Environmental Effects of Ozone Depletion: 1991 Update.* Nairobi, Kenya: United Nations Environment Programme (UNEP), 1991.

Journal Articles

Adams, Charles C. and T. L. Hankinson. "Notes on Oneida Lake Fish and Fisheries." *Transactions of the American Fisheries Society* 45 (1916): 154–69.

Abdulali, Humayun. "On the Export of Frog Legs from India." *Bombay Natural History Society Journal* 82: 347–75.

Beebee, T. J. C., et al. "Decline of the Natterjack Toad *Bufo calamita* in Britain: Palaeoecological, Documentary and Experimental Evidence for Breeding Site Acidification." *Biological Conservation* 53 (1990): 1–20.

Beebee, Trevor J. C. "Environmental Change as a Cause of Natterjack Toad *(Bufo calamita)* Declines in Britain." *Biological Conservation* 11 (1977): 87–102.

Bennett, Stephen H., J. Whitfield Gibbons, and Jill Glanville. "Terrestrial Activity, Abundance and Diversity of Amphibians in Differently Managed Forest Types." *The American Midland Naturalist* 103, no. 2 (1980): 412–16.

Blaustein, Andrew. "Ecological Correlates and Potential Functions of Kin Recognition and Kin Association in Anuran Larvae." *Behavior Genetics* 18, no. 4 (1988): 449–64.

———, and Richard K. O'Hara. "An Investigation of Kin Recognition in Red-legged Frog *(Rana aurora)* Tadpoles." *Journal of Zoology* 209 (1986): 347–53.

———. "Kin Recognition in *Rana cascadae* Tadpoles." *Behavioral and Neural Biology* 36 (1982): 77–87.

Blaustein, Andrew, and David B. Wake. "Declining Amphibian Populations: A Global Phenomenon?" *Trends in Ecology and Evolution* 5 (1990): 203–04.

Blumthaler, Mario, and Walter Ambach. "Indication of Increasing Solar Ultraviolet-B Radiation Flux in Alpine Regions." *Science* 248 (1990): 206–07.

Bradford, David F. "Allotopic Distribution of Native Frogs and Introduced Fishes in High Sierra Nevada Lakes of California: Implication of the Negative Effect of Fish Introductions." *Copeia* 1989: 775–78.

———. "Mass Mortality and Extinction in a High-elevation Population of *Rana muscosa*." *Journal of Herpetology* 25, no. 2 (1991): 174–77.

———. "Winterkill, Oxygen Relations, and Energy Metabolism of a Submerged Dormant Amphibian, *Rana muscosa*." *Ecology* 64, no. 5 (1983): 1171–83.

Brown, Herbert A. "Reproduction and Development of the Red-legged Frog, *Rana aurora*, in Northwestern Washington." *Northwest Science* 49, no. 4 (1975): 241–52.

Burke, Russell L. "Relocations, Repatriations, and Translocations of Amphibians and Reptiles: Taking a Broader View." *Herpetologica* 47, no. 3 (1991): 350–57.

Burton, Thomas M., and Gene E. Likens. "Salamander Populations and Biomass in the Hubbard Brook Experimental Forest, New Hampshire." *Copeia* 1975: 541–46.

Bury, R. Bruce. "Difference in Amphibian Populations in Logged and Old Growth Redwood Forest." *Northwest Science* 57 (1983): 167–78.

————. "Santa Cruz Long-Toed Salamander: Survival in Doubt." *Herpetology Review* 4, no. 1 (1972): 20–21.

————, and Roger A. Luckenbach. "Introduced Amphibians and Reptiles in California." *Biological Conservation* 10 (1976): 1–14.

Caldwell, J. P., J. H. Thorp, and T. O. Jervey. "Predator-Prey Relationships Among Larval Dragonflies, Salamanders, and Frogs." *Oecologia* 46 (1980): 285–89.

Calef, George Waller. "Natural Mortality of Tadpoles in a Population of *Rana aurora.*" *Ecology* 54, no. 4 (1973): 741–58.

Carey, Cynthia. "Hypothesis Concerning the Causes of the Disappearance of Boreal Toads from the Mountains of Colorado." *Conservation Biology* 7, no. 2 (1993): 355–62.

Cecil, Stephen G., and John J. Just. "Survival Rate, Population Density and Development of a Naturally Occurring Anuran Larvae *(Rana catesbeiana)."* *Copeia* 1979: 447–53.

Clarkson, Robert W., and James C. deVos, Jr. "The Bullfrog, *Rana catesbeiana* Shaw, in the Lower Colorado River, Arizona-California." *Journal of Herpetology* 20, no. 1 (1986): 42–49.

Clarkson, Robert W., and James C. Rorabaugh. "Status of Leopard Frogs *(Rana pipiens* Complex: Ranidae) in Arizona and Southeastern California." *The Southwestern Naturalist* 34, no. 4 (1989): 531–38.

Cook, Robert P. "Effects of Acid Precipitation on Embryonic Mortality of *Ambystoma* Salamanders in the Connecticut Valley of Massachusetts." *Biological Conservation* 27 (1983): 77–88.

Cooke, A. S. "Indications of Recent Changes in Status in the British Isles of the Frog *(Rana temporaria)* and the Toad *(Bufo bubo)*." *Journal of Zoology* 167 (1972): 161–78.

Corn, Paul Stephen, and R. Bruce Bury. "Logging in Western Oregon: Responses of Headwater Habitats and Stream Amphibians." *Forest Ecology and Management* 29 (1989): 39–57.

Corn, Paul Stephen, and James C. Fogleman. "Extinction of Montane Populations of the Northern Leopard Frog *(Rana pipiens)* in Colorado." *Journal of Herpetology* 18, no. 2 (1984): 147–52.

Crump, Martha L. "Possible Enhancement of Growth in Tadpoles Through Cannibalism." *Copeia* 1990: 560–64.

———, Frank R. Hensley, and Kenneth L. Clark. "Apparent Decline of the Golden Toad: Underground or Extinct?" *Copeia* 1992: 413–20.

Crump, Martha L., and J. Alan Pounds. "Lethal Parasitism of an Aposematic Anuran *(Atelopus varius)* by *Notochaeta bufonivora* (Diptera: Sarcophagidae)." *Journal of Parasitology* 71, no. 5 (1985): 588–91.

Cummins, C. P. "Effects of Aluminum and Low pH on Growth and Development in *Rana temporaria* Tadpoles." *Oecologia* 69 (1986): 248–52.

Dodd, C. Kenneth, Jr. "The Status of the Red Hills Salamander *Phaeognathus hubrichti,* Alabama, U.S.A., 1976–1988." *Biological Conservation* 55 (1991): 57–75.

———, and Richard A. Seigel. "Relocation, Repatriation, and Translocation of Amphibians and Reptiles: Are They Conservation Strategies That Work?" *Herpetologica* 47, no. 3 (1991): 336–50.

Dunson, William A., and Richard L. Wyman, eds. "Symposium: Amphibian Declines and Habitat Acidification." *Journal of Herpetology* 26, no. 4 (1992): 349–442.

Fishwild, Thomas G., et al. "Sibling Recognition by Larval Frogs (*Rana pipiens, R. sylvatica,* and *Pseudacris crucifer*)." *Journal of Herpetology* 24, no. 1 (1990): 40–44.

Freda, Joseph. "The Effects of Aluminum and Other Metals on Amphibians." *Environmental Pollution* 71 (1991): 305–28.

———. "The Influence of Acidic Pond Water on Amphibians: A Review." *Water, Air and Soil Pollution* 30 (1986): 439–50.

———, and William A. Dunson. "Effects of Low pH and Other Chemical Variables on the Local Distribution of Amphibians." *Copeia* 1986: 454–66.

———. "Field and Laboratory Studies of Ion Balance and Growth Rates of Ranid Tadpoles Chronically Exposed to Low pH." *Copeia* 1985: 415–23.

———. "Sodium Balance of Amphibian Larvae Exposed to Low Environmental pH." *Physiological Zoology* 57, no. 4 (1984): 435–43.

Frisbie, Malcolm Pratt, and Richard L. Wyman. "The Effect of Environmental pH on Sodium Balance in the Red-spotted Newt, *Notophthalmus viridescens*." *Archives of Environmental Contamination and Toxicology* 23 (1992): 64–68.

———. "The Effects of Soil pH on Sodium Balance in the Redbacked Salamander, *Plethodon cinereus,* and Three Other Terrestrial Salamanders." *Physiological Zoology* 64, no. 4 (1991): 1050–68.

Fritts, Thomas H. "Differential Predation on Tadpoles." *Copeia* 1966: 594–98.

Glynn, Peter W. "El Niño-Southern Oscillation 1982–83: Nearshore Population, Community, and Ecosystem Responses." *Annual Review of Ecological Systems* 19 (1988): 309–45.

Hammerson, Geoffrey A. "Bullfrog Eliminating Leopard Frogs in Colorado?" *Herpetology Review* 13, no. 4 (1982): 115–16.

Harte, John, and Erika Hoffman. "Possible Effects of Acidic Deposition on a Rocky Mountain Population of the Tiger Salamander *Abystoma tigrinum*." *Conservation Biology* 3, no. 2 (1989): 149–58.

Hayes, Marc P. "Predation on the Adults and Prehatching Stages of Glass Frogs (Centrolenidae)." *Biotropica* 15, no. 1 (1983): 74–76.

————, and Mark R. Jennings. "Decline of Ranid Frog Species in Western North America: Are Bullfrogs *(Rana catesbeiana)* Responsible?" *Journal of Herpetology* 20, no. 4 (1986): 490–509.

Hayes, M. P., and M. M. Miyamoto. "Biochemical, Behavioral and Body Size Differences Between *Rana aurora aurora* and *R. A. draytoni*." *Copeia* 1984: 1018–22.

Hayes, Marc P., and Michele R. Tennant. "Diet and Feeding Behavior of the California Red-legged Frog, *Rana aurora draytonii*." *The Southwestern Naturalist* 30, no. 4 (1985): 601–05.

Hedges, S. Blair. "Global Amphibian Declines: A Perspective from the Caribbean." *Biodiversity and Conservation* 2 (1993): 290–303.

Heyer, W. Ronald, et al. "Decimations, Extinctions, and Colonizations of Frog Populations in Southeast Brazil and Their Evolutionary Implications." *Biotropica* 20, no. 3 (1988): 230–35.

Hinshaw, Steven H., and Brian K. Sullivan. "Predation on *Hyla versicolor* and *Pseudacris crucifer* During Reproduction." *Journal of Herpetology* 24, no. 2 (1990): 196–97.

Honegger, Rene E. "List of Amphibians and Reptiles Either Known or Thought to Have Become Extinct Since 1600." *Biological Conservation* 19 (1980–81): 141–58.

Jacobson, Susan K., and John J. Vandenberg. "Reproductive Ecology of the Endangered Golden Toad *(Bufo periglenes)." Journal of Herpetology* 25, no. 3 (1991): 321–27.

Jennings, Mark R., and Marc P. Hayes. "Pre-1900 Overharvest of California Red-legged Frogs *(Rana aurora draytonii):* The Inducement for Bullfrog *(Rana catesbeiana)* Introduction." *Herpetologica* 41, no. 1 (1985): 94–103.

Kats, Lee B., and James W. Petranka, and Andrew Sih. "Antipredator Defenses and the Persistence of Amphibian Larvae With Fishes." *Ecology* 69, no. 6 (1988): 1865–70.

Kauffman, J. Boone, and W. C. Krueger. "Lifestock Impacts on Riparian Ecosystems and Streamside Management Implications . . . A Review." *Journal of Range Management* 37, no. 5 (1984): 430–36.

———, and M. Vavra. "Effects of Late Season Cattle Grazing on Riparian Plant Communities." *Journal of Range Management* 36, no. 6 (1983): 685–91.

———. "Impacts of Cattle on Streambanks in Northeastern Oregon." *Journal of Range Management* 36, no. 6 (1983): 683–85.

———. "Some Responses of Riparian Soils to Grazing Management in Northeastern Oregon." *Journal of Range Management* 38, no. 4 (1985): 378–81.

Kirk, James J. "Western Spotted Frog *(Rana pretiosa)* Mortality Following Forest Spraying of DDT." *Herpetology Review* 19, no. 3 (1988): 51–53.

Kruse, Kipp C., and Michael G. Francis. "A Predation Deterrent in Larvae of the Bullfrog, *Rana catesbeiana.*" *Transactions of the American Fisheries Society* 106, no. 3 (1977): 248–52.

La Marca, Enrique, and Hans Peter Reinthaler. "Population Changes in *Atelopus* Species of the Cordillera de Merida, Venezuela." *Herpetology Review* 22, no. 4 (1991): 125–27.

Lawton, Robert, and Valerie Dryer. "The Vegetation of the Monteverde Cloud Forest Reserve." *Brenesia* 18 (1980): 101–16.

Lewis, William M., Jr., and Michael C. Grant. "Acid Precipitation in the Western United States." *Science* 207 (1980): 176–77.

Licht, Lawrence E. "Breeding Habits and Embryonic Thermal Requirement of the Frogs, *Rana aurora aurora* and *Rana pretiosa pretiosa*, in the Pacific Northwest." *Ecology* 52, no. 1 (1971): 116–24.

———. "Unusual Aspects of Anural Sexual Behavior as Seen in the Red-legged Frog, *Rana aurora aurora.*" *Canadian Journal of Zoology* 47 (1969): 505–09.

———. "Survival of Embryos, Tadpoles, and Adults of the Frogs *Rana aurora aurora* and *Rana pretiosa pretiosa* Sympatric in Southwestern British Columbia." *Canadian Journal of Zoology* 52 (1974): 613–27.

Mahon, Robin, and Karl Aiken. "The Establishment of the North American Bullfrog, *Rana catesbeiana* (Amphibia, Anura, Ranidae) in Jamaica." *Journal of Herpetology* 11, no. 2 (1977): 197–99.

Moore, Frank L. "Amphibian Model System for Problems in Behavioral Neuroendocrinology." *The Journal of Experimental Zoology Supplement* 4 (1990): 157–58.

Morey, Steven R. "Microhabitat Selection and Predation in the Pacific Treefrog, *Pseudacris regilla.*" *Journal of Herpetology* 24, no. 3 (1990): 292–96.

Moyle, Peter B. "Biodiversity Loss in the Temperate Zone: Decline of the Native Fish Fauna of California." *Conservation Biology* 4, no. 3 (1990): 275–84.

———. "Effects of Introduced Bullfrogs, *Rana catesbeiana,* on the Native Frogs of the San Joaquin Valley, California." *Copeia* 1973: 18–22.

———. "Fish Introductions in California: History and Impact on Native Fishes." *Biological Conservation* 9 (1976): 101–18.

Murphy, Michael L., and James D. Hall. "Varied Effects of Clearcut Logging on Predators and Their Habitat in Small Streams of the Cascade Mountains, Oregon." *Canadian Journal of Fishery and Aquatic Science* 38 (1981): 137–45.

Nyman, Stephen. "Mass Mortality in Larval *Rana sylvatica* Attributable to the Bacterium *Aeromonas hydrophila.*" *Journal of Herpetology* 20, no. 2 (1986): 196–201.

O'Hara, Richard K., and Andrew R. Blaustein. *"Rana cascadae* Tadpoles Aggregate With Siblings: An Experimental Field Study." *Oecologia* 67 (1985): 44–51.

Olson, Deanna H. "Predation on Breeding Western Toads *(Bufo boreas).*" *Copeia* 1989: 391–97.

———, Andrew R. Blaustein, and Richard K. O'Hara. "Mating Pattern Variability Among Western Toad *(Bufo boreas)* Populations." *Oecologia* 70 (1986): 351–56.

Pechmann, Joseph H. K., et al. "Declining Amphibian Populations: The Problem of Separating Human Impacts from Natural Fluctuations." *Science* 253: 892–95.

Pierce, Benjamin A. "Acid Tolerance in Amphibians." *Bioscience* 35, no. 4 (1985): 239–43.

Porter, Kenneth R., and Dean E. Hakanson. "Toxicity of Mine Drainage to Embryonic and Larval Boreal Toads (Bufonidae: *Bufo boreas*)." *Copeia* 1976: 327–31.

Pounds, J. Alan, and Martha L. Crump. "Amphibian Declines and Climate Disturbance: The Case of the Golden Toad and Harlequin Frog." *Conservation Biology* (in press).

————. "Harlequin Frogs Along a Tropical Montane Stream: Aggregation and the Risk of Predation by Frog-eating Flies." *Biotropica* 19, no. 4 (1987): 306–09.

Rabb, George B. "Declining Amphibian Populations." *Species* 13–14 (1990): 33–34.

Rand, A. Stanley, Michael J. Ryan, and Katherine Troyer. "A Population Explosion in a Tropical Tree Frog: *Hyla rufitela* on Barro Colorado Island, Panama." *Biotropica* 15, no. 1 (1983): 72–73.

Reinert, Howard K. "Translocation as a Conservation Strategy for Amphibians and Reptiles: Some Comments, Concerns, and Observations." *Herpetologica* 47, no. 3 (1991): 357–63.

Savage, Jay M. "An Extraordinary New Toad *(Bufo)* from Costa Rica." *Revista de Biologia Tropical* 14, no. 2 (1966): 153–67.

Schulz, Terri Tucker, and Wayne C. Leininger. "Differences in Riparian Vegetation Structure Between Grazed Areas and Exclosures." *Journal of Range Management* 43, no. 4 (1990): 295–99.

Scott, Norman J., Jr. "The Abundance and Diversity of the Herpetofaunas of Tropical Forest Litter." *Biotropica* 8, no. 1 (1976): 41–58.

Shebley, W. H. "History of the Introduction of Food and Game Fishes Into the Waters of California." *California Fish and Game* 3, no. 1 (1917): 3–12.

Sherman, Cynthia Kagarise, and Martin L. Morton. "Population Declines of Yosemite Toads in the Eastern Sierra Nevada of California." *Journal of Herpetology* 27 (1993): 186–98.

Sjogren, Per. "Extinction and Isolation Gradients in Metapopulations: The Case of the Poof Frog *(Rana lessonae)*" *Biological Journal of the Linnean Society* 42 (1991): 135–47.

Stolarski, Richard, et al. "Measured Trends in Stratospheric Ozone." *Science* 256 (1992): 342–49.

Storer, Tracy I. "Frogs and Their Commercial Uses." *California Fish and Game* 19, no. 3 (1933): 203–13.

———. "The Eastern Bullfrog in California." *California Fish and Game* 8 (4) (1922): 219–24.

Taylor, Daniel M. "Effects of Cattle Grazing on Passerine Birds Nesting in Riparian Habitat." *Journal of Range Management* 39, no. 3 (1986): 254–58.

Tyler, Michael J. "Declining Amphibian Populations—A Global Phenomenon? An Australian Perspective." *Alytes* 9, no. 2 (1991): 43–50.

Wake, David B. "Declining Amphibian Populations." *Science* 253 (1991): 860.

Welsh, Hartwell H., Jr. "Relictual Amphibians and Old-Growth Forests." *Conservation Biology* 4, no. 3 (1990): 309–19.

Weygoldt, Peter. "Changes in the Composition of Mountain Stream Frog Communities in the Atlantic Mountains of Brazil: Frogs as Indicators of Environmental Deteriorations?" *Studies on Neotropical Fauna and Environment* 243 (1989): 249–55.

Woolbright, Lawrence L. "The Impact of Hurricane Hugo on Forest Frogs in Puerto Rico." *Biotropica* 23, no. 4a (1991): 262–67.

Wyman, Richard L. "Soil Acidity and Moisture and the Distribution of Amphibians in Five Forests of Southcentral New York." *Copeia* 1988: 394–99.

―――. "What's Happening to the Amphibians." *Conservation Biology* 4 (1990): 350–52.

―――, and Dianne S. Hawksley-Lescault. "Soil Acidity Affects Distribution, Behavior, and Physiology of the Salamander *Plethodon cinereus.*" *Ecology* 68, no. 6 (1987): 1819–27.

General Press Articles

Amato, Ivan. "From 'Hunter Magic,' a Pharmacopeia." *Science* 258 (1992): 1306.

Barry, John. "Croaking." *Tropic,* 5 May 1991.

Bishop, Hugh. "The 1991 Pet Retail Sales and Profit Picture." *PSM—Pet Supplies Marketing,* June 1992.

Blakeslee, Sandra. "Scientists Confront an Alarming Mystery: The Vanishing Frog." *The New York Times,* 20 February 1990.

Blaustein, Andrew R., and Richard K. O'Hara. "Kin Recognition in Tadpoles." *Scientific American,* January 1986: 108–16.

Booth, William. "Frogs, Toads Vanishing Across Much of World." *The Washington Post,* 13 December 1989.

Burns, Melinda, et al. "Up the Creek." Two-part series on the Los Padres National Forest. *Santa Barbara News-Press,* 25–26 July 1993.

Cave, Shane. "The El Niño Phenomenon and the Planet's Climate." *Our Planet* 3, no. 6 (1991): 12–13.

Coit, Michael. "Agencies Quarrel Over Trail's Impact on Toad." New York *Daily News,* 11 December 1991.

Cowan, Ron. "Brooding Over Australian Frogs." *Science News* 137: 142.

———. "Tales From the Froglog and Others." *Science News* 137: 158.

———. "Vanishing Amphibians: Why They're Croaking." *Science News* 137: 116.

Dolan, Maura. "Ozone Levels Over U.S. Drop to New Lows." *Los Angeles Times,* 23 April 1993.

Duellman, William E. "Reproductive Strategies of Frogs." *Scientific American,* July 1992: 80–87.

Finn, Terry. "Declining Frogs: The Croak of Doom?" United Press International, 1 May 1990.

Florence, Mari. "Ribbetsville Redux." *Los Angeles Times Magazine,* 25 October 1992: 12.

"Frog Shortage Possible This Winter." *Science* 178 (1972): 387.

"Frogs for Funds." *Environment* 33, no. 2 (1991): 21–22.

"Frogs, Toads Are Dying by the Millions." Scripps Howard News Service, 28 November 1991.

Frost, S. W. "The Amphibian in Art and Literature." *Scientific Monthly* 34 (1932): 369–75.

Hair, Jay D. "Mysterious Dying Sounds an Alarm." *Santa Paula News Chronicle,* 10 September 1992.

Hale, Ellen. "Scientists Worried by Amphibians' Decline." *USA Today,* 19 February 1990.

Jorgenson, Amanda. "Biologists Express Concern for Huge Trade in Bullfrogs." *Traffic (U.S.A.)* 6, no. 2 (1985): 25–26.

Kay, Jane. "Manhandling Nature." *San Francisco Examiner Image,* 25 August 1991: 18–23, 30–31.

Kisken, Tom. "County Frogs Fading Fast." Ventura, California, *Star-Free Press,* 27 June 1993.

Knox, Pamela Naber. "A Current Catastrophe: El Niño." *Earth,* September 1992: 31–37.

LaFee, Scott. "Slip-Sliding Away." *The San Diego Union-Tribune,* 14 April 1993.

" 'Laughing Frogs,' Under Police Protection, Keep French Awake." Associated Press, 5 July 1991.

Livermore, Beth. "Amphibian Alarm: Just Where Have All the Frogs Gone?" *Smithsonian,* October 1992: 113–20.

Miller, Joanna. "Bikers Compete With Rare Toad Over Stream Bed." *Los Angeles Times,* 9 December 1991.

———. "Piru Creek Motorcycle Trail to Reopen." *Los Angeles Times,* 10 December 1991.

"Mosquitoes Save Frogs." *Traffic (U.S.A.)* 8, no. 1 (1988): 21.

Nevaer, Louis E. "Fate of Brilliant Orange Golden Toad Linked to Costa Rica Climatological Change." Pacific News Service, 24 May 1991.

Niekisch, Manfred. "The International Trade in Frogs' Legs." *Traffic Bulletin* 8, no. 1 (1986): 7–10.

Nullis, Clare. "U.N. Agency Says Ozone Depletion Running at Record Levels." Associated Press, 23 November 1992.

O'Brien, James P. "Amphibians Under Siege." *Outdoor California,* May–June 1992: 1–4.

Pennisi, Elizabeth. "Pharming Frogs." *Science News* 142 (1992): 40–42.

Phillips, Kathryn. "Frog Man." *Los Angeles Times Magazine,* 2 September 1990: 18–19, 22–23, 37–39.

———. "Frogs in Trouble." *International Wildlife,* November–December 1990: 4.

———. "Where Have All the Frogs and Toads Gone?" *Bioscience* 40, no. 6 (1990): 422–24.

Pounds, J. Alan. "The Secret Sahara." *BBC Wildlife,* June 1991: 381.

"Recent Trends in U.S. Skin Imports." *Traffic (U.S.A.)* 5, no. 2 (1983): 6–7.

Reed, Mack. "New Route to Protect Rare Toad Proposed." *Los Angeles Times,* 4 September 1992.

Sherman, Cynthia Kagarise, and Martin L. Morton. "The Toad That Stays on Its Toes." *Natural History,* March 1984: 72–78.

"Special Issue: Frogs and Toads." *Terra—The Members Magazine of the Natural History Museum of Los Angeles County* 13, no. 4 (1975).

Spencer, Cathy. "One Giant Leap: Frogs and Other Amphibians Are Telling Us Something About Our Environment—They're Croaking." *Omni,* October 1990: 25.

Stauth, Dave. "The Smell of Death." *Oregon's Agricultural Progress,* Summer–Fall 1992: 12–17.

Stern, John. "Space Aliens Stealing Our Frogs!" *Weekly World News,* 17 April 1990: 21.

Stevens, William K. "Researchers Find Acid Rain Imperils Forests Over Time." *The New York Times,* 31 December 1989.

———. "Ozone Loss Over U.S. Is Found to Be Twice as Bad as Predicted." *The New York Times,* 5 April 1991.

Stolzenburg, William. "What Are the Toads Telling Us?" *Colorado Outdoors,* March–April 1989: 24–27.

Thoele, Mike. "Scientists Race to Solve Mystery." Eugene, Oregon, *Register-Guard,* 17 January 1993.

Tugend, Alina. "Decline of Frogs May Be Environmental Warning." *The Orange County Register,* 20 February 1990.

Vogel, Shawna. "Under the Ozone Hole." *Earth,* January 1993: 30–35.

Weart, Spencer. "From the Nuclear Frying Pan Into the Global Fire." *The Bulletin of the Atomic Scientist,* June 1992: 19–27.

Weiss, R. "Historic Priapism Pegged to Frog Legs." *Science News* 139 (1991): 6.

Weisskopf, Michael. "First Summer Thinning Found in Ozone Layer." *The Washington Post,* 22 October 1991.

———. "Ozone Study Predicts Increase in Cataract, Skin Cancer Risks." *The Washington Post,* 21 November 1991.

Yoffe, Emily. "Silence of the Frogs." *The New York Times Magazine,* 13 December 1992: 36–39, 64–66, 76.